Changing Roles in Social Work Practice

TITLE
X X

Changing Roles in Social Work Practice

Edited by
Francine Sobey

Temple University Press
Philadelphia

Temple University Press, Philadelphia 19122
© 1977 by Temple University. All rights reserved
Published 1977

Printed in the United States of America
International Standard Book Number: 0-87722-092-1 cloth; 0-87722-096-4 paper
Library of Congress Catalog Card Number: 77-70327

Contents

361
So 677

102841

Preface

DURING a remarkably short time significant changes have taken place in social work practice. These changes continue to occur in almost every type of setting in which social workers are employed. New demands upon the field have led to the creation of new kinds of service structures within long established organizations and whole new kinds of agencies built in response to redefined functions and goals. Drawing upon generic and specialized knowledge and skills, new methods are emerging to help "at-risk" populations cope with their problems in functioning in a troubled, postindustrial society.

Radical changes in staffing patterns, which I documented in *The Nonprofessional Revolution in Mental Health,* have already taken place in human service programs across the nation, inside and outside of the profession of social work. Even the most traditional agencies that held firm against this development are now moving to employ a wider range of social work personnel—from community peer-helpers to doctorate level social workers. Inevitably, different team structures have developed to combine a range of personnel no longer limited to the single Master of Social Work level. As a result, new helping roles and conceptions of practice have been emerging from these changing new divisions of responsibility. Selected roles and skills formerly performed at one educational level are being redefined upward. Thus, personnel with the two-year Associate degree in a social work program of study perform many roles formerly done by the baccalaureate degree social worker, who, in turn, has redefined his roles upward. The MSW degree worker is pressed on one side to develop the crucial new educator role needed for training purposes, and on the other side to upgrade his therapeutic skills. All this has great implications for future training and practice.

Confronted by the unsettling effects of change both inside and outside the social work world, the practitioner, the administrator, the university-based educator, and especially the student all need from the social work profession clear knowledge for their helping purposes. The primary goal of this book is to bring together knowledge of recent developments in selected fields and settings to help prospective or established social work practitioners with the problems of their particular client groups—problems made increasingly complex by changing social values and the ubiquitous processes of societal change. The practitioner is in a strategic position to expand helping roles and methods by testing out concepts taught in the classroom and by generating new ones. This book is intended to join practitioner with educator in seeking a more effective configuration of organizational program, team structure, tasks, roles, and skills.

This book illustrates recent significant steps that have been taken in this relatively young social work profession. Following Bartlett's historic lead, generic principles are being applied to practice in specialized fields. Generic models—the life model for instance—are being found more compatible with real life experience in a rapidly changing society. Help is beginning to be made available when, where, and how it is needed by particular social groups. Lifestyle is emerging as a crucial variable in tailoring programs to these groups within a holistic, human-ecological systems perspective. On the path to integration, practitioners are combining policy awareness with their practice approaches, touching client and organization alike. Action-oriented, short-term treatment, crisis intervention, milieu, behavioral, and educational methods are in the ascendant.

Among the questions raised in the book are: What is the nature of practice in some of the newer or remodeled service systems? What knowledge is now required? What attitudes are imperative for successful results? How does one function in these newer helping roles and team structures? And, most crucial in the new age of "accountability," What evidence of successful outcome is available? What remains to be worked upon?

I do not pretend to have compiled a comprehensive array of social work practice with representative samples from across the nation. This volume is as much an illustration of the gaps as of the riches of social work practice in the regions, the voluntary, the public, and the private sectors of urban America. The selection represents some of my key interests and experiences in my roles of social work practitioner, researcher, and educator. My experience in teaching social work practice and in developing course work on professional-paraprofessional roles in mental health and social work practice at the Columbia University School of Social Work and in conducting staff development seminars for social welfare and mental health personnel is reflected in the book's content. The book also represents my convictions regarding certain current educational priorities required to improve practice. Among these is focus on the entire life cycle and a more equal emphasis on preventive, health-promoting roles (anticipatory counseling, parent education, and child and aged policy advocacy), compared with more traditional clinical social work roles within well-established pathologies.

The chapters have been prepared by authors following new directions as practitioners, administrators, and research and social work scholars. The points of reference were an outline which organized the major themes and suggested questions posed in this preface, the background of my previous publication, *The Nonprofessional Revolution in Mental Health,* and considerable discussion and cross-fertilization of ideas and relevant bibliographic sources between the editor and chapter authors and their associates. As a result of this process and rapidly changing events that crystallized thinking and obsolete data, several of the book's chapters were rewritten. Yet, each author, professionally competent in his or her own right, has been free to deal with the suggested framework in an individual way compatible with the particular subject matter.

In the introduction, I view changing directions for practice in the selected fields and programs represented in the book's chapters. As a guide to the particular changes highlighted, I have prepared headnotes to precede each chapter. The body of the book presents changes primarily at the organizational policy level that have affected large populations in the fields of child welfare, health care, mental health, the aging, alcoholism, and so on. Also illustrated are developments characteristic of the newer ecological perspective—that is, changes that pervade organizational policy and direct practice with individuals, small groups and community—in chapters on industrial social welfare and child treatment services. Changes at the individual and small group level of practice are exemplified in programs such as the adolescent mental health walk-in center, the group home, the abortion counseling clinic, and the hospital-based community mental health service.

No chapter in this book is to be considered a perfect model for practice in this period of experiment and growth. Case and policy illustrations have been given to open the minds of students and professionals to some newer significant developments in social work practice. My intention has been to provide a base for more specialized study of discrete problems and fields of the reader's choosing. The book is addressed to conceptual and practical career development needs for social workers with an ever-widening range of educational and work backgrounds and interests. It is intended for use in university programs of social work study with diverse tracks and titles—social work practice with individuals and groups, social planning, community organization and administration, social treatment, interpersonal interventions, and clinical counseling. Within university undergraduate and graduate social work programs, it should introduce the student to some key aspects of modern social work practice, which is moving toward broader frameworks, redirecting attention from single to multi-methods, from solo to team practice, and from limited to broader views of the complex interrelationships between practice, policy, and program. At the undergraduate level, it should harmonize well with social work practice courses placed within the newer schools of human ecology.

Specifically, this book is intended for use in undergraduate social work programs and Master's programs as students begin to consider particular career choices. It is also intended for use in continuing education and inservice training programs, and it is hoped that it will stimulate agencies to venture into offering new services as well as enhancing existing services. The informed citizen-volunteer, the student, and the instructor of allied human services programs may also find it of value.

Many educators and practitioners helped and encouraged me to fulfill the purposes of this book. Shirley Hellenbrand was generous in providing substantive comments and helpful feedback; she also assisted with editorial tasks. Bernice Shepard, at the National Association of Social Workers, also gave specific editorial help in addition to preparing a chapter for the book. Connie Buckley and Carel Germain read early drafts of the book, gave cogent suggestions, and practical editing aid. Donald Feldstein provided critical commentary from the viewpoint of the undergraduate social work educator. Throughout, many colleagues helped practically and conceptually—among them Alfred Kadushin at the University of Wisconsin, Elaine Rothenberg, Dean at Virginia Commonwealth University School of Social Work, Joan Hunter at the School of Social Administration, Dundee, Scotland, and Hyman Weiner, Dean at New York University School of Social Work. At Columbia University, the Dean of the School of Social Work, Mitchell Ginsberg, and members of the newly-titled Social Work Practice faculty encouraged me to address the need for bibliographic sources for newer curricula developing in social work programs of study throughout the country. Finally, at Temple University Press, David Bartlett responded humanly to the content of this book and brought it to life. To all who have helped, I express our deepest gratitude.

Francine Sobey
Columbia University

Contributors

Francine Sobey, DSW, is Associate Professor of Social Work Practice, Columbia University School of Social Work, and Social Work Training Consultant.

Bernice Q. Madison, Ph.D., is Professor of Social Work, San Francisco State University.

Milton Wittman, DSW, is Chief, Social Work Education Branch, Division of Manpower and Training Programs, National Institute of Mental Health, Alcohol, Drug Abuse and Mental Health Administration, U.S. Department of Health, Education, and Welfare, Rockville, Maryland. This paper reflects his own opinions and does not represent policy of HEW.

Barbara Berkman, DSW, is Special Lecturer, Simmons College School of Social Work, Boston; Adjunct Assistant Professor, Community Medicine (Social Work), Mount Sinai School of Medicine, City University of New York; and Research Associate, Social Service Department, Mount Sinai Hospital, New York City.

Margaret E. Hartford, Ph.D., is Director, Leonard Davis School of Gerontology, University of Southern California, Los Angeles.

Mary M. Seguin, DSW, is Director, Older Volunteer Project, Andrus Gerontology Center, University of Southern California, Los Angeles.

Shirley C. Hellenbrand is Associate Professor, Columbia University School of Social Work.

Roslyn Yasser is Associate Administrator, District Council 37, Health and Security Plan, American Federation of State, County, and Municipal Employees.

James K. Whittaker, Ph.D., is Professor in the School of Social Work and Coordinator of Child Welfare Project at University of Washington, Seattle, Washington. His chapter is adapted from a paper in *Journal of Autism and Childhood Schizophrenia* 5 (Sept. 1975) and appears here by permission of the original publisher.

Morris Black, ACSW, is Director of the Manhattan–West Side Office of Mental Health Services, Jewish Board of Guardians, New York City.

Mary Funnye Goldson is Associate Professor, Columbia University School of Social Work and Chief Consultant, Lower East Side Family Union, a community-based child welfare agency.

Atkins Preston is Associate Executive Director, Henry Street Settlement Urban Life Center, and Executive Director, Henry Street Children's Services, Inc.

Florence Haselkorn is Professor of Social Work, Adelphi University School of Social Work, Garden City, Long Island.

Bernice Shepard, ACSW, is Director, Alcoholism Consultation Service, and Staff Consultant, National Association of Social Workers.

Sue Matorin, ACSW, is Chief of Social Work Training, Washington Heights Community Service, New York State Psychiatric Institute.

Part I. Overviews

1

Orientation to Changing Roles in Social Work Practice

FRANCINE SOBEY

THIS book is about change—change as it affects the practice of the urban professional social worker in selected fields and specialized programs. No longer can practice be based on enduring patterns repeated year after year. The profession must now constantly respond to a changing society. Certainties either of knowledge or values become fewer and farther between. When the runaway pace of present-day living results in confusion and estrangment, as it all too often does, people long for breathing space, for a sense of rootedness in place, for timely, respectful contact with familiar, helpful places and persons. Paradoxically, social work practitioners must meet society's expectation that they will stay close to people, helping them to adapt to and cope with the diverse changes demanded of them, by making explosive changes in their own services and settings. At the same time society looks to the social worker for leadership in creating yet more changes in services and settings to which all must eventually adapt.

As social work in the United States enters the 1980s, the former social work settings—child welfare agencies, settlement houses, hospitals and clinics for the physically or mentally ill—have become, partly through governmental impetus, the hubs of large fields of practice, systems within networks of systems. They have spun off new organizational environments—such as adolescent walk-in centers, abortion clinics, work-site counseling services, and many others—all struggling to put down roots and establish effective relationships with the rest of the fast-evolving service-systems.

In response to the pressures of life in a crisis-ridden society, social work tasks inevitably will continue to expand. New roles are being shared inside and outside the profession. Multiple methods are being used in interventions with individuals, groups, communities, and institutions. Amid the diversity, a common base (or generic framework) of values, purposes, knowledge, and method is being developed and applied.

Along with the features held in common, however, variations and/or specializations must develop. Practice is always specific; as each individual is unique, so are there unique elements that distinguish the problems and practices of one field from another, one specialty from another—the child welfare field from the mental health field, or the helping repertoire of the counselor-therapist in a children's residential treatment center from that of the social work planner in the medical clinic.

It is no simple task now to understand what social work encompasses, to grasp the range of opportunities that await the student in a particular field or program; information is urgently needed to gain a sense of the whole in order to make career choices. While the service fields presented in this book are not and can not be complete, the sample chosen reflects major professional concerns. A growing repertoire of helping roles, tasks, and methods that cuts across many fields is presented for study. And the distinctive features of each changing service field are emphasized within each chapter and in the editor's headnote preceding each chapter.

For those readers already established in a particular social work career, the contents of this book should broaden their knowledge base and provide a fresh perspective on recent, changing directions in the field. (So many of us were trained in a single method, in solo practice, and in the sickbed of society!)

The book's chapters take the reader into some natural life-spaces—the workplace, the home, the neighborhood—and into some agency structures such as the hospital and neighborhood facility where social workers have recently altered their ways of helping people to solve particular problems. The focus is on selected human problems—for example, those of children in troubled families, adolescents in need of mature guidance, alcoholics, the aged, and the physically and mentally ill. These are age-old problems increasingly being met in new contemporary contexts. That is, they are more and more being seen within the circular and interrelated systems of individual, family, and community, and within a broad ecological systems perspective. The word *ecology,* derived from the Greek *oikos* meaning a house or place to live, is frequently invoked in this book's chapters to express the practitioner's growing understanding of the relationship of individuals and groups to their environments.[1] Some encouraging approaches are suggested to improve that vital mutual relationship. There is concern with understanding transactions among all known elements in the person's lifespace.[2] Thus, in addition to the home, the work-world, friends, leisuretime activities, and many other influences must now be reckoned with along with our former concern with what was going on within the person.

Changing Populations and Problems

Some of the problems and populations described in this book have only recently been brought into the sphere of social work—the blue-collar worker with job, home, and consumer credit problems; the over-80 retired person living alone; the adolescent or adult woman unwillingly pregnant and able to consider the option of legal abortion; and the teenage or adult person turning increasingly and detrimentally to alcohol.

To help with the problems of these groups, social workers must learn to adapt their knowledge and programs. For example, the blue-collar worker is still wary of the "head-shrinker."[3] He responds to a different definition of his problems than does the individual who goes to a clinic with some perception of disorder. He defines his problems in a practical way that highlights the need for financial benefits or discipline for his children rather than straightening out by a psychiatrist. For him retaining his job is paramount. Interventive objectives that he formulates with the social worker must be consistent with his priorities. The social worker must learn more about the client's world of work and about social work methods that fit this milieu.[4] (See chapter 6 in this book.)

Another previously neglected population, whose problems are increasingly becoming the concern of the social worker, is the alcoholic.[5] Alcoholic disorders account for 42 percent of all United States county and state mental hospital admissions among patients aged 35–44 years, and 40 percent of those aged 45–64 years.[6] Because of its current visibility, alcoholism has moved high among national health priorities, even superseding the importance formerly accorded to mental illness. The finding of the National Institute on Alcoholic Abuse and Alcoholism that a third of the country's 9 million alcoholics are women triggers special attention and planning for this group. Another group—teenagers and preteenagers—are increasingly reported drunk and needing to be sent home from school.[7] Thus, the social worker needs to learn more about alcohology to become more effective in delivering services to prevent or treat this illness among both sexes and in the many developmental periods in which it is emerging.

Not only populations seen by social workers but also types of problems are changing. The overt types of neuroses seen commonly at the turn of the twentieth century appear to have decreased in frequency, and anxiety-depressive syndromes have become the dominant psychiatric disorder in the North American culture, with character pathology a close second.[8] The latter makes treatment with children, and especially the growing number of behaviorally disturbed adolescents in residential care and community facilities, much more difficult.[9] (See chapters 7, 8, and 9 in this book.) For the social worker's purposes, however, more important than changing psychiatric diagnoses is the trend to see disturbed children and adult problem populations not as patients but as people who need to develop social, educational, and vocational competence. The same goals apply to more recent physiological diagnoses—for instance, "minimal brain dysfunction" in hyperkinetic and developmentally disturbed children, adolescents, and adults.[10] Key theoretical contributions of White, Erikson, and Heinz Hartmann, among others, are being utilized to formulate objectives for these vulnerable groups.

Even the bricks and mortar of social structures are changing. The group home is now the support chosen for the angry 12-year-old, who previously would have been sent to an ambivalent foster home or an impersonal institution. The mental health walk-in clinic is available for the alienated central city adolescent. Both the newer and the traditional structures (hospitals, residential treatment centers, foster homes) are represented in this book. The concept of "new" is relative, however, for very little is totally new (without antecedents). Moreover, new organizational structures quickly become old ones.[11] They too are inevitably superseded by concepts more compatible with the advancing times.

Emerging with these newer care structures for population groups with contemporary problems is a sweeping change in divisions of labor and responsibility within a newly reconstituted helper system. The rise of new team-colleagues and the role changes of the late 1960s (reported in *The Nonprofessional Revolution in Mental Health*)[12] will continue to influence social work staffing patterns into and well beyond the 1980s. A variety of interprofessional and multidisciplinary staff patterns are developing in so-called primary settings in which social workers are the major profession (for example, child welfare) and in secondary settings (health, mental health, and industrial social welfare) in which other professions and occupational groups preceded social work and are considered hosts. The nature of that development—whether teams predominate, who belongs to the team, and how tasks and roles are differentiated among newer and traditional helping structures—became a central issue requiring data from the practice world. Team issues and differential manpower usage will be addressed in each of the book's chapters. A brief orientation will be given later in this chapter.

Prevention and New Modes of Intervention

In marked contrast with manpower developments, the changes in practice toward preventing pathology and promoting social and emotional health can hardly be called sweeping. One study after another documents the lack of community based preventive services for at-risk families, followed by pronouncements that highest priority must be assigned to the task of developing them.[13] There are, however, some encouraging signs reported in this book's chapters.

1. New fields of practice, such as family planning, focus on primary prevention as defined within the public health model. More practiced in picking up the pieces than in preventing something from happening, social workers were not prominent in the forefront of this development. They are now moving more confidently, however, and adapting their practice to settings in which, first, family planning and, second, "abortion counseling" are

available for many target populations across the nation. (See chapter 10.) Key primary preventive programs—for example, lead poisoning prevention—are also engaging the social worker's attention in work with recently identified at-risk populations.

2. There is painfully little evidence that we are learning more effective ways to prevent the tragic problems of children. However, chapter 2 describes the potential for transforming an outmoded, ineffective child care system into a tool for early resolution of problems—the essence of secondary prevention. Furthermore, cybernetic and systems knowledge is increasingly available for harnessing to improve the quality of life for all age groups in all social work practice systems. Computerized data also has key implications for enriching and streamlining the whole process, from planning the worker's social study, assessment, and intervention to evaluating feedback and practice outcome.[14] Crisis and other short-term interventions where timing is important have moved to first place in work with people of all ages and problem categories.

3. Even in fields which have been discouragingly slow to move toward preventive emphases, such as health care, recognition of this serious deficit is at least a step in the right direction. Chapter 4 points out that in the many newer components of the developing health care network, social workers, even where included in the health care team, have rarely moved into case-finding activities, but rather have continued to depend on referrals from public health nurses and physicians. Independent case-finding activity by social workers is imperative to bring help to more people at an earlier stage of their troubles. Defining the situations with which they can help would also bring social workers into closer relationship with the needs perceived by the social work profession and by community citizens.[15]

4. In the fields and practice settings described in this book, there is a perceptible shift from exclusive reliance on the medical disease model to the broader ecological perspective that works with the positive growth and life developmental forces within the individual's environment—for example, using self-help groups among alcoholics and peer groups among the aging and utilizing school and community structures to reach populations otherwise isolated.

Informal and formal education harnessed to specific social

work purposes is also part of the new shift in fields such as consumer education, education on substance abuse, and foster and natural parent education. Teaching clients to anticipate and prevent crises in their lives is being accorded its rightful status in our interventions, in contrast to traditional clinical treatment. This "teaching" is not to be associated with a traditional class-room, subject matter approach. Here, the learner observes, imitates, rehearses behaviors, or makes social decisions—interacting with social workers and others in real-life or role-play situations.[16]

The rediscovered educational role for the social worker, who is called a "life-space educator" in some chapters, increasingly makes use of social learning theory and cognitive and behavioral emphases, in addition to modern ego psychology.[17] Earlier psychodynamic emphases—on resistance and underlying conflict, for instance—have not vanished. They tend, however, to be recast for handling at the wider range of practice levels with which social workers are now engaged.[18]

For well over a decade, in-house critics have fired ascerbic barbs at the solo social work practitioner (read caseworker, now "clinical" social worker) who was so intraperson oriented that he neglected the larger dimensions of real life and any objectives other than personality change through psychoanalytically based insight.[19] While some of the strident voices have stirred unnecessary professional and political divisions within the social work profession and perhaps slowed the process of change, in the long run there has proved to be at least a kernel of truth in some of the attacks on practice.

Certainly the charge cannot be denied that practice tended to be too pathology oriented and was thereby limited to "treatment" of diagnosed patients and clients; there was no effort to employ a range of interventions for ordinary citizens who needed increased competence in dealing with daily life. Anticipatory counseling and preventive intervention before and throughout life cycle crises—from the crisis of first parenthood to retirement from the work force, on through aging and dying—are urged in this book's chapters as requiring much more social work focus.[20] The literature reports increasing success with these crisis interventions—planned short-term, task-centered, and other problem-solving interventions—to promote health and thereby prevent, cut short, or contain human dysfunctions.[21] Some of these interventions occur at the individual or group level, others at administrative, legislative, and social policy levels. Since staff at many educational and experience levels perform these interventions, differential theoretical and practice content for the many levels has become available for use.[22]

The Framework of the Helping Situation

The notion of what constitutes the helping situation was broadened and reconceptualized in the early 1970s.[23] A number of variables previously undervalued are now being considered more prominently. For the purposes of this book, the entire helping situation can be considered to consist of the following complex and interrelated features.

1. Practice milieu and structures: the agency organization. This includes (1) the smaller decentralized settings, such as group homes and work-site counseling services; (2) the larger agency structures within networks of complex practice fields, such as large urban hospitals in health care and industrial and labor union organizations responsible for coordinating services for thousands of children and their families within voluntary and public sectors; and (3) special informational and other functional systems created for use within the agency organization, such as the child welfare tracking system described in chapter 2 and the problem-oriented health care record system in chapter 4.
2. Populations at risk and their key problems. This includes the populations already referred to and the changing definitions of their problems.
3. Helper system. This includes the social worker as a prominent member of a team structure with community input and implications for managing many new relationships.
4. Helping processes and interventions. This includes the planning and management of objectives, helping tasks, methods to be used, and relationships of clients with other organizations and institutions.

Of the four features described above, which broadly define the helping situation, two have even in the recent past been insuffi-

ciently highlighted in both social work education and practice—
the practice-milieu and structure, and the helper system. Let us
discuss the implications of each for the social worker's practice
interventions.

Practice Milieu and Structure

Since the term *milieu* is so loosely bandied about, its meaning
should first be clarified. It is, in fact, defined loosely even in
various dictionaries as "environment," "setting," "surroundings," or more precisely, "spatial locale." Its literal meaning is
"the center." All of these aspects of the definition will apply to
our understanding of the rationale for the milieu and its interventions.

In all this book's chapters there is consensus that the agency's
milieu and organization determines to a large extent what the
practitioner will do. The newer practice milieus with their smaller, decentralized units have impressive predecessors (settlement
houses, home visitations) within social work's earliest history
and in the milieu focus of Sullivan, Stanton and Schwartz, and
Cummings' writings on the mental hospital ward.[24] Interest
shifted from hospital to community milieus with the geographic
catchment areas concept of the community mental health center
legislation and the decentralized neighborhood concept of the
antipoverty programs of the 1960s.

Let us now locate some of those settings in which the milieu is
utilized as a central tool in the helping situation. The mental
health walk-in clinic for adolescents could hardly differ more in
appearance from its psychiatrically defined predecessor located a
few blocks away on an upper floor in a traditional office building.
The storefront is located on the street, next to the school attended
by its consumers, easily accessible, and visible to neighborhood
residents. It looks like a place one would want to attend after
school hours—not a recreational center, but an unpretentious
building out there among the neighborhood hangouts, stores, and
homes of one's neighbors. The group home, too, provides a
home-like atmosphere in its residents' community with links to
familiar places, persons, and things. In line with our understanding of the developmental stages of youth, the atmosphere is tuned
midway between the often excessive intimacy of the typical nu-

clear family situation (foster or natural) and the impersonality of
the large institution for youth.

Other structures in which the milieu is particularly important
include the health center in a low-income housing project of
urban Boston that operates in a small radius of center office,
clients' homes, and neighboring health and community facilities,
emphasizing twenty-four-hour-a-day service, including home
care.[25] Another milieu-oriented structure is the emergency
homemaker center of a vast child welfare network monitored by
social workers who assign homemakers to go in to care for needy
children at any hour of the day or night. And still another is the
twenty-four-hour telephone and go-to-the-scene outreach of the
network of alcoholism and abortion counseling crisis services.

The services described above embody a philosophy of helping
and caring which highlights meeting human needs in a variety of
locations, fitting structures to people and to places where they
live at the precise times when they are coping with stressful
events. Formerly, agencies did not assign as much priority to
clients' needs and convenience as do these newer structures. A
large number of these structures are placed in the center of low-
income neighborhoods in an effort to give more nearly equal care
to the poor as compared with the previously better serviced middle class. The developmental needs of each age group are considered in designing the specific milieu, and the populations are
defined epidemiologically as "populations-at-risk." The need to
humanize practice settings and programs that had grown cold and
impersonal is being recognized.

There are, of course, some serious gaps in the humanistic am-
biance of many social service milieus. The recent rediscovery of
the elderly population of all classes, but especially the poor, has
revealed shockingly inhuman nursing homes and other ware-
house-type facilities so uncaring that they have become national
scandals. With the aid of other professional and community
groups, social workers are in the forefront of planning radical
changes in these less than savory milieus. Because so many social
work clients are involved at one time or another with public welfare, the inhuman and institutional insanities of this milieu, bril-
liantly portrayed in the Frederick Wiseman documentary film,
Welfare, is also relevant to the social worker concerned with
critical analysis of milieu in helping interventions.

At this point, critical questions come to mind. If, as Haselkorn indicates in chapter 10, maladaptive responses to the abortion experience appear related more significantly to the societal and service milieu than to personality factors, why are we still failing to place more equal emphasis on environmental factors?[26] Is it because, difficult as it is to change behaviors of people by any method, it is infinitely more difficult to assess systematically the influence of "setting" and the interactions of people within a situational context? At another level, we might ask why do we not utilize some of the more constructive newer milieus as "social utilities" for middle-class populations, if in fact they have a humane edge over the older customary facilities? Are there hidden reasons for limiting some of these newer milieus to use among poor people?[27] Or are there valid differences between socioeconomic groups in their attitudes toward satellite center services that make accessibility, for instance, a less crucial consideration for more comfortable middle-class populations?

Beyond ecological, philosophical, and humanistic values, what is the potential in these milieus for shaping more practical objectives and tasks? Chapter 7, on children's residential care, illustrates the development of specific social skills and behaviors for increased intra- and interpersonal competence among some of our most seriously regressed and poorly functioning members of society. Some social welfare settings, such as the industrial union's Personal Service Unit, have built-in explicit structures that encourage the formulation and achievement of objectives within limited time periods. The union's grievance machinery (which includes timetables, deadlines for action) spurs the social worker to act as promptly as possible on mutually defined objectives with the union member, thereby maintaining accountability to him, to the sponsoring organization, and to professional standards.

A more task-oriented, time-limited approach tends to flow from formulation of more specified objectives. See the case vignette about Susan at the conclusion of chapter 8: a potential career is sought for the urban ghetto teenager whose family is not equipped to guide her toward a much needed adult occupational identity.

In looking more at the functioning of people in everyday milieus, there is new opportunity to see them as members of small and large groups and communities rather than as isolated iden-

tities. Thus, the small group method has spread rapidly throughout both the newer and the more traditional practice settings. The
pre- and postabortion groups, the informal meeting at the end of
each day for children placed in group homes, and the groups for
the elderly are illustrative. Drawing on small group behavior
theory, these groups tend to strengthen the demand for behavior
and attitude change by unifying people into cohesive systems—
peers, family, staff. The very speed with which the many varieties of the group method have in many places superseded the
individual method, however, leads one to question whether the
one-to-one relationship has not been prematurely and inappropri-
ately discarded in some instances.

There are additional factors to be considered in the shift from
individual to group method. Some of the groups reported in the
various chapters suggest a somewhat unstructured, totally experiential quality. Research findings do not yet establish their
effectiveness. That in itself should not deter further experimentation, but it does suggest that we be more critical in forming groups
and in evaluating their purposes and progress, especially vis-à-vis
alternative methods.[28]

Other problems of the milieu result from the new tensions that
arise when the social worker or team member is thrust more
deeply into real life situations. At Columbia Point Health Care
Center in Boston, not only the professional social worker but also
the nurse and the physician found that although in principle they
appreciated the values of working in the heart of the client's
environment, the actual work there was depleting and stressful.[29]

The knowledge explosion notwithstanding, we do not have a
solid base for intervening with special populations. Our understanding of the complex interrelationships of poverty, ethnicity,
personality, health, and social behavior are as yet tentative and
not integrated with our core of knowledge or practice theory in
social work.[30] Thus, a key advantage of milieu programs is that
they may use the delivery of episodic care to introduce the
client-population to the possibility of basic, broader changes in
their physical and social milieu—changes that might break the
cycle of poverty and ill health. But before this opportunity can be
exploited, there will have to be much greater practical experience
in these newer milieus and increased social worker involvement
in epidemiological research focused on these special populations.

If the milieu concept has been loosely used, its derivative, "milieu therapy" or "therapeutic milieu," is even more nebulous. In the literature of many helping professional disciplines, these terms seem commonly to serve as smokescreens for the practitioner's favored intervention, whether it is drug therapy, establishment of token economies in behavioral interventions, or psychoanalytically-based treatment! While it is understandable that one's philosophy would influence one's choice of interventions in the milieu and the extent of its use, still "milieu therapy" is not properly the title of one or another particular technique. It conveys a much broader view of each milieu as a microcosmic society in which all social interactions are therapeutically significant. This includes interactions between and among staff and target populations as well as interactions with the outside community that are aimed at producing changes in persons and their environment.[31]

The emphasis on milieu as a locale or geographic location may appear from one point of view to be untimely or even regressive. It could be correctly argued that the smaller community units in which we live are increasingly dominated by state and national systems. During the 1970s, the ties to these extracommunity systems have become even stronger. Technological changes have vastly reduced space between people and institutions and set the stage for a further strengthening of this vertical pattern, named the "Great Change" by Roland Warren in *The Community in America*.[32] Functions are constantly being transferred from the small geographic community to the national unit of government. Chief among these is funding, the lifesource of social service programs in all places. Despite revenue-sharing, the direction of development is increasing toward control by the federal government.[33] If this vertical pattern (from nation to smallest geographic unit) is constantly being strengthened, thereby weakening the small units in which we live, is it not fruitless to focus on a particular geographic unit?

The answer would have to be that this inordinate dependence on decisions made outside the client's lifespace, inevitably implemented in ways that create frustration for people, is in itself a frequent source of conflict for people. One way of addressing the conflict is to strengthen the community's horizontal patterns—by systematically developing the service milieu and the linkages between meaningful social institutions within the client's geographic community and extracommunity networks.[34] (See chapter 6 for an illustration.)

The concept of milieu, seen within the larger frame of systemic interdependence, leads us to another major mechanism for helping people to develop mutually beneficial relationships with other people and institutions. It is the new, expanded team.

The Team Helper System

This team may be interprofessional within social work, or it may be composed of people from many disciplines, including the community at large. It may be a combination of both. The size and the composition of the team in each setting also varies, depending on the philosophy of the particular setting, the problem on which the team works, and the purposes, the resources, and the interventions available to each team. The new team is inevitably enlarged under the philosophy that all persons related to the problem at issue should be included in it. Reference is made in this book to the formal inclusion of children's parents on the team in roles that minimize the formerly sharp distinctions between staff and client group. The concepts of family-centered, comprehensive care and continuity of care have led to the creation of many new team members in roles recently enacted only in the client's home (such as home health aide and mental health agent) and in social institutions (patient care representative, ombudsman). The notion of the team as providing a realistic life model for people with particular problems—for instance, alcoholism—results in teams balanced between recovered alcoholics and nonalcoholics. (See chapter 11.)

That the new manpower not only augments previously limited helping resources but also expands help in different directions has recently been documented. There was great resistance both inside and outside the social work profession to moving from the solo social work practitioner (in primary settings) and the traditional team (in secondary settings) to the modern team characterized in most of this book's chapters. On the basis of my special research interest in manpower, I wish to underscore the point— that despite the sweeping changes in the helping system recorded in this book, significant resistance to the new team still exists.[35]

The objective student and practitioner should study this phenomenon and its complex educational, social, and political implications. Only then will the continuing complaint of "lack of teamwork" be understood in the face of the real data about existing teams and team possibilities.[36]

A major rationale for the alliances described in this book between many professional, paraprofessional, and lay community groups is that the limitations of the solo practitioner and the older team have recently become more evident. In addition, the proliferation of rights movements, patterned on the concept of civil rights, have led many people other than those with Master's degrees in social work to believe that they have something to contribute in helping people. The evidence from the world at large is that all people, regardless of age, social class, and diagnostic labels, now expect basic respect from care providers. It is not enough to preach respect for the inherent worth and dignity of each individual. These simple long-held humanistic values of social workers must be implemented in the relationships of the helping team.

There is evidence, too, in this book that people are being competently helped by an expanding range of helpers and that on the larger social scene, our alliances with trade unionists, other professionals, and people formerly designated as "clients" (blue-collar union members, foster parents, and natural parents) have potential for strengthening our weak political power base and for helping us become effective in areas where we were previously ineffective. They are especially able to apply pressure on legislators to provide laws that help rather than hinder practice interventions.

At the direct practice level, the advocate (called "social health advocate" or "family outreach worker" in health care and given other titles in other fields) has provided a role model for the professional social worker, as he demonstrated the utility of getting out of one's private office and into the client's lifespace. Much hard work in dealing with problems of housing, welfare, daily life tasks, and community liaison has been and continues to be done by people with no recognized professional credentials. The importance and acceptance of the advocacy role is evident in the fact that "case" and "cause" advocacy is now taught in professional social work education at the highest levels.

During the mid-1970s there was a proliferation of social work educational programs at the Bachelor's and Associate degree levels. The Bachelor of Social Work degree was recognized in 1969 by the National Association of Social Workers as the first professional level, an action not fully accepted by its entire membership. The necessary work in developing rational differential roles and functions within a systemic framework for manpower has hardly begun. The NASW policy statement, *Standards for Social Service Manpower,* represents a beginning step, outlining a six-level classification with suggested levels of practice and preparation. Testing out and feedback from practitioners across the country must follow.[37]

There are two diametrically opposed viewpoints about the new teams illustrated in this book. One, espoused by Madison in chapter 2 on child welfare, is that there should be very clear distinctions in expectations, tasks, and roles between the various team members within mutually defined service goals. In this model, the MSW is the team leader or manager and has primary responsibility for team operations. The second team pattern, illustrated in chapter 8 on the adolescent walk-in clinic, prefers undifferentiated roles to match the informal working style of the milieu. The personality and maturity of the helping person is considered primary. The "case" is no longer assigned formally through hierarchical channels from supervisor to worker. The adolescent consumer exercises his right to select from among the team of potential helpers in a milieu in which the personal style and methods of each helper are visible to colleagues and consumers alike. Peer-group review is built into regular staff meetings among the helper system, with safeguards for poor fit between client and helper. Professionals and paraprofessionals are trained together in the milieu with the goal of developing a mutual support system for staff.

Even in the less differentiated team structures, however, there are divisions of labor, sometimes of an informal nature. The important function of providing information and referral (termed access services) is usually performed by community members, volunteers, and others lacking formal AA, BSW, or MSW credentials. At the other end of the continuum, critical decisions in the client's life, requiring complex professional judgments based on skilled assessment, tend automatically to be referred to the

most highly trained personnel available within all team structures. Understandably, in newer settings, roles are at first quite
blurred. It takes time to evolve rational differentiation, divested of
considerations marked by bias and vested interest.

Perhaps the greatest influence on team composition and division of labor and responsibilities is the number of social workers
available and their distribution by educational level within each
field and major method. The latest overview of social service
manpower for 1980 predicts considerable continued growth of
master's degree and baccalaureate programs, with employment
conservatively estimated at 402,000, an 85 percent increase over
the actual 217,000 employed in 1970. Between 1960 and 1970,
there was massive expansion of Bachelor's and Associate degree
programs and of programs for personnel with less than a college
education ("New Careers," for example). Despite contraction in
many areas during the past few years and severe limitations in the
current data on employment by educational level and field, continuing expansion is anticipated, especially in mental health, aging, and all fields associated with health care delivery.[38] The
distribution of social service workers still varies from field to
field, with significant differences in the ratio of MSW to Bachelor
degree workers and Associate degree workers performing direct
service to clients. A large proportion of direct service interventions to clients is now performed by the Bachelor's degree
worker, for example, in the welfare, alcoholism, and health care
fields.

Bachelor's level workers need new knowledge for their service
interventions—specialized knowledge, such as alcohology in alcoholism, and core knowledge, such as the impact of illness and
hospitalization on patient and family. (See Berkman's classification in chapter 4.) Logically, the MSWs practicing in these and
other fields need greater core and specialized knowledge, too.
Haselkorn's reference to the complex social and psychological
dynamics of the abortion recidivist leaves no doubt of the "clinical" knowledge and skills necessary for this work. In addition,
there is a disturbing need for the professional to act as staff educator, trainer, team manager, and coordinator—and the recent
consensus is that the roles should be filled by the MSW.[39] Even in
fields where there is a high ratio of MSWs to workers at other
levels (as in community mental health)[40] and therefore fields in

which the MSW can stay with direct service functions, social workers are moving towards administrative management and team leadership. Indeed, recently the MSW was recognized as being formally qualified to become director of community mental health centers, a post formerly limited to physicians.

Thus, regardless of team composition, division of labor, or role definition, the new team constitutes a fundamental change in the world of practice. The social worker practitioner has become a formal educator for staff as well as lifespace educator for clients. Even the private practitioner, supported by third party payments, tends to be an educator and a consultant for some service, working in tandem with indigenous aides and representatives of other professional disciplines. No one has escaped involvement in a working team.

Effective training programs must be devised. Knowledge of the group process, of learning-teaching concepts, generic principles of supervision, curriculum building, and of andragogy—the science of adult learning—requires translation into goal and task oriented training procedures tailored to program goals and projected personnel needs.[41] The would-be social work educator must use all the sensitivity he possesses in work with clients, become aware of his own biases, and develop imaginative nonhurting ways of opening nontraditionally trained colleagues to those prejudices that disrupt their good work with clients. Here one treads on delicate ground, especially with so-called indigenous staff who often have much in common with clients to be helped and often predict clients' real-life behavior more accurately than their "professional" educators do.[42] Similarities (of race, religion, social class, neighborhood residence, or background of illness or social dysfunction) can be used positively to develop empathy between client and helper. Knowledge born of this empathy can be shared with those helping persons who come from dissimilar backgrounds. But some of those very attitudes and problems with which the professional helper is trying to help the client may exist among the indigenous workers, too, and this is known to compound the professional's helping and training efforts. Nor are we unaware of the phenomenon of antitherapeutic group processes that are beginning to blight some of our newly hallowed teams and peer-helper groups. Especially in large hierarchical organizations, there is danger of diffusion of responsibility and creation of an anarchic ambience for the client. The team idea can become a nightmarish abstraction if not one qualified person is available at the right moment and truly accountable for making important decisions for needy patients, or if too much risk is spread lightly over several partially responsible heads. An appropriate balance must be found between the old rigid linear hierarchy between social work supervisor and supervisee and the more mature, autonomous functioning encouraged by the new style team's collegial milieu.

Interdependence and Integration

Thus, the team helper system must be seen in terms of its consequences for becoming more accountable to clients; it must also be seen within the larger frame of systemic interdependence. The more that programs and fields grow, differentiating and specializing one from another, the more they need mechanisms of integration. This is especially true as modern technology makes us increasingly interdependent—one person upon another, person to person, group to group, profession to profession, and communities to nations.

In the aggregate, the interdependent changes reported in this book are not radical. No truly large-scale systems changes have taken place. Some are anticipated—for instance, national health insurance and welfare reform—based on political changes. Understandably, we have no illusions about instituting broad-scale social change through the medium of social work services and practice. Nor do we harbor illusions that revolutionary changes have taken place at the direct service level. With the exception of the social impact of contraceptive and cybernetic technologies, the changes reported in this book are more evolutionary than revolutionary. The case illustrations suggest that little steps are still as much as most clients can take. No miracles have been wrought by proliferating group, family, and team-community approaches. The newer acceptance of the therapist's right to a personal style of work (under Gestalt influence), coupled with the conviction that the helper at every educational level must be human rather than a blank screen on which the client projects his problems, has wrought subtle changes in relationship. The use of communications theory and technology in training staff and in helping target populations has resulted in greater emphasis on observing not only what is being said, but tone of voice and facial and bodily expressions in experiential transactions between people. Yet, observational, communicational, and other skills central to social work practice, are gained only over time and with repeated and sustained experience.

Thus a steady, highly modest, and long overdue beginning is being made by practitioners and policy makers alike in recasting their conceptions of both larger and smaller frames for practice and in realizing the implications of these for facilitating constructive changes within the client's lifespace. Admittedly, the gaps in implementation are disturbingly larger than the successful demonstrations.

Gaps in Implementation of Change

Realistic deficits—lack of funding or categorically restricted funding, lack of planning or power base, gaps in the profession's knowledge base and methodology—clearly delay the processes of constructive change.[43] And the contemporary scene provides many illustrations of reversals of constructive change in a society that is struggling to learn how to manage contraction rather than boundless growth. For example, the fate of many existing local community structures, such as the adolescent mental health storefront, currently hang in the balance, victims of inflation and an inhospitable climate toward social services. This is especially true for the newer, more experimental structures, which lack the seniority of the more established ones and, more important, are not income-producing. Preventive programs tend to fall in this category.[44]

If there is controversy about whether, how, or when the social worker should intervene before problems develop, there is little controversy about the necessity for aftercare in the community. Yet in every field and setting, this crucial variable is seriously neglected. The solid consensus in this book, in the professional literature, in the newspapers, and in the field is that what happens to the child, the adolescent, or the adult, once he leaves the hospital, the clinic, or the agency program, will probably be more important than anything that happened to him while under care. Infinitely more significant than the program's theoretical or methodological stance (whether it follows insight therapy or behavior modification or takes an individual or family or small group approach) is what happens after the social worker's intervention is completed.

Another glaring need is for more comprehensive feedback on change efforts—including client feedback.[45] Whittaker points out that evaluation need not be highly sophisticated. The new expanded team, interprofessional and multidisciplinary, could provide a rich setting for planning ongoing action research. Hard data for assessment is scarce, since much of the practice is too recent to have benefited from research. Nor was research evaluation built into programs from their inception, as is necessary in order to begin to realize the concept of accountability, mentioned frequently in this book. It is also true that many of the newer values—right to treatment, equity of care, comprehensive care, continuity of care, all prominent in newer programs—show social work's influence in shaping philosophy and practice in the diverse, specialized fields addressed. Yet the profession cannot take for granted a rigorous implementation of these values into the 1980s.

Practice Change Within Larger Social Change

To set the stage for viewing structural and ideological change at any given time, the reader should keep in mind that our practice changes are only tiny parts of large waves of social and political change, sometimes referred to as social and humanitarian movements. Characteristic of each such humanitarian movement are four distinct periods—innovation, peaking, criticism, and retrenchment. The first is a period of innovation or new ideas. The peak occurs soon after implementation as problems dim enthusiasm. This pattern was evident in the community mental health and antipoverty social programs between 1965 and 1970. Waves of criticism, in part brought about by overloading the system for implementing the new trend, are followed by a time of retrenchment. This, in turn, stimulates problemsolving and planning before a new and lengthier period of innovation can be entered.

Thus, to maintain a sense of perspective concerning contemporary changing practice critical questions must be asked. Are we separating the wheat from the chaff of change? Can we distinguish the valuable new ideas that deserve to be put to use from fleeting slogans and gimmicky therapies that decline for lack of a sustaining scientific base? Yet more to the point, has time-tested knowledge been prematurely discarded in this fast-moving, throwaway society?

The responses to these questions constitute this book's complex subject. I do not promise that questions will be answered evenly and comprehensively. The reader should be mindful that each chapter contributor's choice of changes to be emphasized is influenced by many factors, including the individual's own philosophical stance, employment experience, and geographic location. Compared with the social work educator, who typically must spend a large proportion of time reading the literature, the full-time practitioner in the field forms a somewhat different, more pragmatic world view. Similarly, practice on the East Coast has a longer and stronger psychoanalytic tradition, making it at first more receptive to modern ego psychology, Gestalt and ecological systems developments than to behavior modification theory. In contrast, other parts of the country moved towards behavioral psychology and other frames much earlier, introducing ego psychological and ecological emphases only recently. "Generic" social work practice was adopted earlier and became more prevalent in the Midwest than in other parts of the country.

Despite these differences, it should be noted that many practice operations differ more in semantics than substance, since practice is highly pragmatic. Siporin notes this in his discussion of the newer pluralistic eclectic character of social work practice:

Psychoanalytic insight is called discrimination learning in sociobehavioral theory; supportive and motivating techniques are understood as reinforcement, personality may be referred to as a behavioral repertoire or potential. The psychoanalytic procedures of making maladaptive behavior ego-dystonic may also be understood as introducing cognitive dissonance or aversive behavior. A frequent helping action of the social worker is to demonstrate and to teach clients what is variously called interpersonal sensitivity, interpersonal competence, empathy or compathy.[46]

Nonetheless, it is real rather than semantic diversity which is addressed in this book's chapters. Practice-milieu and team are now seen as the core of intervention. Imaginative uses of these and other elements of the helping situation are the tools of the creative practitioner who is flexible and adaptable enough to respond to societal change with appropriate interventive changes at multiple case and policy levels. Newer milieus developed to fit technological advances will provide laboratories for future interventions. In recent conferences and symposia, some referred to in this book, there are harbingers of improved collaboration between allied disciplines and their diverse methods (for example between the behaviorist and the psychotherapist), based on the growing realization that eclectic practice approaches provide more rapid, efficient, and inexpensive interventions than do distinctly separated and mutually exclusive ones.[47]

Clearly, the practice procedures of what Germain identifies as the "ecological-systems paradigm" for social work are not yet fully defined. Human ecology within a systemic framework is considered more likely to hold potential to respond to societal change and thereby to strengthen social work practice in the long run, however, than are narrowed and more parochial paradigms.[48]

We want to enable man to live in better harmony with his changing environment; this entails trying to understand what is changeable and what is permanent in human life.[49] With this lofty and ambitious purpose in mind, the chapters of this book have been written. The reader is invited to join with chapter authors in their modest efforts to understand and to help people more effectively in this changing society of ours.

Notes

1. Carel B. Germain, "An Ecological Perspective in Casework Practice," *Social Casework* 54 (1973): 323–30. For an introduction to this perspective in social work practice, see Max Siporin, *Introduction to Social Work Practice*. (New York City: Macmillan Co., 1975). For illustration of the ecological field and its problems, see Lynn Hoffman and Lorence Long, "A Systems Dilemma," in *Family Process* 8 (Sept. 1969): 211–34, reprinted in Allen Pincus and Anne Minahan, eds., *Social Work Practice: Model and Method* (Itasca, Ill.: F. E. Peacock Publishers, 1973), pp. 309–29. For derivation of the concept of ecology, see Amos Hawley, *Human Ecology* (New York: Ronald Press, 1950), p. 84.

2. Harriett M. Bartlett, "Characteristics of Social Work," in *Building Social Work Knowledge* (New York City: National Association of Social Workers, 1964), pp. 1–5. For philosophical base, see Gordon Hearn, *The General Systems Approach: Contributions Towards a Holistic Conception of Social Work* (New York City: Council on Social Work Education, 1971). Both provide background for understanding this concept.

3. For elaboration of this point, see Levy and Rowitz, *The Ecology of Mental Disorder* (New York City: Behavioral Publications, 1973), p. 143.

4. See *Work in America,* Report of a Special Task Force to the Secretary of HEW (Cambridge, Mass.: MIT Press, 1972). For a nontechnical discussion of real-life attitudes toward working, see Studs Terkel, *Working* (New York City: Pantheon, 1974).

5. Eileen M. Corrigan, *Problem Drinkers Seeking Treatment* (New Brunswick, N.J.: Publications Division, Rutgers Center of Alcohol Studies, 1974).

6. National Institute of Mental Health statistics, based on statistical breakdown of a sample survey in October 1972 of the year's 403,924 admissions.

7. *New York Times,* 20 November 1975, p. 1.

8. Lawrence Kolb, professor of psychiatry, Columbia University Physicians and Surgeons, addressing Annual Symposium of Taylor Manor Hospital, Elliott City, Maryland; reported in "As the economy goes down, so goes the nation's psyche," *Frontiers of Psychiatry* 5 (15 Oct. 1975).

9. See Blanche Bernstein, Donald Snider, and William Meezan, eds., *Foster Care Needs and Alternatives to Placement: A Projection for 1975–1985,* (New York City: New School for Social Research, 1975) for documentation of increasing pathology and behavioral disturbance among adolescents noted in all facilities.

10. For the organic approach, increasingly emphasized in settings where social workers practice, see Camilla Anderson, *Society Pays: The High Cost of Minimal Brain Damage in America* (New York City: Walker and Co., 1972).

11. Harold W. Demone and Dwight Harshberger, *A Handbook of Human Service Organizations* (New York City: Behavioral Publications, 1974), p. 7.

12. Francine Sobey, *The Nonprofessional Revolution in Mental Health* (New York and London: Columbia University Press, 1970); Alan Gartner, *Paraprofessionals and Their Performances* (New York City: Praeger Publishers, 1971); Barker and Briggs, *Using Teams to Deliver Social Services* (New York: Syracuse University Press, 1969).

13. Bernstein, Snider, and Meezan, *Foster Care Needs,* pp. 3–4.

14. Vondracek, Urban, and Parsonage, "Feasibility of an automated intake procedure for human service workers," *Social Service Review* 48 (No. 2, 1974): 271–78.

15. Barbara Gordon Berkman and Helen Rehr, "Unanticipated Consequences of the Casefinding System in Hospital Social Service," *Social Work* 15 (April 1970): 63–70.

16. Genevieve Oxley, "A life model approach to change," *Social Casework* (Dec. 1971); Joanne Gumpert, Beula Rothman, and Gladys Simons, "Natural parents as partner in child care placement," (April 1973), pp. 224–32; Anthony Maluccio, "Action as a tool in casework practice," *Social Casework* (Jan. 1974), pp. 30–36.

17. Howard Goldstein, *Social Work Practice: A Unitary Approach* (Columbia: University of South Carolina Press, 1973), pp. 165–81; D. Jehu, *Learning Theory and Social Work* (London: Routledge and Kegan Paul, 1967). Harold Werner, "Cognitive Theory," in *Social Work Treatment,* ed. by Francis Turner (New York City: Free Press, 1964). Anthony Graziano, *Behavior Therapy with Children* (Chicago: Aldin-Atherton, 1971); Joel Fischer, ed., *Applied Behavior Change* (New York City: Free Press, 1975).

18. For recent textbooks which retain these emphases, see George Wiedeman, *Personality Development and Deviation: A Textbook for Social Work* (New York City: International Universities Press, 1975). Judith C. Nelson, "Dealing with resistance in social work practice," *Social Casework* 56 (Dec. 1975): 587–92.

19. Richard A. Cloward and Irwin Epstein, "Private Social Welfare's Disengagement from the Poor: The Case of Family Adjustment Agencies," in *Social Welfare Institutions: A Sociological Reader,* ed. by Meyer N. Zald (New York City: John Wiley and Sons, 1965), pp. 623–44; Scott Briar, "The Casework Predicament," *Social Work* 13 (Jan. 1968): 5–11; Joel Fischer, "Has Mighty Casework Struck Out?" *Social Work* (July 1973) pp. 107–10.

20. Early theory and models for anticipatory counseling can be found in Irving L. Janis, "Emotional Innoculation: Theory and Research in Effects of Preparatory Communications," in *Psychoanalysis and the Social Sciences* (New York City: International Universities Press, 1958). See also Donald C. Klein and Erich Lindemann, "Preventive Intervention in Individual and Family Crisis Situations," in *Prevention of Mental Disorders in Children,* ed. by Gerald Caplan (New York City: Basic Books, 1961); Gerald Caplan, *Principles of Preventive Psychiatry* (New York City: Basic Books, 1964); Erich Lindemann, "Symptomatology and Management of Acute Grief," in *Crisis Intervention: Selected Readings,* ed. by Howard J. Parad (New York City: Family Service Association of America, 1965).

21. Allen Bergin and Hans H. Strupp, *Changing Frontiers in the Science of Psychotherapy,* (Chicago: Aldine-Atherton, 1972) pp. 6–99. William Reid and Ann Shyne, *Brief and Extended Casework* (New York City: Columbia University Press, 1969); William J. Reid and Laura Epstein, *Task-Centered Casework* (New York City: Columbia University Press, 1972). Reported success with task-centered casework models has led to its application to work with groups; see for example, Charles Garvin, "Task-Centered Group Work," *Social Service Review* 48 (No. 4, Dec. 1974): 494–507.

22. J. P. Zweig and J. Z. Csank of Sir George Williams University, Montreal, report successful stress-prevention intervention at the large

organization level in their "Effects of Relocation on Chronically Ill
Geriatric Patients of Medical Unit," *Journal of Geriatric Society* 23
(1975): 132–36. For background, see D. C. Aquiler and J. M. Messick,
Crisis Intervention: Theory and Methodology (St. Louis: C. V. Mosby
and Co., 1974); E. Schulman, *Intervention in Human Services* (St.
Louis: C. V. Mosby and Co., 1974).

23. Max Siporin, *Social Work Practice,* pp. 159–349.

24. Mary Richmond, *Friendly Visiting Among the Poor; A Handbook
for Charity Workers* (New York City: Macmillan Co., 1899). See Arthur
Fink, *The Field of Social Work,* 6th ed. (New York City: Holt, Rinehart
and Winston, 1974), especially "Origins of Social Settlements," pp.
43–48, and bibliography. See Harry Stack Sullivan, "Socio-psychiatric
research: its implications for the schizophrenia problem and for mental
hygiene," *American Journal of Psychiatry* 10 (1931): 977–91; Alfred H.
Stanton and Schwartz, *The Mental Hospital* (New York City: Basic
Books, 1954); Elaine Cumming and John Cumming, *Ego and the Milieu*
(New York City: Atherton Press, 1962).

25. For full discussion of this milieu, see H. Banta and Renee C. Fox,
"Role Strains of a Health Care Team in a Poverty Community (The
Columbia Point Experience)," in *Social Science and Medicine* 6 (Great
Britain: Pergamon Press, 1972): 697–722.

26. Davies Martin, "The assessment of environment in social work
research," *Social Casework* 55 (Jan. 1974): 3–12.

27. Richard Brandon, "Social Pathology or Class Victimization," in
Handbook of Evaluation Research 2, ed. by Elmer Struening and Marcia
Guttentag (Beverly Hills, Calif.: Sage Publications, 1975).

28. E. Pattison, University of California at Irvine, evaluated various
types of groups and found those with specific behavioral aims (e.g.,
Alcoholics Anonymous) or a definite service to perform to be more
effective than highly accessible drop-in centers (e.g., Golden Age Clubs)
or rap groups that do not make specific demands or structure frameworks for helping. Reported in "Goal-less mental health groups score
low in therapeutic potency," *Frontiers of Psychiatry* 5 (No. 17, 15 Oct.
1975).

29. Banta and Fox, "The Columbia Point Experience."

30. To illustrate, an extensive study of Japanese men living in the San
Francisco Bay area found that those who have become westernized have
a heart disease rate 2.5 times higher than those who cling to traditional
ways (the latter have the same low incidence of heart disease that men in
Japan do). The stresses of the American lifestyle, especially competition
and haste, seem to account for the differences, rather than factors such
as diet, smoking, etc. Preliminary findings reported in "Study of
Japanese Americans Indicates Stress Can Be a Major Factor in Heart
Disease," *New York Times,* 5 August 1975.

31. Gene Abrams, "Defining Milieu Therapy," *Archives of General
Psychiatry,* vol. 21, no. 5.

32. Roland Warren, *The Community in America* (Chicago: Rand
MacNally, 1963).

33. National Goals Research Staff, *Towards Balanced Growth: Quantity and Quality* (Washington, D.C.: U.S. Government Printing Office, 1970), p. 175.

34. Warren, *Community in America,* 2nd ed. (1972), p. 320.

35. See Margaret Purvine, ed., *Educating MSW Students to Work with Other Social Welfare Personnel* (New York City: Council on Social Work Education, 1973), especially chapters by Thomas Briggs, "Social Work Manpower: Developments and Dilemmas of the 1970s" and Francine Sobey, "New Educational Content for a Changing Social Work Practice: Focus on Manpower"; see also Ira M. Steisel and William Adamson, "The Use and Training of Allied Mental Health Workers in Child Guidance Clinics," *The Journal of Child Psychiatry,* vol. 13, no. 3 (Summer 1974).

36. Lack of teamwork was a major complaint voiced at the 27th Annual Institute of the American Psychiatric Association, Washington, D.C., Oct. 1975: opening address by Alyce C. Gullattee, Chairperson of Program Committee.

37. National Association of Social Workers, *Standards for Social Service Manpower* (Washington, D.C.: NASW, 1974); see also Chauncey A. Alexander, "Implications of the NASW Standards for Social Service Manpower," *Journal of Education for Social Work* 11 (Winter 1975): 3–8.

38. Sheldon Siegal, *Social Service Manpower Needs: An Overview to 1980* (New York City: Council on Social Work Education, 1975), p. 17. In recognition of the expected expansion, a new journal appeared in Feb. 1976, specializing in medical and psychiatric social work, *Social Work in Health Care.*

39. Siegel, *Manpower Needs,* p. 17.

40. Based on figures given by Carl Taube, National Institute of Mental Health.

41. William Dyer, *Modern Theory and Method in Group Training* (Washington, D.C.: NTL Learning Resources Corp., 1972); M. Miles, *Learning to Work in Groups* (New York City: Columbia University Press, 1959). E. R. Hilgard and G. H. Bower, *Theories of Learning* (New York City: Appleton-Century-Crofts, 1966); Beulah Rothman, "Perspectives on Learning and Teaching in Continuing Education," *Journal of Education for Social Work* 9 (Spring 1973); Mary L. Somers, "Contribution of Learning and Teaching Theories to the Explication of the Role of the Teacher in Social Work Education," *Journal of Education for Social Work* 5 (Fall 1969). See Edwina T. Leon, "The MSW as Supervisor of Paraprofessionals," in *Educating MSW Students,* ed. by Purvine, pp. 38–48. See Purvine, ed., appendix for illustrations of curriculum-building; see also E. Brawley and R. Schindler, eds., *Community and Social Service Education in the Community College: Issues and Characteristics* (New York City: Council on Social Work Education, 1972), chapter on curriculum; Schulman, *Intervention in Human Services* (St. Louis: Mosby, 1974). Malcolm Knowles, "Innovations in Teaching Styles," *Journal of Education for Social Work* 8 (2): 32–39.

42. This data is reported in Sobey, *The Nonprofessional Revolution;* for specialized research, see Victor B. Cline, "Ability to Judge Personality Assessed with a Stress Interview and Sound-Film Technique," *Journal of Abnormal and Social Psychology* 50 (1955): 183–87.

43. For realistic problems, see Robert R. Alford, *Health Care Politics* (Chicago: University of Chicago Press, 1974); for gaps in the profession's knowledge base, see Alfred Kadushin, "Assembling Social Work Knowledge," in *Building Social Work Knowledge,* pp. 1–5.

44. Urie Bronfenbrenner, "Is Early Intervention Effective?" in *Handbook of Evaluation Research* 2.

45. See approach of John E. Mayer and Noel Timms, *The Client Speaks: Working-Class Impressions of Casework* (New York City: Atherton Press, 1970).

46. Max Siporin, *Social Work Practice,* p. 155.

47. Report of APA Task Force on Behavior Therapy in Psychiatry, reported in *Frontiers of Psychiatry,* 15 Nov. 1973, p. 8.

48. Carel Germain, "Ecological Dimensions of Space and Time in Social Work Practice," unpublished address, Staff Institute, Division of Family Counseling, Center for Human Services, Cleveland, Ohio, 7 Dec. 1973.

49. Rene Dubos, *Beast or Angel?: Choices that make us human* (New York: Scribner and Sons, 1974); see also previous writings of Rene Dubos, *So Human An Animal* and *A God Within,* for the holistic and humanistic philosophy underlying the modern purposes of social work and allied professions.

2

Changing Directions in Child Welfare Services

BERNICE Q. MADISON

*Child welfare services must be seen as systems and not as
discrete programs if social workers are to meet children's
needs more effectively. The practical implications of this
view, both in relation to society's policies as they affect
children and families and the internal policies of agencies
serving children and families, are presented in this
chapter.*

*The author's conviction is that social work practice and
objectives will more fully utilize the worker's skills once
key elements of modern organizational and managerial
technology are applied to information, delivery, and
management systems in child welfare. Ways of improving
communication, decision making, and teamwork between
agency, client, and community are presented. New and
more flexible interventions to keep children in their own
homes and to improve foster care and adoption are
considered.*

*The inter–social work and the multidisciplinary team
model for improving the quality of services to children is
highlighted as having major potential for this field of
practice.*

IN the field of child welfare, practice during the past decade
has been affected by a number of changes—some already widely
implemented, others as yet in the experimental or testing stage,
and still others proposed or actively discussed. There is space
here to examine only those innovations that appear to have the
greatest promise.

Delivering and Managing Child Welfare Services

Social work skills cannot be fully utilized to benefit children
within an outmoded, cumbersome, and ineffective system of de-

livering and managing child welfare services. Practitioners have increasingly deplored the uneven, uncoordinated, and improperly organized delivery of services in ways often misunderstood by the intended beneficiaries, with the result that they are minimally used and supported. The system now in operation can be transformed into a powerful tool for improving the quality of life for children, however, through the use of elements of modern organizational and managerial technology already being adapted to improve other human services. The two major areas awaiting such technology are the information system and the delivery and management system.

Information system

There is universal agreement that the child welfare field lacks "sound, up-to-date data on characteristics of children in care, services being offered, and the functioning of the system"[1]—and that "existing information retrieval systems as well as information processing methods are not meeting current day requirements."[2] These lacks and inadequacies are exacerbated by the vagueness surrounding legal definitions of key concepts, such as "neglect," leading to differences in interpretation among practitioners. Yet, considerable consensus exists on the kind of consistent, comprehensive information that should be available. Several innovative projects are especially promising.

1. ARENA. On a national level, one such undertaking is the Adoption Resource Exchange of North America, established by the Child Welfare League of America (CWLA) in 1967 as a clearinghouse to help agencies in the United States and Canada place children with special needs. It was developed as an additional resource for the forty-two state and regional exchanges, operated for the most part by state departments of public welfare, as well as for individual adoption agencies. ARENA gathers photographs and information about children awaiting adoption in different parts of the continent and makes them available to would-be adoptive parents. Its operation also improves the level of adoption practice by broadening the perspective of agencies, helps to standardize practices and procedures, and works to identify and eliminate legal barriers to interstate placement.[3]

In 1973, 827 agencies were registered with ARENA. This number included one or more agencies in all 50 states, the District of Columbia, Puerto Rico, the Virgin Islands, and 7 Canadian provinces. Between 1967 and 1973 it had facilitated the placement of 1,283 children.[4] In 1976, ARENA was incorporated into the North American Center on Adoption (NACA), which was created to increase public awareness of the large numbers of children, perhaps as many as 100,000, waiting for adoption and to help remove legal and other obstacles to placing them.

2. Michigan Tracking System. At present, this system takes in the private agency, institution, court, and state children in Michigan who live outside their own homes and whose parental custody has been disturbed by court action. By means of computerized and centralized arrangements, it stores and prepares monthly and other summary reports on the status of each child. These reports provide the basic initial documentation, revised and updated, needed for comprehensive reporting and require little clerical effort. Since the documentation is received by each agency and court concerned, it provides a tracking system for monitoring movement of a child from one court or agency jurisdiction to another. The system also produces summary statistical reports that fulfil court and state reporting requirements. Objectives of the system are (1) to assure that realistic plans are made for all children as quickly as possible after they enter care; (2) to facilitate achievement of these plans at the earliest possible time; (3) to identify areas of need for program improvement, expansion, or modification; and (4) to provide a base for social service and fiscal planning. Overall, the system hopes "to improve child care programs, encourage more rational decision making and thereby provide a means of optimizing available human and financial resources,"[5] The establishment of similar systems in each state, if intercompatible, would create a national tracking system.

3. The Social Service Information System (SSIS) of the East St. Louis Region of the Illinois Department of Children and Family Services. This system has been tested, assessed, and developed during the past four years and is by now implemented statewide. It responds to the need for "a reporting system that functions on an ongoing basis, is relatively simple in execution and takes into account staff time, caseloads, measurable staff accomplishments and operating costs." The system provides a realistic and helpful picture of the manner in which direct service staff allocate their time in relation to defined productivity meas-

ures and operating costs. The entire process is geared to helping set goals consistent with the "management-by-objectives" approach to administration. While the SSIS was not intended to be a vehicle for qualitative review, "much of the information it provides is useful for this purpose."[6]

4. CHILDATA. This system emanated from collaboration over a three-year period among sixteen child care agencies in the Chicago area and the Council for Community Services Research. They decided that "agencies not only have a right to good data systems, but an obligation to the community that supports them to maintain modern and efficient record systems that will improve their services and accountability." The system contains four types of information: client, family, service, and outcome data. One of its objectives is to incorporate "information for management to help monitor agency service systems, rather than build a statistical package only."[7]

5. The Nashville-Davidson (Tennessee) Linkage System. This is an integrated information system on a county level that links court, welfare, and institutional records of children who enter the child care network. Data have been collected for the years 1969 to 1973 and will continue to be collected for the duration of a three-year program that is being tested for its effects on improving the delivery of services to neglected and dependent children.[8]

6. The Edwin Gould Services for Children Management Information System. Developed within one agency, this system substitutes technology for the traditional manual method of collecting data. It is designed to accumulate a large and potentially useful data base on each child, to eliminate the use of "standard report forms," and to focus on outcomes as well as on service input. The latter is done by requiring caseworkers "to designate a planned goal for each child and estimate a date for achieving it." The system represents a method to relate the day-to-day operations of the agency to the increasing demand for program and service accountability.[9]

Delivery and management system

Among key elements that must be considered in modernizing such a system and making it responsive to changing needs are the following.

1. Organizational structure and relationships. Fragmented organization of child welfare services—separate units for day care, foster care, adoption, protective services, and so forth, some enjoying higher status than others—often results in fragmenting the child; that is, viewing him in relation to the needs of the bureaucracy rather than his own needs. Fragmentation leads to breakdowns in coordination, lack of cohesiveness in services, and rigidity in approaching what has to be done and how best to do it.

Crucial as well is the ranking of child welfare services within the agency's hierarchy—whether the element charged with child welfare is at the agency's highest administrative level or diffused among lower echelons.

Lack of organizational and staff coordination between the child welfare element and other elements within the agency is another widespread deficiency. This often results in disparate plans for the same child and in records that lack essential information. For example, records of foster children do not always indicate what, if any, medical care was made available, even when both welfare and health services are located within the same agency.

Failure to coordinate the efforts of a given agency or child welfare staff with other agencies involved also diminishes the effectiveness of services. Overly informal working relationships among various bodies may lead to coordination failures and misunderstanding about which agency should act on some critical responsibility. Formal working relationships are necessary, but it is equally important to avoid rigidity and to cultivate clear understanding and mutual support among all parties.

2. Promptness and accessibility of services. Substantial agreement exists that when a child requires services, he ought to get them in relation to his sense of time, rather than to an adult's sense of time—that is, as quickly as is compatible with competent decision making:

> The child's-sense-of-time guideline would require
> decisionmakers to act with "all deliberate speed" to
> maximize each child's opportunity either to restore stability
> to an existing relationship or to facilitate the establishment of
> new relationships to "replace" old ones. Procedural and
> substantive decisions should never exceed the time that the
> child-to-be-placed can endure loss and uncertainty.[10]

Yet, practice in child welfare is rife with delays that reflect adults' sense of time. That many of them are generated by outmoded laws is widely recognized.[11] Many stem from inadequate financing, funding that favors some programs over others, inadequate in both quantity and quality. Unnecessary delays may result from indecision about the potential of certain types of care for benefiting children or unexplicated differences in practice concepts. In many cases there is a lack of research on how well or poorly different types of care do in fact serve children and parents. Some delays may be caused when agency resources such as supervision, peer discussions, and psychiatric and other consultation are used in order not to have to make a decision.

Abuse of the child's sense of time often occurs when the administrative structure lacks devices for systematic case review. Early planning is frequently hampered by inaccessibility of service to those who require it. Hence, many children do not get needed services at all; others, by the time they reach the agency, are in emergency situations. To facilitate case finding and to avoid preventable emergencies, it may be desirable to decentralize services to neighborhoods; but this kind of decentralization may be costly.

3. Availability and relevance of services. As well as being prompt and accessible, services must meet individual needs. Services for children should represent a full range that begins with assistance to parents to sustain their parental role and ends with adoption. The agency's responsibility is to assure that the child is offered or referred to the appropriate type of service in this continuum. To avoid fragmentation, all services should be closely interrelated so that options are possible and the plan of choice is accessible. This again emphasizes the importance of thorough planning and coordination of the different agencies' services, as well as fixing responsibility for specific actions when referrals to other agencies are involved.

Also essential for a full continuum is the creation of new forms of services and the use of those already available in a differential framework. In relation to foster care, for example, Maluccio notes:

At the very least, it is possible to classify each foster home on the basis of the major purpose for which it is most suited.

The range of different types includes:
Temporary foster homes: for emergencies or for placement of infants.
Long-term homes: for children needing care indefinitely but who have meaningful relationships with their parents.
Permanent foster homes: for children whose parents are unavailable and for whom legal adoption is impossible or contra-indicated.
Treatment foster homes: for children with emotional disturbance.
Group homes: for children who are unable to tolerate the intimacy of a small family but who do not need the structure of an institution.
Work homes: for older adolescents on semiindependent status.[12]

Foster family group homes may be differentiated into agency-owned family group homes; agency-rented, family-owned group homes; group homes for low-functioning children; visiting foster home programs; and medical foster homes.[13] In adoption, diversified programs include regular adoption, quasi adoption, subsidized, single-parent, and transracial adoptions.[14]

Because children and their families increasingly need a variety of services, depending on their individual requirements, it can only restrict the options available to label some services as "best" while others are rated only as "good," "fair," or "poor." If a family or child does not need adoption, adoption is not the "best" solution for it. Rather, every service on the continuum must be seen as one service among many, and it is the quality of all services, their planned nature, their availability and accessibility when needed that are the crucial elements.[15]

4. Duplicating and overlapping services. Resource limitations often dictate centralization of services and facilities to cut down overhead and administrative costs while service accessibility may seem to dictate decentralization. In centralization, the duplication of facilities and services is diminished or eliminated, while decentralization brings up the problems of providing accessibility and availability of services without duplication and overlap. Some have argued that overlapping of services is not necessarily an evil, and that different organizational elements

may focus on different types of intervention for the same case. Others point out that governmental funds go only where comprehensive planning can be shown. Undoubtedly, some middle ground exists. The solution, perhaps, is better coordination rather than complete elimination of overlapping services.

5. Continuity and flow of services. That "continuity of relationships, surroundings, and environmental influence are essential for a child's normal development" is known and accepted.[16] Decentralization and organizational fragmentation may bring with them the danger of disruption of services which may, in turn, interrupt the continuity of the child's relationships and surroundings. Not only the child loses when continuity is interrupted. Even the most intensive and skilled services may be largely wasted if a fragmented bureaucracy is permitted to pull a child out of a carefully constructed plan, or if decentralization is interpreted to mean that follow-up of a child to maintain a permanent benign living situation is not necessary.

Again, it seems clear that the solution lies in a unified organizational structure and in improved coordination and communication among agencies and between different elements within an agency.

6. Involving the community. Failure to involve the community in providing services is likely to hinder the introduction of improvements in services or to make difficult their implementation. Genuine and continuing involvement is often able to strengthen services both quantitatively and qualitatively and to maintain them at a high level. The child welfare field will severely limit what it can accomplish unless it examines child-related issues in the larger social context. For example, in discussing black adoption, Madison and Schapiro wrote:

> Agency efforts to increase and improve adoption for black children, however genuine and persistent, take place within larger societal forces—social, economic, and psychological—which exert a powerful influence and which are not subject to agency control. In addition to the continuing insufficient number of black persons seeking children to adopt in relation to the number of black children available and the continuing high illegitimacy rates among

blacks—one cannot ignore the slow and uneven nature of the decline in poverty and the relative stability of the indexes of family breakdown and dependency. All this is aggravated by spreading megalopolises, social upheavals, a deteriorating environment, and institutional racism that is still of destructive proportions.[17]

Community involvement is taking place at federal, state, and local levels, by groups diversified in composition and organizational patterns. For example, a new foster care constituency has been created by the emergence of foster parent organizations on both local and national levels. At the first National Foster Parent Conference, held in May 1971, there were 851 delegates; at the fourth, held in April 1974, there were 2,000 delegates and every state was represented.[18] In California, a symposium on services to children and youth, initiated and supported by the state assembly, determined "that the basic problems are only partially within the structure of the system" and went on to propose a wide-ranging series of legislative initiatives.[19] An effort to stimulate one type of community involvement at the municipal level is the recently created Assembly Select Committee on San Diego foster care programs. During hearings its chairman noted, "In Sacramento there are 537 registered lobbyists all up there to protect business and to make sure the 537 loopholes are written in. There is only one lobbyist for kids. I think this is one of the problems."[20]

At the level of particular agencies, the principal forms of community involvement have been advisory committees composed of representatives of various lay and professional groups, and the use of indigenous and community workers as social service staff. These forms have not been uniformly effective, which suggests a need to develop new forms of community participation. There is a compelling need for a more direct, on-going involvement of consumers in the everyday delivery of services.

7. Producing measurable results. In child welfare, as in other areas of social work practice, failure to produce results stems not only from definitional vagueness in defining children's problems but also from an inability to state objectives so that outcomes can be measured in quantified terms. To some, setting clear and pre-

cise parameters and stating goals in measurable terms would tend to put program focus on results rather than processes, on output rather than input—and this, they feel, would have a narrowing effect. Others believe that improved definitions are essential to long-range planning, priority-setting, cost analyses, statistical systems, studies of expenditures, definition of work-load standards, and measurement of effectiveness.[21] The latter view is certainly more compatible with the growing insistence by Congress and various levels of administration for more accountability in social service programs. HEW has urged the states to require reporting on the effectiveness of *"results"* of services and the establishment of "goal-oriented" social services systems, characterized by consistency in definition, by systematic and reliable tools for measuring effectiveness, and by program and budget accountability. The old criteria for effectiveness in social work was whether clients were able to reduce their dependence on state aid. With services and funding now operating at quite separate levels, the services must be justified. There is an urgent need for a more consistent and successful response to the requirement for accountability. Dilemmas encountered in making such responses are well understood.[22] Ways of dealing with them are being developed.

With the possible exception of ARENA, all of the information systems described earlier contribute to improved accountability. Michigan's tracking system, by monitoring reviews and actions, makes possible centralized accountability control over each case. The entire SSIS, and especially its review and evaluation features, are accountability-oriented. The CHILDATA system was designed to improve accountability as well as services. The management information system developed by the Edwin Gould Services for Children has assisted program directors, supervisors, and caseworkers "in meeting more effectively the needs of their clients, and in evaluating the overall results of their efforts, thereby adding a valuable dimension to the agency's program and service accountability."[23]

8. Staffing. The most important changes in staffing patterns seem to have come about as a result of complaining less about shortages of qualified manpower—a persistent theme until the mid-1960s—and concentrating more on what is now seen as a chronic maldistribution and malutilization of personnel. It is now

recognized that while the trained and experienced professional is still the key resource for child welfare work, the total manpower system requires proper utilization and distribution of people with varying degrees and varieties of skills—an appropriate mix of skills. Programs are using social workers with MSW degrees in combination with those who have earned BA degrees in social work and those with a lesser amount of social work education or with none at all. The organizational structure of the agency and the scope and nature of its operations determine the appropriate mix.

The distinction between activities that ought to be the exclusive province of the MSW and those appropriate for people with lesser amounts of social work education or with no such education is a difficult one. Various attempts to draw lines have been attempted and various manpower utilization patterns have been suggested.

Some attention has also been given to the need for a more direct, ongoing involvement of social work consumers in the everyday delivery of services. This has been recognized, for example, in making foster parents participants in decision-making, that is, bringing them into the process as colleagues, persons of equal station and importance. Writes Reistroffer:

> Engagement in planning and decision making on a collegial basis would require major adjustments in the colleagues' self-perceptions, as well as costly practice adjustments. It would require all to surmount the high hurdles of contention, mistrust and bias, and to begin to work together. Clearly, the high rate of failure and replacement in foster family care demands this level of communication and effective efforts.[24]

A successful effort to develop effective communication and teamwork between foster parents and agency staff, reported by Daniels and Brown, describes one important outcome:

> The awareness they gained of the constraints which were placed on the agency by other institutions was one of the more positive developments which occurred. . . . As they began to see the total system in which the agency operated, they began to think in terms of system change.[25]

There is also considerable agreement that it is essential to involve natural parents, including fathers of children born out of wedlock, but the effort in their case is to help them "to work toward being a part of a plan to resolve foster care for their child,"[26] or to increase the "ability of the parent and the child to maintain family identification and feelings of closeness during placement,"[27] or to participate in permanent planning for their children. In other words, agencies are exploring ways of involving natural parents more actively in treatment rather than—as in the case of foster parents—encouraging them to become colleagues.

A modern management system

Perhaps one of the most comprehensive attempts to deal with these crucial issues is contained in the report of a three-year research and demonstration project, published in 1973. One of this project's three objectives was to design a model for achieving improvement in the delivery and management of child welfare services—specifically, in a county department of social services, but applicable, with modifications, to voluntary agencies and larger governmental systems as well. The findings

indicate that the issues that currently frustrate the efficient delivery of child welfare services . . . are common to all large organizations charged with providing services to people, whatever their nature. Consequently, it was possible for the management consultants affiliated with the Project to apply to the model they designed for a delivery system for child welfare services, the knowledge and experience gained in other large public service operations. The design process included appropriate adaptations, to enhance the usefulness and relevance of the model in its particular setting. Each issue is addressed in some detail and, in addition, example applications show *how* to create and apply the model in "real life." For this purpose, detailed illustrative materials are furnished which show how modern, dynamic management systems can be applied in child welfare organizations. At this point in the turbulent evolution of public social services, one special interest is how to establish "goal-oriented" social service systems, characterized by consistency in services, by systematic and reliable tools for measuring the effectiveness of services, and by program and budget accountability.[28]

The research team that produced the model hopes that agencies will undertake intelligent experimentation to test it in real life, to modify it as necessary, and to use it effectively. They stress that

> underlying [this] service model is the concept of dynamic management . . . [This concept] implies that administration is not stabilized but alert to new developments and to new requirements. As a minimum, it is necessary to clearly define the mission of the agency, establish the policies and goals needed to accomplish the mission, and organize operations for maximum effectiveness and coordination of effort. Such a system also must include a functional management control system to plan, program and budget for effective use and control of resources.[29]

In regard to staffing, after an exhaustive review of the literature and a careful study of the implications of employing a variety of manpower utilization patterns as they relate to the entire delivery system, the project's research team concluded that by far the best results are promised by proper use of social service teams. Substituting the team concept for the currently prevalent hierarchical pattern, with its demonstrated weaknesses, would significantly improve the quality of services and appreciably increase caseload capacity—to say nothing of providing more adequate service to the multiple-problem family. Experimentation with teams has already produced a considerable amount of information on the team concept itself, the structural and operational aspects of the team, the team-client and team-community relationships, team model decision making, team meetings, case reviews, recording procedures, and variants of the team pattern.[30]

As most practicable for child welfare, the report proposes a team model in which the leader identifies the special skills and areas of expertise possessed by individual members. Each member is available, on call by other team members, to provide expert advice and assistance in his designated skill area on particular cases and problems. Cases are assigned to the team, with the team leader designating which member is to be the "case coordinator" with primary responsibility for contacts with the families or child and other agencies involved. Only after clearing with the case coordinator do other team members make such contacts. Diagnosis and decisions on outcome goals are made through case reviews by the entire team under the guidance of the leader. The case coordinator is responsible for calling on other members or outside agencies for expert advice and case support, as determined by the team's review and as special problems arise.

The team staffing model proposed in the report consists of a leader, social workers, community worker, consumer member, and secretary. Their qualifications are described and the responsibilities of each member are carefully spelled out. A team model delivery system is delineated in detail, showing how it operates internally and how it ties into the total system for delivering and managing child welfare services in a given agency.[31] The following excerpts illustrate some of the suggested approaches.

The Consumer Member. The inclusion of the consumer member, to participate in team service in a quasi-official capacity, is based upon the vital need to involve the community in the daily, direct team service to its clientele. The consumer member is an individual who has been (or still is) a recipient of social services. He works directly with the team members, participates in team decision-making, and is responsible for advice and assistance that make explicit client interests and aspirations. He might be a natural, foster or adoptive parent, a representative of a consumer organization (such as the local branch of the Foster Parents Association or of the local Welfare Rights Organization), or a former foster child, or an adult who was an adopted child, or a former consumer who is a member of some non–social-service oriented organization (Women's Liberation, for example) which, the team believes, might help in developing needed resources, etc. A consumer member would not serve on a full-time, continuing basis; rather, he would be called in periodically, when his special involvement was important. This means that over a period of time, a sizable number of consumers, representing hopefully, a full range of consumer interests, would contribute to the work of the team.

The consumer member is to be paid on a *per diem* basis.

The Team Secretary. In addition to the traditional clerical functions, the individual occupying this position may act in limited fashion as a social worker as well. For example, the secretary provides information to clients about appropriate procedures, works directly with clients in helping them fill out forms, contacts clients by telephone and obtains needed information requested by other team members, etc.

Supportive activity of this type frees the professional and other team members of time-consuming routine matters, and permits them to devote their energies to the necessary professional aspects of the case. To assure full integration as a member of the team, the secretary attends team meetings and participates in training programs.

Concepts, Modalities, and Techniques

In contrast to the considerable ferment in information, delivery, and management systems, the philosophic bases of child welfare have for the most part undergone reassessment in the light of social change and new knowledge. Innovations in practice have focused on refining rather than changing longstanding principles and on implementing them more decisively and consistently. These refinements are attempting to respond more effectively to the emergence of a number of living styles among American families—living groups, single parent households, two-parent families united by a social rather than a legal contract, and others different from the traditional two-parent nuclear family. They are also taking into account the more pronounced movement of women into the labor force, into educational settings, and into political, social, and cultural activities, as well as the rising rate of divorce and separation that currently characterizes all modern societies.

Concepts

The principle enunciated by the first White House Conference in 1909—that children should not be deprived of home life with their own families except for urgent and compelling reasons—remains unchallenged. In real life, however, many children have been removed from their own homes—almost 327,000 children were in foster care in 1970. Because of disillusionment with the inadequate and extremely costly services provided as alternatives to parental failure, many innovative modalities are concerned with decreasing the number of removals.[32] Deeper insight has also served to strengthen adherence to two other principles—the essentiality of safeguarding the child's continuity of relationships, and the importance of attuning all services to the child's, rather than the adult's, sense of time. A third principle is almost as basic—that the child's physical and psychological well-being are equally important and that any sharp distinction between them is artificial. Parents must give the child adequate physical care and at the same time must fulfil his psychological needs.

Not so clear is the validity of the position that social work intervention should be related to the needs of the child rather than the needs of any others involved in the situation—a notion traditionally stated as "the best interests of the child" or in the newer phraseology as "the least detrimental available alternative."[33] Practitioners know that meeting the needs of the child inevitably produces an impact on the child's family and on the community in which both live. How to serve the child in a total situation context and to treat his needs as paramount poses many dilemmas not resolved by the "drive for children's rights" or by proposals for a system of child advocacy designed to protect children in their relationships to parents, families, schools, courts, and society.[34]

Perhaps the major value of explicating and clarifying the rights of children in a fast-changing society—as well as the rights of foster children, the rights of young people, the rights of foster parents, and so on—is to state aspirations entertained by sizable segments of the population and thus to suggest broad guidelines for action. This may lead to the development of more realistic and sound policies and mechanisms for implementation that will translate rights into a way of life.

Since legal provisions and requirements profoundly influence what society undertakes to do for children, it is likely that if current proposals for changes become law, they will contribute importantly to redirecting or modifying child welfare practice. Among several proposals being discussed, those made by Goldstein, Freud, and Solnit, and by the Childhood and Government Project,[35] are receiving wide attention.

One of the key positions taken by Goldstein, Freud, and Solnit is a "preference for privacy" or minimal state intervention:

> To safeguard the right of parents to raise their children as they see fit, free of government intrusion, except in cases of

neglect and abandonment, is to safeguard each child's need for continuity.[36]

Parents are addressed by these authors as "psychological parents," stressing their conviction that the child's physical and psychological needs are indivisible. At the same time, they take the view

> that the law must make the child's needs paramount. This preference reflects more than our professional commitment. It is in the society's best interests. Each time the cycle of grossly inadequate parent-child relationships is broken, society stands to gain a person capable of becoming an adequate parent for children of the future.[37]

The minimal state intervention advocated by the Childhood and Government Project is even more restricted since it appears to minimize the importance of psychological parenting.[38] Mnookin writes:

> A state may remove a child from parental custody without parental consent only if the state first proves: a) there is an immediate and substantial danger to the child's health; and b) there are no reasonable means by which the state can protect the child's health without removing the child from parental custody.[39]

And he adds, "On balance, I think 'health,' should be limited to 'physical health,' although this is a very difficult issue and requires more thought." Nor is Mnookin prepared to support unequivocally the view that the law must make the child's needs paramount, arguing,

> One obvious objection to the best interests of the child test is that by its very terms it ignores completely the interests of the parents. Obviously a child's parents have important interests at stake when the state seeks to intervene; a parent can derive important satisfactions and pleasures from a relationship with a child, and the destruction of this relationship can have an enormous effect on the parent quite apart from benefits or losses to the child.[40]

In reviewing the Goldstein, Freud, Solnit work, Polier makes several incisive points. She warns of the

> danger that the position taken by the authors that there
> should be only minimal state intervention will be
> misconstrued to support the rejection of psychological
> parents despite the inability of the natural parents to fulfill
> this role. Courts required to make immediate and final
> decisions on custody may conclude, in the words quoted
> from a judge, that "our inability to predict or solve (the
> uncertainties of life) anchors us closely to nature's
> intendment."[41]

She notes that the authors do not make clear how the courts are
to determine which adults are so extremely unfit as to necessitate
state interference.

> How courts or legislatures are to determine which are or are
> not "extreme cases" remains as uncertain as the guidelines
> traditionally invoked to determine what was in the best
> interest of the child. The limitation of removal to "extreme
> cases" is at odds with the emphasis placed on a child's need
> for loving, feeling loved, valued, wanted as essential to the
> development of healthy self-esteem, and the consequences
> predicted for later life when there is failure to meet such
> needs.[42]

She points out that the authors' focus on children where custody
is being contested does not deal with the major problems involved; and she hopes that

> there will be a further volume in which the wisdom of
> psychoanalytic theory will develop guidelines for society's
> treatment of children for whom no adults battle. It is in this
> vast arena, shrouded by apathy and burdened by hostility
> toward welfare, that guidelines for achieving psychological
> parenting to which this book contributes so much are most
> desperately needed.[43]

Modalites

1. Innovations in practice designed to keep children in their
own homes. In order to avoid unnecessary placements, agencies
are reexamining ways in which they have traditionally worked
with biological parents. Experimentation by one agency resulted

in modified guidelines for its program of home services—accept-ance of long-term treatment as inevitable in most cases; placing treatment emphasis on fostering family members' strengths, a focus that requires, in addition to counseling and psychotherapy, education and development of individual skills and personal growth; including the "parenting" of children and parents in the agency's job, that is, meeting their physical, medical, economic, educational, recreational, and social needs; using volunteers to form kinship systems for the families; helping some parents to accept the fact that they are capable of being partial parents only; and helping children to understand their parents and to "make peace" with their deficiencies as mothers and fathers.[44] A parent-ing continuum scale has been developed for use as an intake tool for evaluating parental capacities. It has been found that talking it out in treatment is frequently secondary to living it out with the parents—accompanying them to appointments, teaching them household management and menu planning, and helping them understand children's needs.

There are other pioneering programs in this context whose promise has been carefully tested. In "five-day foster care," children live with and receive care from foster parents during five days a week; on weekends, holidays, and vacations, they live with their parents.[45] "The five-day week" in residential treat-ment centers for latency-age children combines weekends at home with intensive family therapy.[46] Day treatment programs allow "the child to maintain his relationship with his family," thus "minimizing the severe separation trauma many children endure with full residential placement."[47]

Efforts to avoid unplanned emergency removals of children from their own homes have also generated a considerable amount of experimentation. One such effort, reported by the Children's Aid Society and the Society for Prevention of Cruelty to Children (SPCC) of Buffalo, was initiated in 1966 to provide "emergency parents" for children left alone at night. Where emergency homemakers usually enter the home when there is a family member with whom to work, the emergency parents come when there is no such member.[48]

Another and a much more comprehensive experiment in Nashville-Davidson County, Tennessee, was preceded by a thor-ough analysis of the county's system of services for neglected and abused children. The purpose of the experiment was "to reduce the number of children removed precipitously from their homes, reduce the number of children who have to go through the legal system unnecessarily, to plan orderly placements for those children who must be placed, to set goals for children who come into emergency care with decisions to return to their parents or relatives made within a reasonable time [two weeks to one month], and develop placements that more nearly meet the needs of children who must remain in care." It was launched in 1971 under the supervision of the County Department of Welfare as a three-year project supported by the Office of Child Development. The new services added to the system by the project included a twenty-four-hour emergency intake with personnel available to screen calls and refer emergencies to appropriate caseworkers; emergency caretaker service with people available to be summoned to serve as temporary guardians until the return of parents; twenty-four-hour emergency homemaker service for crisis situations where parents cannot exercise their parental responsibility; and emergency foster homes to provide temporary care where children cannot be maintained in their own home by a homemaker, or where other situations arise, such as regular foster home placements breaking down.[49]

Another experiment with some potential for decreasing children's removals from their own homes is a neighborhood multiservice center, created by the Juvenile Protective Association in Chicago, that includes day care, homemaker services, and a tutorial program.[50] A program that may prevent the removal of children from their own homes at a later date was launched by the Spence-Chapin Services to Families and Children in October 1976. Called "The Children's House," it offers counseling services to families whose children are developmentally impaired. The focus is on two groups: babies two years old and younger, and children of nursery school age.

2. Innovations in practice designed to facilitate permanent solutions for children within a relatively short period of time. Some agencies are developing emergency foster homes for children in crisis situations or for those who need to be separated from their parents for protective purposes. The long-range plan for these children is either return to their own homes or placement in permanent foster or residential homes—within a reasonable time.

Emergency placements pose special problems for foster parents, not only for their own family relationships but also vis-à-vis relationships with the community, the natural parents, and the agency. One foster father writes: "We found that in crisis situations, the caseworker did not have time to evaluate the child's total needs. The foster family then played a part in communicating the child's apparent needs to the agency."[51]

Some agencies, rejecting foster care as a permanent solution for any child, see only two roads to permanence: rehabilitating the natural parents or family, or helping them to free the child for adoption. In working with the parent, the worker makes definite proposals with clear purposes in mind:

"We will help you assess your ability to fulfil parenting responsibilities and the reality of your plan to resume care of your children"—focus on the demands of parenting.

"If you are unable to achieve your goals within the time you have set, perhaps some alternate plan such as adoption should be considered"—use of time.

"We will accept whatever your capacities are and we will not blame you if you cannot meet your child's needs"—recognizing the parent as a person with needs.

"If this limited parenting is hard for you, total parental responsibility will be even harder. Perhaps we should consider adoption as an alternative so that your child may have the opportunity to have a new family of his own"—interposing adoption as a leverage.

"The parent who abandons his child abdicates his role as parent. A three-month period of no contact with your child is viewed as abandonment by the laws of the state. We will use this law if necessary"—allowing the parent to abandon the child.[52]

This approach assumes that adoption is a realistic alternative for the older child—a position questioned by many practitioners.[53]

Other efforts to achieve a "resolution" of foster care—instead of making it "as good as possible"—have taken the form of special group counseling programs for parents.

The purpose is to enable parents to discuss their concerns about foster care and to encourage them to work toward being a part of a plan to resolve foster care for their child. The group sessions allow parents to tell each other about their specific situations and to address themselves to how each is moving toward a solution to foster care.[54]

It is hoped that this kind of counseling, buttressed by supportive and supplementary services, will return the child to his own home—the most obvious permanent arrangement. If this does not happen, then the agency works with parents toward releasing the child for adoption, regular or subsidized—a solution facilitated, it believes, by taking a broader view about what kinds of children are adoptable.*

3. Innovations in practice designed to facilitate adoption. In order to maximize the possibility of adoption for children who are not legally free at the time of placement and to eliminate the "damage of interim foster placement," some agencies are developing "foster care–adoptive family" programs. The families involved must commit themselves to adoption while accepting the risk that the children may not become legally free. Careful selection and preparation of these adoptive parents and emotional support during placement are essential. Although these programs encounter a number of special problems, they can be effective.[55]

Efforts to facilitate the adoption of older children focus on well-established concepts and principles "to develop a conscious, systematic approach in preparing older children for adoption." These children, their foster families, and the adoptive families are seen as "the system of attention, and as interacting units in adoption planning." Issues that arise in working with this three-component system and techniques that are effective in achieving sound adoption are being clarified and refined.[56]

Adoption of Black and other minority children has been facilitated by changes in practice that have affected all adoptions. The

---

* The movement to plan and carry out permanent solutions for children in foster care within a relatively short period of time either through discharge to their families or through adoptive placement has been speeded up in New York by a law enacted in 1971. It provided a mandated judicial review of those children who had been in foster care continuously for twenty-four months. See Festinger, Trudy Bradley, "The New York Court Review of Children in Foster Care," *Child Welfare* 54, no. 4 (April 1975): 211–46; and the same author's "The Impact of the New York Court Review of Children in Foster Care: A Followup Report," *Child Welfare* 55, no. 8 (Sept.-Oct. 1976): 515–47.

new modalities in this segment include ARENA, quasi adoption, family-resources programs, long-term and permanent foster family care, subsidized adoption, single-parent adoption, and transracial adoption. Quasi adoption is placement of children in families who are neither adoption applicants nor prospective foster parents in the conventional sense. The parents in these families are given assurance that the agency's total services are available to help child and family grow together and that, should they delay in deciding about adoption, they can be reclassified as permanent foster parents and continue to receive payment for the child's expenses. In addition, the adoption process was shortened, requirements in selecting adoptive parents were made more flexible, and a broadened definition of adoption was developed. Casework methods were modified to become more effective in working with blacks, and more Black workers have been employed in order to bring to the agency knowledge of Black culture and to improve communication with the Black community.[57]

While almost all of these new modalities have encountered resistance from child welfare practitioners, some were and still are beset by acrimonious debate. This is especially true of transracial adoptions. A recently completed three-year study of adoption of Black or part-Black children by White parents revealed a success rate of 77 percent, "approximately the same as that of a number of other studies that have examined conventional White infant adoptions as well as adoptions of older children and other racial groups." But the design of the study concentrated on the parents' reports about their children so that "one is never sure whether one is dealing with a fact or the parents' perception of a fact."[58] The controversy is continuing, pointing to the need for more evaluative research and more analysis of tested experience.[59]

4. Innovations in practice designed to make foster care as good as possible. Most practitioners recognize that in certain situations even the best efforts will not bring about children's return to their own homes or adoption. In such instances, four approaches are receiving renewed attention.

First, agencies will work with the natural parents to enable them to maintain a mutually satisfactory relationship with their child, while living apart. Recently, some agencies have accepted the concept of part-time parenting "as a viable possibility, to be nurtured and supported through a new child care structure."[60] This structure involves natural parents in a variety of activities with their placed children, such as attendance at a preplacement luncheon, participation in medical examinations required by the agency, buying clothing for their children with the agency clothing allowance; planning and carrying out projects for themselves and their children, and using the agency's residence as a temporary shelter for themselves and siblings at times of crisis. The agency's objective is to obtain from natural parents a more direct and meaningful impact on the daily lives of their children than is usual in such cases—to the end of improving the children's general functioning and increasing the ability of the parent and the child to maintain family identification and feelings of closeness during placement.

Second, long-term and permanent foster family homes will be developed for those children whose placement is expected to be permanent. In recent years, several scholars have discussed the problems that have beset this type of care and ways of drastically improving its quality so that it does not create a "limbo state" for the child in which emotional growth is almost impossible.[61] Among major difficulties have been delays and ambiguities in planning or outright absence of planning because foster care was considered a "temporary" arrangement—despite all evidence to the contrary. Another block has been the unwillingness or the inability of staff to make timely decisions involved in permanent arrangements—decisions which often require taking risks, since our capacity to predict is limited.[62]

Some agencies, nevertheless, have made considerable progress in planning. Rothschild describes how her agency has moved to define the types of plans that are possible, identifying those characteristics of parents and children that determine which plan should be instituted for a given child and evaluating outcomes of placements in relation to what is known about children and their optimum development. She notes that while more children would have been adopted in the past if biological parents had been more willing to surrender their parental rights and that more would be adopted in the future if laws were changed to shift emphasis from the rights of biological parents to the rights and welfare of the child, "return to biological parents and adoptive placement are not the sole criteria for evaluation of foster care service."[63]

Long-term foster care provided by her agency has met a variety of important human needs.

Third, differential use of foster homes is possible. Mention has already been made of the variety of functions that foster homes may be called upon to perform to meet individual needs of placed children. Especially important in this context is the use of group homes, halfway houses, and group homes in alliance with larger institutions. These may serve adolescent and preadolescent children, sibling groups, physically and mentally handicapped youngsters, those with emotional disturbances, and those who are ready to be discharged from an institution but are not ready to return to their own homes, or who have no homes to return to. A group home may be the foster parents' own home or it may be an agency-operated home, staffed by personnel employed by the agency. In both instances, it is a facility located in the normal community, with all that this implies for participation in community activities. (See chapter 9 in this book.) Some group homes serve as many as fifteen children; others are built on a foster home model. Group homes can provide a stable and consistent environment in which an adolescent may live and mature in the community; an atmosphere in which the young person can work through the emancipation of adolescence while living in a healthy and emotionally undemanding group and family setting; an arena where he can discover and test new ideas and experience different ways of relating to others; or a transitional setting for those coming out of institutions.[64]

Group homes, halfway houses, and other community services as alternatives to custodial institutions, whose development has been gathering momentum since the early 1960s, are part of the concept of "juvenile diversion," which has been gaining acceptance because of disillusionment with a juvenile justice system that has neither controlled delinquency nor halted its continuing rise.[65] Many child welfare practitioners sympathize with the deinstitutionalization concept for children who have been placed for want of appropriate alternate facilities, who do not need the special services of an institution, or who have found themselves in unhelpful institutions. It is also pointed out that some recent deinstitutionalization movements, under the guise of humanitarian effort, have made it possible for economy-minded budget cutters "to utilize deinstitutionalization rhetoric to destroy facilities without establishing viable alternatives."[66] Writing at the end of 1974, Gula noted that only about a dozen states had established real alternatives for dependent, retarded, delinquent, or disturbed children.[67]

Fourth, clarification of the role and status of foster parents may lead to improvement in practice. Some writers emphasize that there has always been confusion regarding the role of foster parents, since they fill different roles in different agencies; they have been seen as clients, as colleagues, as employees, or as surrogate parents. This uncertainty obviously has a negative effect on their relationship with the foster child.[68] Other writers, however, believe that this problem has been overstated. Kline and Overstreet maintain that the situation of foster parents "is not unlike that of individuals in other service structures in which a system of interpersonal relationships is the medium for producing the service."[69] If the agency adheres to clear and consistent programs and policies, foster parents will not be confused by being simultaneously, surrogate parents, agency employees, and, at some points, temporary clients. In the view of these authors, foster parents' primary role is that of surrogate parents, all other roles being played, if necessary, for the purpose of enabling them to discharge the primary one.

While there is no universal agreement, there is no doubt that seeing them as professional surrogate parents is the concept that is gaining acceptance. It is noted that if only children who in fact require foster care are placed, they will be youngsters with serious problems. "Consequently, foster parents will be expected to perform as professionals and should be trained and paid as professionals."[70] Professional competence is also considered essential for foster parents in group homes serving adolescents. The demand for training, strengthening the movement toward professionalization, is strongly voiced by the foster parents' associations. Undoubtedly, this will lead to considering foster parenthood as a career that makes a needed contribution to the community, and this in turn will result in more meaningful participation of foster parents in the entire placement process—involving as it does the larger social fabric, policy and decision making, and the planning and carrying out of plans for specific children.

Special considerations have influenced practice with foster

parents whose children have been placed with them for long terms or permanently. In some states, the agency delegates to them all responsibility for nurturing and parenting. The child does not "belong" to the agency; rather, he is cared for only by the foster parents and belongs to the foster family. The agency is only supportive, performing the necessary legal tasks and working with the parents as called for. In other states, the agency retains guardianship after approving permanent placement because it believes that it is helpful to foster parents and child for the agency to stay in the picture throughout the child's minority. The purpose of supervision is to help the child establish his identity and to help foster parents become involved in their total responsibility for the child. In still other states, guardianship is given to the foster parents, while the agency retains only residual rights.[71]

Techniques

No fundamental changes in techniques have been generated by the child welfare field in recent years. The knowledge and skills considered essential for competent practice in the past are still indispensable. While behavioral modification techniques are being used by some practitioners, there is no indication that this is taking place on a wide scale.[72] As in other areas of practice, child welfare workers are using a variety of techniques, selecting them for their special efficacy in given situations.

If there is a tendency, it is to deal with everyone involved in the child welfare network in a systems or ecological perspective; that is, to see the client not only as an individual but also as a member of small and large groups and of the total community.

There is also a pronounced trend to rely on an eclectic or multi-methods approach, that is, combining a variety of interventive techniques in most situations. It appears also that group work is being more frequently used in more settings. Small groups have been found effective in residential programs for adolescents. They strengthen the demand for behavior and attitude change by unifying staff and adolescents into more cohesive interactive systems; they contribute to improvements in overall living conditions; and they teach adolescents to see certain situations not as staff problems but as group problems.[73] Techniques to improve the therapeutic impact of the group leader's activities are widely practiced, backed up by a deeper grasp of the unique properties of groups and their varying effects on different kinds of children and youth.[74]

As already noted, child welfare workers are finding that the use of environmental and financial supports (hence the importance of the availability and accessibility of these resources) immeasurably strengthens the efficacy of intervention. This tends to place psychoanalytically-oriented techniques in a more balanced perspective. This tendency is also bolstered by a conscious recognition of the role of ethnic and cultural factors in the helping process; they illumine the needs of the individual client and the manner in which and by whom services ought to be offered.

The use of teams to deliver child welfare services may also be considered innovative. To what has been said already, it may be added that the diversified team personnel is often able to gain readier access to the many-faceted milieu in which all clients live than one worker ever could, however well-trained.

The multidisciplinary approach (not a new technique since it has been used by child welfare workers in many situations in the past) gained special importance with the passage of the Child Abuse and Neglect Act in January 1974. It is widely recognized that for its solution, the problem of the abuse and neglect of children requires the involvement and services of the health, law enforcement, social work, and education professions, among others. Social workers have been strengthening and developing their interdisciplinary skills in order to create and maintain systems that link a number of discrete service providers into an integrated and coordinated method for the delivery of services to this group of children and their families. The very need to define abuse and neglect more precisely and meaningfully, a need that presents many dilemmas, also stresses the primary importance of common understandings among the various professionals involved. The multidisciplinary approach is also essential in day care, a service that has seen substantial growth in the past decade.

The possibilities of offering effective informational service and counseling without face-to-face contact have been developed by devices such as "Operation Peace of Mind," a telephone hotline established in Houston in September 1973 and the National Telephone Hotline service for runaway youths established in August 1974 in Chicago. There are now local and state hotlines in various parts of the country. An important feature is that the young runaways who use hotlines have complete control over what information they wish to give and what information, if any, is relayed to their families. No pressure is applied to them, so that if reunions between parents and children occur, it is because both want to reunite.

Assessment

Preliminary indications are that the information systems described in this chapter are fulfilling their major objectives to a significant extent. There is little doubt, for example, that ARENA has made adoption possible for some children who, without it, would have remained in foster care. The Nashville-Davidson system has linked the information available on each child under care, replacing a disjointed series of data with an integrated record. Important as well are the benefits generated by these systems which go beyond the contributions made by their informational features. Thus, the CHILDATA system, while it does not include direct measures of quality, does supply facts that make assessment possible. The SSIS has helped staff recognize that reporting of elements is more relevant to service delivery than other methods of reporting. The Edwin Gould system showed that

> presentation of cost information in a format that allows administrators to determine the exact cost of care for each child according to meaningful cost categories has tremendous implications for decision making in the child care field. In the short run, such information can facilitate intake and staffing decisions, can lead to more rational budget-reduction processes and can help the agency move to a more decentralized system of child care, with full spending power (and thus full accountability) in the hands of each child care team.[75]

Furthermore, the mounting and management of these systems has increased the ability and willingness of agencies to work together. Their staffs are being provided valuable experience in using modern technology to facilitate and make more effective their everyday activities on behalf of children, as well as an opportunity to contribute meaningful input to the functioning of this technology.

The model for improving the delivery and management of child welfare services, discussed earlier, may hold great promise. It deals with issues common to all large organizations charged with providing services to people and, because the basic concepts it incorporates have already been tested elsewhere, there is good reason to believe that the model can be successfully applied in the child welfare field. One element of this model, the team approach to staffing, has been tested by social work practitioners in several social service settings. While some unresolved or only partially resolved areas remain, overall experience with this staffing pattern has been clearly positive.[76]

Unfortunately, assessment of innovative modalities and techniques, closely associated with the requirements of accountability, continues to be sporadic or inconclusive. As a minimum, the assessment process requires the spelling out of concepts, definitions, and objectives in a relevant form; the mounting of appropriate statistical and other procedures; and the presentation of an evaluative statement that not only shows the extent to which stated objectives had been achieved, but equally important, also illuminates the extent to which this achievement is responding to the changing needs of clients and society—a dynamic, action-oriented evaluation that permits a circular movement between the past, the present, and the future. This kind of assessment in child welfare is relatively rare. Statements such as, "As yet, little or no systematic follow-up or evaluation has been conducted to determine the effectiveness of group homes in performing any of these functions," are all too common.[77] Aside from the procedural and technical difficulties involved (including the problem of quantification mentioned in connection with accountability), the child welfare field is still handicapped by lack of built-in systems of feedback able to furnish essential data in a consistent and usable form.

The need for such feedback, as an integral element of service, is becoming apparent to more professionals and others involved in child welfare. For example, the experimental project concerned with natural parents as partners in child care placement conducted evaluative research throughout its existence. It tested hypotheses "related to two lines of inquiry: the effectiveness of the Family Residential Center in facilitating contact between children and their natural parents and the effects of such increased contact upon the behaviors and attitudes of the children and their natural parents.''[78] The experimental group was compared with two controls. Overall findings sustained the hypotheses positively in regard to both lines of inquiry, and most strikingly in regard to the positive value of parent involvement. Parents with severe problems were able to increase, sustain, and improve their parenting role with children in placement.

A program designed to reduce foster placements, which did not include evaluation as an ongoing part of service, did undertake evaluative research after sizable experience had been gained. It addressed questions such as: "How successful is our program in alleviating a child's problems and difficulties, as compared to programs which place children in foster homes and group residences? How do the parents and children selected for services in their own homes differ diagnostically from families whose children were selected—during the same time period—to be placed outside their homes?"[79] So far, the agency has learned that fewer than 5 percent of the children served have required separation from their parents, but that gains among the children and families are achieved slowly and turnover of cases is low. An important contribution to more accurate decision making—who stays home and who stays in placement—has been the development of a parenting continuum scale as an intake tool.[80]

An evaluation of the first of two operational years of the new child care system in Metropolitan Nashville-Davidson County, Tennessee—especially impressive for clarity, incorporation of realistic limitations, and technical competence in handling large amounts of data—has been completed by an independent group of researchers employed for the purpose. The evaluation is output rather than process oriented: objectives and criteria for their attainment are carefully spelled out and progress toward achieving them is delineated quantitatively. Some of the highlights of this progress include: the number of neglect and dependence petitions filed in the Davidson County Juvenile Court declined from 687 in 1969–70 to 365 in 1972–73; the number of children institutionalized declined from 247 in 1972–72 to 22 in 1972–73; especially encouraging is the impact of this reduction in children under the age of six—from 190 to 2; in 1972, 882 referrals involving 2,104 children were received by the emergency service unit of DPW, but screening by this unit showed that only 454 referrals warranted emergency intervention. An examination of the case load of the caretaker, homemaker, and emergency foster home units also provides insights into program performance. Although some performance aspects need further study (for example, it is not clear why the number of foster home placements shows large fluctuations), the evaluators' preliminary conclusions are that "there is little doubt that the new system is achieving the objectives."[81]

Limited assessment is available concerning the performance of group homes in preparing children to leave residential treatment and return to their own homes or begin independent living. One study indicates that many children can use group homes successfully in this context. For them, this transitional experience fulfils one or more of the following needs:

Provides a home when their own is not available or is temporarily unavailable;

Provides an opportunity to live in the community and receive further treatment services;

Provides a transitional protective environment where their still rather fragile egos can gain support and strength;

Enables them to get reacquainted with their parents on a more realistic basis than the institutional climate permits;

Represents a further motivation for progress for both parents and children.[82]

Conclusion

Perhaps the most promising innovations stem from the growing realization that child welfare services must be seen as systems rather than as discrete programs. This kind of view has far-reaching implications, both in relation to society's policies as they affect children and families and the internal policies of agencies serving children and families. In this context, the importance of community supports in maximizing the effects of therapeutic interventions, in enabling agencies to provide for the child what he actually needs for as long as he needs it, is emerging with renewed urgency. Similarly, the wisdom of using modern technology to create informational and delivery and management systems to serve children and families more effectively is becoming obvious. Included in the development are efficient built-in monitoring and evaluation devices that will enable the field to come to grips constructively with the problems of assessment and accountability—the latter undoubtedly a force in moving society toward benign and relevant policies.

Equally promising appears to be the team model in staffing. Not only is the team better equipped to see the child as a whole person instead of fragmenting him to fit the needs of the bureaucracy but it is also likely to bring about more genuine access to and involvement of the community—to say nothing of relieving individual team members of the heavy weight of responsibility for making crucial decisions alone. Stressing collegial rather than hierarchical relationships between members and emphasizing ability to use modern organizational and management techniques, the team model has far-reaching implications for the education and training of social workers:

> [Social workers] must be taught how to participate in a team atmosphere—with all that this implies in knowledge and appreciation of basic team management concepts and the ability to apply them appropriately. In addition to "human growth and environment," social workers must learn how to manage their workloads, how to use their time for most effective results, how to keep current in regard to the progress of each case within their jurisdiction, and how to utilize feed-back as a constructive tool in the movement toward goals. Management skill will need to be recognized just as client relationship skill has been.[83]

Along with learning to use science and technology, it remains imperative for child welfare practitioners to gain increasingly more profound understanding of people and societies and to develop an ever deeper commitment to serving children with the best knowledge and skills at their disposal. It is this combination that will bring about genuinely nurturing services for all children in the coming decade.

Notes

1. Shirley Jenkins, *Child Welfare in New York City* (New York City: Praeger Publishers, 1971), p. 33 (Vol. 1 of *Priorities in Social Services: A Guide for Philanthropic Funding)*, p. 33.
2. Michigan State Department of Social Services, *Child Care and Placement Information System,* draft for training use (DSS T/A 210–3–72–OYS). See also Marvin R. Burt and Louis H. Blair, *Options for Improving the Care of Neglected and Dependent Children* (Washington, D.C.: The Urban Institute, March 1971), p. 30; California State Social Welfare Board, *Report on Foster Care: Children Waiting* (Sacramento: State Health and Welfare Agency, March 1974), p. 2; Bernice Q. Madison and Michael Schapiro, *New Perspectives on Child Welfare: Services, Staffing, Delivery System* (1973), p. 10; this report is available from the Frederic Burk Foundation, 75 Southgate Ave., Daly City, Calif.
3. Bernice Q. Madison and Michael Schapiro, "Black Adoption—Issues and Policies: Review of the Literature," *Social Science Review* 47 (Dec. 1973): 531–60.
4. Arlene L. Nash, "Reflections on Interstate Adoptions," *Children Today* 3 (July –Aug. 1974): 7–11.
5. Michigan, *Child Care Information System,* p. 1.
6. Jack H. Donahue, Elizabeth Angell, Aloyisus J. Becker, Judith Cingolani, Marilyn Nelson, and George E. Ross, "The Social Service Information System," *Child Welfare* 53 (April 1974): 243, 253.
7. Ann M. Rothschild and Jean E. Bedger, "A Regional CHILDATA System Can Work: An Exchange of Letters," *Child Welfare* 53 (Jan. 1974) 56–57.
8. Marvin R. Burt and Ralph Balyeat, *A New System for Improving the Care of Neglected and Abused Children* (unpublished manuscript prepared for Children's Bureau, Office of Child Development, HEW, and Tennessee Dept. of Public Welfare, under OCD Contract ODC-CB-91, 15 Oct. 1973).
9. Similar requirements are included in the Michigan tracking system; see Michigan, *Child Care Information System,* p. 15. See also Robert H. Mnookin, "Foster Care—In Whose Best Interest?" *Harvard Educational Review* 43 (Nov. 1973), and David W. Young, "Management Information Systems in Child Care: An Agency Experience," *Child Welfare* 52 (Feb. 1974): 105.
10. Joseph Goldstein, Anna Freud, and Albert J. Solnit, *Beyond the Best Interests of the Child* (New York City: Free Press, 1973), p. 2.
11. Ibid., p. 25.
12. Anthony N. Maluccio, "Foster Family Care Revisited: Problems and Prospects," *Public Welfare* 31 (Spring 1973): 15–16.
13. Elizabeth A. Lawder, Roberta G. Andrews, and Jon. R. Parsons, *Five Models of Foster Family Group Homes: A Systemic View of Foster Care* (New York City: Child Welfare League of America, 1974).
14. Madison and Schapiro, "Black Adoption," pp. 533–45.

15. Madison and Schapiro, *New Perspectives on Child Welfare,* p. 173.

16. Goldstein, Freud, and Solnit, *Beyond the Best Interests of the Child,* p. 31.

17. Madison and Schapiro, "Black Adoption," p. 554.

18. *Children Today* 3 (Sept.–Oct. 1974), p. 24; Madison and Schapiro, *New Perspectives on Child Welfare,* pp. 24–25.

19. California Assembly Symposium on Services to Children and Youth, *California Children: Who Cares?* (Sacramento: Assembly Office of Research, March 1974), p. 11; idem, *Legislative Proposals* (April 1974).

20. California Assembly, *Report on Status of San Diego Foster Care* (Sacramento: Assembly Office of Research, June 1973), p. iii.

21. Robert Elkin, *A Conceptual Base for Defining Health and Welfare Services* (New York City: Child Welfare League of America, Family Service Association of America, Travelers Aid Association of America, 1967).

22. George Hoshino, "Social Services: The Problem of Accountability," *Social Service Review* 47 (Sept. 1973): 373–83.

23. Young, "Management Information Systems," p. 110.

24. Mary E. Reistroffer, "Participation of Foster Parents in Decision-making: the Concept of Collegiality," *Child Welfare* 51 (Jan. 1972): 29.

25. Robert Daniels and John A. Brown, "Foster Parents and the Agency," *Children Today* (May-June 1973) p. 26.

26. Irving W. Fellner and Charles Solomon, "Achieving Permanent Solutions for Children in Foster Home Care," *Child Welfare* 52 (March 1973): 182.

27. Gladys Simmons, Joanne Gumpert, Beulah Rothman, "Natural Parents as Partners in Child Care Placement," *Social Casework* 54 (April 1973): 231.

28. Madison and Schapiro, *New Perspectives on Child Welfare,* p. 171. See also pp. 113–36 and appendix B.

29. Ibid., pp. 176–77.

30. Ibid., pp. 139–49.

31. Ibid., pp. 149–58. The following quotations are from pp. 152–53.

32. David Fanshel and Eugene B. Shinn, *Dollars and Sense in the Foster Care of Children: A Look at Cost Factors* (New York City: Child Welfare League of America, 1972).

33. Goldstein, Freud, and Solnit, *Beyond the Best Interests of the Child.*

34. *White House Conference on Children 1970* (Washington, D.C.: U.S. Government Printing Office, 1971), pp. 345–69, 389–97.

35. This project is being conducted by Robert H. Mnookin and his associates at the University of California, Berkeley, and is being supported by grants from the Ford Foundation and the Carnegie Corporation of New York.

36. Goldstein, Freud, and Solnit, *Beyond the Best Interests of the Child,* p. 7.

37. Ibid.

38. Mnookin, "Foster Care," pp. 617–18.

39. Ibid., pp. 631.

40. Ibid., pp. 614–15.

41. Justine Wise Polier, review of Goldstein, et al., *Beyond the Best Interests of the Child,* in *Child Welfare* 53 (March 1974): 195–96.

42. Ibid., pp. 196.

43. Ibid., pp. 198.

44. Harriet Goldstein, "Providing Services to Children in Their Own Homes," *Children Today* (July–Aug. 1973) pp. 2–3.

45. Bessie Loewe and Thomas E. Hanrahan, "Five-Day Foster Care," *Child Welfare* 54 (Jan. 1975): 7–18; Myrtle Astrachan, "The Five-Day Week: An Alternate Model in Residential Treatment Centers," *Child Welfare* 54 (Jan. 1975): 21–26.

46. *Children Today* 3 (5, Sept.–Oct. 1974), p. 27.

47. Andrew L. Ross and Lawrence J. Schreiber, "Bellefaire's Day Treatment Program: An Interdisciplinary Approach to the Emotionally Disturbed Child," *Child Welfare* 54 (March 1975): 183–94.

48. Norman W. Paget, "Emergency Parent—A Protective Service to Children in Crisis," *Child Welfare* 46 (July 1967): 403–09.

49. Burt and Balyeat, *A New System,* p. 5.

50. G. Lewis Penner, *The Protective Services Center* (Denver: American Humane Association, 1968).

51. John F. Simonds, "A Foster Home for Crisis Placements," *Child Welfare* 52 (Feb. 1973): 89.

52. Leon W. Chestang and Irmgard Heymann, "Reducing the Length of Foster Care," *Social Work* 18 (Jan. 1973): 88–89.

53. Madison and Schapiro, "Black Adoption."

54. Fellner and Solomon, "Achieving Permanent Solutions," p. 183.

55. Margaret Gill, "The Foster Care/Adoptive Family: Adoption for Children Not Legally Free," *Child Welfare* 54 (Dec. 1975): 712–20.

56. Leon W. Chestang and Irmgard Heymann, "Preparing Older Children for Adoption," *Public Welfare* 34 (Winter 1976): 35–40.

57. Madison and Schapiro, "Black Adoption," pp. 532–46.

58. Lucille J. Grow and Deborah Shapiro, *Black Children–White Parents: A Study of Transracial Adoption* (New York City: Child Welfare League of America, 1975).

59. Amuzie Chimezie, "Transracial Adoption of Black Children"; D. Lincoln Johnson, "Transracial Adoption: Victim of Ideology," *Social Work* 20 (July 1975): 296–301.

60. Simmons, Gumpert, and Rothman, "Natural Parents as Partners," p. 225.

61. Bernice Madison and Michael Schapiro, "Permanent and Long-Term Foster Family Care as a Planned Service" *Child Welfare* 49 (March 1970): 131–36; idem, *New Perspectives on Child Welfare,* pp. 20–65; Kermit T. Wiltse and Eileen Gambrill, "Foster Care 1973: A

Reappraisal," *Public Welfare* 32 (Winter 1974): 7–15, and "Foster Care: The Use of Contracts" (with Theodore Stein), *Public Welfare* 32 (Fall 1974): 20–25.

62. Goldstein, Freud, and Solnit, *Beyond the Best Interests of the Child,* p. 51.

63. Ann M. Rothschild, "An Agency Evaluates Its Foster Home Service," *Child Welfare* 53 (Jan. 1974): 49.

64. St. Paul (Minn.) Metropolitan Council Staff Report, *A Survey of Group Homes in the Metropolitan Area* (Oct. 1971, mimeographed), p. 2; Chestang and Heymann, "Preparing Older Children for Adoption."

65. Alan R. Coffey, *The Prevention of Crime and Delinquency* (Englewood Cliffs, N.J.: Prentice-Hall, 1975), p. 111.

66. Joseph H. Reid, "On 'Deinstitutionalization,' " *Child Welfare* 54 (April 1975): 295–97.

67. Martin Gula, "Community Services and Residential Institutions for Children," *Children Today* 3 (Nov.–Dec. 1974): 15–17.

68. Maluccio, "Foster Family Care Revisited," p. 17.

69. Draza Kline and Helen-Mary Forbush Overstreet, *Foster Care of Children: Nurture and Treatment* (New York City: Columbia University Press, 1972), p. 220.

70. California Assembly, *California Children: Who Cares?* pp. x–35.

71. Madison and Schapiro, *New Perspectives on Child Welfare,* pp. 35–36.

72. Theodore J. Stein and Eileen D. Gambrill, "Behavioral Techniques in Foster Care," *Social Work* 21 (Jan. 1976): 34–39.

73. Max L. Scott, "Small Groups—An Effective Treatment Approach in Residential Programs for Adolescents," *Child Welfare* 49 (March 1970): 163.

74. Arthur Greenberg and Morris F. Mayer, "Group Home Care as an Adjunct to Residential Treatment," *Child Welfare* 51 (July 1971): 423–35; see also the special issue on groups and group methods, *Child Welfare* 50 (Oct. 1972).

75. David W. Young, "Case Costing in Child Care: A Critical Step Toward Increased Accountability in Social Services," *Child Welfare* 52 (May 1973): 303.

76. Madison and Schapiro, *New Perspectives on Child Welfare,* pp. 146–49.

77. St. Paul (Minn.) Metropolitan Council, *Survey of Group Homes,* p. 2.

78. Simmons, Gumpert, and Rothman, "Natural Parents as Partners," p. 231.

79. H. Goldstein, "Providing Services to Children," p. 7.

80. A longitudinal research program to assess key elements of foster care has been completed at the Columbia University School of Social Work. Begun in 1964 and funded by HEW, the program selected a sample of 624 children from birth through age 12 who came into foster care in New York City between January and November 1966 and remained in care at least 90 days. The components of the research program include

the family, child, and agency; one book on the family research was published in 1972 and a second volume is in preparation. See Bernice Madison, "Essay Review: A Study of Filial Deprivation in Foster Care Placement," *Child Welfare* 52 (Nov. 1973): 615–22.

81. Burt and Balyeat, *A New System,* p. 20.

82. Greenberg and Mayer, "Group Home Care," pp. 434–35.

83. Madison and Schapiro, *New Perspectives on Child Welfare,* p. 176.

Bibliography

Astrachan, Myrtle, "The Five-Day Week: An Alternate Model in Residential Treatment Centers," *Child Welfare,* Vol. LIV (January 1975), 21–26.

A Survey of Group Homes in the Metropolitan Area, Staff Report, Metropolitan Council, Saint Paul, Minnesota, October 1971 (Mimeographed).

Burt, Marvin R., and Louis H. Blair, *Options for Improving the Care of Neglected and Dependent Children,* Program Analysis Applied to Local Government (The Urban Institute: Washington, D.C., March 1971).

Burt, Marvin R., and Ralph Balyeat. *A New System for Improving the Care of Neglected and Abused Children.* An unpublished manuscript prepared for Children's Bureau, Office of Child Development, Department of HEW and Tennessee Department of Public Welfare, under OCD Contract Number ODC–CB–91. October 15, 1973.

California Children. Who Cares? A Progress Report on The California Assembly Symposium on Services to Children and Youth (Sacramento: Assembly Office of Research, March 1974).

California State Social Welfare Board. *Report on Foster Care: Children Waiting* (Sacramento, California: State of California Health and Welfare Agency, Department of Social Welfare, September 1972).

Chestang, Leon W. and Irmgard, Heymann. "Reducing the Length of Foster Care," *Social Work,* Vol. 18, No. 1 (January 1973), 88–92.

Chestang, Leon W. and Irmgard Heymann. "Preparing Older Children for Adoption," *Public Welfare,* Vol. 34, No. 1 (Winter 1976) 35–40.

Child Care and Placement Information System. Draft for Training Use. (Michigan State Department of Social Services, March 9, 1972. DSS T/A 210 (3–72) OYS).

Children Today, Vol. 3, No. 5 (September–October 1974), 27.

Chimezie, Amuzie. "Transracial Adoption of Black Children," *Social Work,* Vol. 20, No. 4 (July 1975), 296–301.

Coffey, Alan R. *The Prevention of Crime and Delinquency.* New Jersey, Prentice-Hall, 1975, p. 111.

Daniels, Robert and John A. Brown. "Foster Parents and the Agency," *Children Today* (May–June 1973), 25–27.

Donahue, Jack H., Elizabeth Angell, Aloyisus J. Becker, Judith Cingolani, Marilyn Nelson, George E. Ross. "The Social Service Information System," *Child Welfare*, Vol. 53, No. 4 (April 1974), 243–57.

Elkin, Robert. *A Conceptual Base for Defining Health and Welfare Services* (New York: Child Welfare League of America, Family Service Association of America, Travelers Aid Association of America, 1967).

Fanshel, David and Eugene B. Shinn. *Dollars and Sense in the Foster Care of Children. A Look at Cost Factors* (New York: CWLA, 1972).

Fellner, Irving W. and Charles Solomon. "Achieving Permanent Solutions for Children in Foster Home Care," *Child Welfare*, Vol. 52, No. 2 (March 1973), 178–187.

Gill, Margaret. "The Foster Care/Adoptive Family: Adoption for Children Not Legally Free," *Child Welfare*, Vol. LIV, No. 10 (December 1975), 712–20.

Goldstein, Harriet. "Providing Services to Children in Their Own Homes," *Children Today* (July–August 1973), 2–7.

Goldstein, Joseph, Anna Freud, Albert J. Solnit. *Beyond the Best Interests of the Child* (New York : The Free Press, 1973).

Greenberg, Arthur and Morris F. Mayer. "Group Home Care as an Adjunct to Residential Treatment," *Child Welfare*, Vol. 51, No. 7 (July 1972), 423–35.

Grow, Lucille J. and Debrah Shapiro. *Black Children –White Parents: A Study of Transracial Adoption*. New York: Child Welfare League of America, 1975. Pub. No. A–37.

Gula, Martin. "Community Services and Residential Institutions for Children," *Children Today*, Vol. 3, No. 6 (November–December 1974), 15–17.

Hoshino, George. "Social Services: The Problem of Accountability," *Social Service Review*, Vol. 47, No. 3 (September 1973), 373–383.

Jenkins, Shirley. *Priorities in Social Services: A Guide for Philanthropic Funding*. Vol. 1: *Child Welfare in New York City* (New York: Praeger Publishers, 1971), p. 33.

Johnson, D. Lincoln. "Transracial Adoption: Victim of Ideology," *Social Work*, Vol. 21, No. 3 (May 1976), 241–43.

Kline, Draza and Helen-Mary Forbush Overstreet. *Foster Care of Children. Nurture and Treatment* (New York: Columbia University Press, 1972).

Lawder, Elizabeth A., Roberta G. Andrews, Jon R. Parsons. *Five Models of Foster Family Group Homes: A Systemic View of Foster Care,* (New York: Child Welfare League of America, 1974).

Legislative Proposals. California Assembly Symposium on Services to Children and Youth (Sacramento: Assembly Office of Research, April 1974).

Loewe, Bessie and Thomas E. Hanrahan. "Five-Day Foster Care," *Child Welfare,* Vol. LIV (January 1975), 7–18.

Madison, Bernice Q. and Michael Schapiro. "Permanent and Long-Term Foster Family Care as a Planned Service," *Child Welfare,* Vol. 49, No. 3 (March 1970), 131–36.

Madison, Bernice Q. and Michael Schapiro. *New Perspectives on Child Welfare: Services, Staffing, Delivery System* (San Francisco, 1973). This Report may be obtained by writing to the Frederic Burk Foundation, 75 Southgate Ave., Daly City, California.

Madison, Bernice Q. and Michael Schapiro. "Black Adoption—Issues and Policies: Review of the Literature," *Social Service Review,* Vol. 47, No. 4 (December 1973), 531–560.

Maluccio, Anthony N., "Foster Family Care Revisited: Problems and Prospects," *Public Welfare,* Vol. 31, No. 2 (Spring 1973), 12–17.

Mnookin, Robert H. "Foster Care—In Whose Best Interest?" *Harvard Educational Review,* Vol. 43, No. 4 (November 1973).

Nash, Arlene L. "Reflections on Interstate Adoptions," *Children Today,* Vol. 3, No. 4 (July–August 1974), 7–11.

Paget, Norman W. "Emergency Parent—A Protective Service to Children in Crisis," *Child Welfare,* Vol. 46, No. 7 (July 1967), 403–409.

Penner, G. Lewis. *The Protective Services Center* (Denver: American Humane Association, 1968).

Polier, Hon. Justine Wise, Review of Goldstein, Freud and Solnit, *Beyond the Best Interests of the Child* in *Child Welfare,* Vol. 53, No. 3 (March 1974), 195–98.

Reid, Joseph H. "On 'Deinstitutionalization,' " *Child Welfare,* LIV, No. 4 (April 1975), 295–97.

Reistroffer, Mary E. "Participation of Foster Parents in Decisionmaking: the Concept of Collegiality," *Child Welfare,* Vol. 51, No. 1 (January 1972), 25–29.

Report on Status of San Diego Foster Care (Sacramento: Assembly Office of Research, June 1, 1973).

Ross, Andrew L., and Lawrence J. Schreiber. "Bellefaire's Day Treatment Program: An Interdisciplinary Approach to the Emotionally Disturbed Child," *Child Welfare,* Vol. LIV, No. 3 (March 1975), 183–194.

Rothschild, Ann M., and Jean E. Bedger. "A Regional CHILDATA System Can Work: An Exchange of Letters," *Child Welfare,* Vol. 53, No. 1 (January 1974) 51–57.

Rothschild, Ann M. "An Agency Evaluates Its Foster Home Service," *Child Welfare,* Vol. 53, No. 1 (January 1974), 42–50.

Scott, Max L. "Small Groups—An Effective Treatment Approach in Residential Programs for Adolescents," *Child Welfare,* Vol. 49, No. 3 (March 1970), 161–64.

Simmons, Gladys, Joanne Gumpert, Beulah Rothman. "Natural Parents as Partners in Child Care Placement," *Social Casework,* Vol. 54, No. 4 (April 1973), 224–32.

Simonds, John F. "A Foster Home for Crisis Placements," *Child Welfare,* Vol. 52, No. 2 (February 1973), 82–90.

Special Issue: Groups and Group Methods, *Child Welfare,* Vol. 50, No. 8 (October 1972).

Stein, Theodore J. and Eileen D. Gambrill. "Behavioral Techniques in Foster Care," *Social Work,* Vol. 21, No. 1 (January 1976), 34–39.

White House Conference on Children 1970 (U.S. Government Printing Office: Washington, D.C., 1971).

Wiltse, Kermit T., and Eileen Gambrill. "Foster Care, 1973: A Reappraisal," *Public Welfare,* Vol. 32, No. 1 (Winter 1974) 7–15. "Foster Care: Plans and Activities," *ibid.,* Vol. 32, No. 2 (Spring 1974), 12–21; and same authors and Theodore Stein, "Foster Care: The Use of Contracts," *ibid.,* Vol. 32, No. 4 (Fall 1974), 20–25.

Young, David W. "Case Costing in Child Care: A Critical Step Toward Increased Accountability in Social Services," *Child Welfare,* Vol. 52, No. 5 (May 1973) 299–304.

Young, David W. "Management Information Systems in Child Care: An Agency Experience," *Child Welfare,* Vol. 53, No. 2 (February 1974), 102–112.

3

New Directions for
Social Work in Mental Health

MILTON WITTMAN

This chapter presents recent major policy and structural changes in the nation's mental health service systems and the implications for practice that flow from these changes. Consider the implications of a legal decision that establishes the patient's right to treatment in mental institutions, and the increasingly accelerated movement of patients from mental institutions into the community!

Mental health is being integrated into a larger national health system outlined in recent health policy legislation. Social workers in health planning, administration, and community organization roles will increasingly be needed for mental health programs. A simultaneous need for clinically skilled social work counselors is occurring now that community mental health centers have a legal mandate to expand programs for many new populations—such as older persons and alcoholics.

A wider range of professional and paraprofessional manpower will be required to expand treatment interventions and correct gaps in our preventive service programs in community mental health.

THIS has been an era of profound changes in the system of mental health services in the United States. These changes have wrought significant modifications in the practice of social workers in mental health. This chapter will review the history of the changes in structure and function of the mental health services, describe the trends in direct and indirect practice of social work attributable to these changes, and forecast the modes for service delivery that can be anticipated in the near future. Also discussed will be the current stage of professional development and the impact of mental health knowledge on social work education and practice.

The Historical Context of Change

The growth and structure of care of the mentally ill in the United States have been marked by an ill-defined series of dramatic shifts and by more clearly described incremental changes. The dramatic shifts occurred after both World Wars, following the passage of specific legislation, the publication of significant reports, and a number of judicial decisions directly bearing on the care, treatment, and rehabilitation of the mentally ill. The practice of social work in relationship to mental health has been greatly affected by these changes, by socioeconomic changes over two decades, and also by new theoretical constructs emerging from the social and behavioral sciences. These have shaken the foundations of the profession and have had an impact on the fields of service which form the milieu of social work.

The First World War produced far-reaching developments in treatment of the mentally ill (psychoanalysis and psychosocial diagnostic formulations), in the structure of service (introduction of child guidance and adult mental health clinics to provide an alternative to hospitalization), and in attitudes toward mental illness (growth of the mental health movement). This was the period when psychiatric social work emerged as a recognized specialization, with an established national organization and accepted standards for education clearly related to the graduate master's degree level of preparation. It was certainly an era of specialization in practice, with strong emphasis on the casework method.

The Second World War brought attention to the stark plight of the mentally ill in state hospitals and the need for more help to the "walking wounded," the ambulatory mentally ill person. A direct result was the National Mental Health Act of 1946 (Public Law 79-487) and the impetus it gave to expand research, training, and services to the mentally ill and to the total population. The effusion of federal funds in the 1940s and 1950s had significant impact on reorganization of state mental health programs. Many moved from rigid structures, such as a state mental hospital system, toward the more comprehensive and multifunctional community

mental health pattern of organization. State staff, multidisciplinary in composition, came into being and took leadership in
promoting new legislation, broader training and research efforts,
and improved public understanding of mental illness and the mentally ill. The advent of psychotropic drugs and their extensive use
reversed the trend in hospital admissions, reducing the patient
populations drastically.

The most significant change in the pattern of service delivery to
the mentally ill followed the 1963 Mental Health and Mental Retardation Centers legislation. This occurred shortly after the first
presidential message on mental health.[1] The law was a direct
reaction to the impact of psychoactive drugs on mental hospital
populations. Its passage followed publication of *Action for Mental Health,* the final report of the Joint Commission on Mental
Illness and Health during the Kennedy administration, which was
seeking new initiatives in mental health. By 1973, ten years later,
over 500 centers had been funded and were operational. The goal
of 1,000 by 1975 and 2,000 by 1980, set early in the program, was
far from attainment. Nevertheless, the impact that mental health
centers have had on patient populations and community services
may yet cause them to be ranked among the leading social inven-
tions of the twentieth century.

The New Thrust in Mental Health Centers

The creators of the comprehensive community mental health
center envisioned a multifunction institution, serving a catchment
area of 75,000 to 200,000, with an interdisciplinary staff capable
of highly skilled clinical services, outreach education, and consultative services. There was to be federally funded mental health
center initiated within the context of a state mental health plan.[2]
The center was expected to offer the five essential services: inpatient and outpatient care, partial hospitalization, emergency services, and consultation-education functions. Not required, but
deemed desirable, were diagnostic, rehabilitative, and pre- and
aftercare services, training, research, and evaluation. These 1963
objectives were extended in 1975 by Public Law 94-63 to require
centers to provide seven additional mandatory services: services
to the aging, to children, to alcoholics, and to drug-addicted populations; and screening for courts and other public agencies,

follow-up care for discharged mental patients, and development of alternative care facilities for mental patients in the community.[3] The last three functions are directed toward the problems which have arisen during the past two decades as the states with the largest hospital populations have moved to deinstitutionalize mental patients as a matter of social policy. The exodus of patients followed in other states as well.

The mission of the mental health services in the United States is closely related to the epidemiology of mental illness and to the efforts to discover, treat, control, and prevent mental breakdown. The growth of specialized institutions was based on objectives of personal care and the protection of society. Personal care became congregate care, and it became apparent that society was being protected well beyond the point of any real danger. The persistence of the advocates for the mentally ill finally produced a series of landmark decisions which materially affected social policy. These have mandated state and local responses not anticipated in the usual budgeting and planning processes.

Of particular import were federal court decisions by Judge Johnson in Alabama, Judge Judd in New York, and *Donaldson* v. *Connors* in Florida (settled by a Supreme Court decision in 1975) which established the right to treatment of patients who remain in mental hospitals, the right to release if they are not considered dangerous, and the right to community care after release.[4] A District of Columbia federal judge ordered the release to community care of a thousand patients in St. Elizabeth's Hospital considered not to need mental hospital care.[5] For social workers in mental health, the implications of these judicial actions are overwhelming. The mental health system is already underfunded, understaffed, and strained by unrealistic and impossible expectations for service delivery. While it is not possible to predict what will be the ultimate effect of these decisions, it is certain that the movement of patients from mental institutions is likely to be much accelerated in the near future. Judge Judd ordered Willowbrook to be reduced from a population of 2,600 mentally retarded patients to 250 over a six-year period. The New York State Department of Mental Hygiene agreed to find 200 community places in a twelve-month period. The implications for manpower deployment are immediately apparent. The resources for community care must promptly be expanded if a commitment of this magnitude is to be met. One important first step is the implementation of improved health planning.

Related Context of Health Planning

As the nation moves inexorably toward a National Health Insurance system, some intermediate steps have been initiated to restructure health resources more efficiently for the immense tasks ahead. The 1974 Health Planning and Health Resource Development Act is an instrument for revising the infrastructure of the health system of services in the United States.[6] The act authorizes one billion dollars over three years for this purpose. New Health Services Areas, each including about 500,000 to 3 million population, will be set up to serve as planning areas. New Health Systems Agencies will take the initiative for all health planning in their respective areas. It can be expected that social workers with preparation in planning, administration, and community organization will be drawn into leadership roles in Health Systems Agencies. Governing boards of the agencies must have a majority of consumers, and the rest providers. Envisioned is a vast facilities construction, modernization, and development program which will especially affect the primary care services for the medically underserved. New institutions, such as health maintenance organizations, will be expanded in scope and numbers. Prevention and research will be encouraged through improved planning and funding.

This new health legislation has a number of critical ramifications for social workers and social work in relation to mental health. It is certain that singular contributions will be demanded of social workers in health planning and resource development. As never before, knowledge about and skill in short and long range planning will be at a premium. Hard issues of multi-institutional integration will need to be faced. Mental health and health services will be forced into congruence as never before. Social planning for the involvement of consumers and diffusion of services to the underserved or unserved populations will be particularly important. It is here that the schools of social work will be put to the test. After two generations of preparing mainly clinical practitioners, training capabilities must now be increased to provide for health planning and administration. The close articulation of mental health services in the public health context becomes especially important.[7] Many social workers rooted in the 1960s poverty programs will be experienced in work in the community health field. The proper coordination of state and local health services is far from achievement. The new legislation (if it works) should provide a vast stimulus to improved health organization.[8]

Changing Social Services Directions

On the day that President Ford signed the National Health Planning and Resources Development Act of 1974 into law, he signed the bill entitled "Social Services Amendments Act of 1974."[9] This new revision of the scope of public social services (Title XX) became effective on October 1, 1975. An important objective of these amendments is to prevent inappropriate institutionalization. Here is a direct link to the new mental health centers legislation. Moreover, the new amendments direct such services as counseling, day care, and home care to be made available not only to people in poverty, but, on a fee-for-service basis, to those who earn less than 115 percent of the median income in the state. Thus it appears that middle or lower middle income families could pay for care to be provided under the auspices of the state in a local social service agency. Casework services, on a fee basis, could be made available to a far wider range of population than now receives them. Public social agencies will need to include staff members who are qualified to offer skilled counseling (casework) services. This would require better education for public welfare staffs through basic preparation (BA or MSW) or through in-service training, staff development, or continuing education. The last offers some hope for furthering the education of the BA graduate who seeks a career in the public social services but has not had basic professional education for social work. For over 250,000 personnel in the public social services, it will become necessary to provide knowledge commensurate with the broadened scope of service responsibility.

The cross-link with health and mental health services becomes clear when it is noted that Medicare and Medicaid services are included under social services and are the direct responsibility of state social services departments.[10] Long-term care of the aged mentally ill increasingly falls to nursing homes. Ochberg reported in 1974 that at the existing rate of increase, there would soon be over a million elderly persons in nursing homes.[11] The great need for services for these elderly persons is still far from being met, and community mental health centers now have a legal mandate to provide programs for older persons. The requirement for more consultation and education in mental health for the elderly will mean that content on geriatrics and gerontology will need to be brought into continuing education for mental health centers staffs.

Modification in Mental Health Practice

One example of the changes in patient care may be found in the trend toward unitization in mental health programs. Unitization is the practice of assigning a ward to a specific county or geographic area in the service boundary of the mental hospital. All staff become oriented to the home environment of each patient so that follow-up in the community can achieve a close integration of services not possible under the old discharge system. Social workers are as frequently in the community as in the hospital. The social worker in this instance serves not only as a therapist but also as a mental health educator, a coordinator of services, and a liaison person. The skills required transcend those employed in straightforward clinical social work.

A second example of changes in care is the use of outpost or outreach facilities. These may be based in an urban store front, as in the West Philadelphia Consortium system of counseling centers, or in a town hotel, as in the Seward, Nebraska, subunit of the Pioneer Mental Health Center, whose main office is in York, Nebraska. Social workers in these outposts conduct groups, provide casework service, carry on community organization activities, and engage in educational and interpretation interventions. In each case, there is a planned effort to have some impact on the general population served, whether in urban or rural environment. In contacts with employers, welfare personnel, general medical practitioners, and others important to the convalescent patient, the social worker must be able to communicate and to interpret the meaning of mental illness and its effect on the individual at home, in foster care, or in an alternate care facility.

The foregoing examples of extended mental health services raise the issue of paraprofessional manpower as a means of enlarging capabilities to cover the population served. Most hospital and mental health center staff now have a complement of trained and untrained paraprofessional staff. Those who are trained may have had a two- or four-year mental health worker training program. These programs produce graduates able to move quickly into the parameters of the community case load that require supportive services or linkage to resources providing partial hospitalization, alternative services, or intermediate care.[12] The network of social and health services includes innovative institutions manned in part by trained volunteers. The free clinics, runaway houses, and counseling centers described in a recent report typify these developments.[13] Hotline and walk-in clinics represent an attempt to provide emergency or crisis services attuned to the ambience of youths in search of new experiences as autonomous individuals. Many suicide prevention centers also make use of volunteers for first contacts. These institutions perform important screening and early detection functions accomplished less well by older forms of institutionalized services.

Social Work Roles in Mental Health

A wide range of total services are conducted by MSW and non-MSW social workers in mental health programs, from direct treatment (casework, psychotherapy, group or family therapy) to indirect service (community liaison, consultation, education, administration). A recent paper classified twenty-seven functions for social workers in community mental health (CMH). These were clustered in four general areas: (1) diagnostic and treatment activities, (2) community activities, (3) supervision and training, and (4) administration, research activities, and others. Workers in agencies with a "*higher* orientation" to community mental health spent 46 percent of their time in diagnosis and treatment, while 60 percent of the time of social workers in facilities with a "*lower* orientation" to community mental health spent their time in these pursuits. There were 18 percent in community activities in the higher group compared with only 5 percent from the lower group. The findings suggest the necessity for good preparation in the community aspects of CMH work. A significant finding was

that many more workers traced their preparation for CMH work
to on-job experience than to education in a school of social
work.[14]

Rural outreach and consultation are part of MHC functions.
Muhlenberger has described the work of a small new mental
health center in a rural Ohio community. It carries on a variety of
outreach activities through use of volunteers and consultations in
public schools, with the welfare department, and with the clergy.
A 1971 report also described work with county welfare personnel.[15] It is obvious that closer links are developing between
the mental health and welfare systems. The interprofessional
team concept prevails in the core structure of CMH services.
Among the criteria for successful functioning of teams of health
professionals, Kane names social work participation as essential
to accomplishment of the team mission.[16] The post-MSW preparation of social workers requires a clear orientation to roles of
the mental health professionals and of the paraprofessionals as
well.[17] It is significant that the experience of team relationships in
CMH continues from training into practice. It means much more
than clinical work with the medical members. Involved is work
with nonmental health and nonmedical staff in the community,
with whom collaborative relationships are essential, especially in
relation to supportive services for the mentally ill.

Future Deployment of Mental Health Services

The HEW Forward Plan for Health: FV 1977-81 lays out the
health status of the United States and points the way for future
organization and delivery of health services.[18] A major section of
this plan deals with prevention; another emphasizes manpower
for health. Most significant is the prediction that national health
insurance is inevitable and will probably emerge at the midpoint
of the planning period (about 1978). The plan gives meaning to the
provisions of Public Laws 641 and 647. Health planning and social services will be even more tightly related to efficiency and
cost-containment in health services. Thus it becomes important
for the social worker at the state or local level of planning to be
well-informed regarding the impending changes in health services
structure. The Health Systems Agencies are now in the process
of formation, organization, and staffing. A parallel operation in

quality assurance, the focal point for which is the Professional Standard Review Organization (PSRO), is operational, or is being planned, to serve as monitor for health services delivery in every region of every state. Social workers are being employed in a number of them. They tend to come from medical or psychiatric social work background. Their participation is important to the success of these organizations.

The Health Maintenance Organization (HMO) is projected as one useful instrument for future delivery of health and mental health services. They are projected as prepaid, group practice arrangements which, in time, could provide primary care health services to the total population. Envisioned in the scope of services would be a range of services from prevention to total provision of medical and health care. This ideal model may be seen as a precursor to the future national health insurance system, and would, in fact, serve as an alternative to the existing private practice model, which seems so generally inefficient in providing full coverage for the sick and the well populations. Not all existing HMOs include mental health coverage, but the intention is that they all would eventually do so. Present patterns for reimbursement for services do not always include funding of preventive services. As these are clearly part of what is done in the service system by mental health personnel, it becomes necessary to make sure that fund allocations cover preventive services on a par with treatment services. For example: a social worker's time spent in work with a parent education group should be funded just as is the time spent in a therapeutic hour with a child in treatment. Good work in parent education is likely to have significant influence on the ultimate need for treatment of children with behavior problems.[19] The long-range plans for HMOs contemplate that they might ultimately be self-supporting, after initial assistance from federal funds. Much would depend on the capacity of the new institution to build the infrastructure needed to provide the full range of services required for its catchment area, its success in building fiscal resources to assure continuity, and its acceptance by the consumer as an effective medical and health need resource.

The high expectations from the updated mental health centers legislation can be realized only with sustained funding and provision for adequate staffing. Their survival as a separate institution will depend on the way in which mental health centers emerge in the next stage of their development. They are not only free-standing institutions, but also are integrated into the health systems network serving the total community. Many of their activities resemble closely the work of family and children's agencies, social settlements, and community organization units in rural and urban settings. This blurring of roles has lead to the development of state and local human services or human resources superstructures that include the complex of social, health, and mental health institutions, agencies, and organizations under a single umbrella arrangement. These new departments have suffered from the growing pains which are inevitable when theory outdistances practice. Institutions also have their turfs, and conflict must result when changes are mandated with little account taken for domain and territoriality. Consolidation can become confusion rather than integration when human services are described (as they usually are) as including health and mental health services.

As an example of the perplexing problems that will emerge in the 1980s, one need only contemplate the possible effect of the judicial and court decisions mentioned earlier in this chapter. Cleland and Sluyter voice some of the fears that the impossible will be expected and the public will gain yet another grievance against the mental health system.[20]

If it is true that community health and mental health centers are taking on some of the functions of social agencies, and that social agencies are beginning more and more to take on some of the work of mental health centers, then it is time to assess the meaning of such combinations and permutations of service structure. It is true that Title XX matching funds, derived from an amendment to the Social Security Act, can be used to fund mental health services for eligible patients. It is clear that many of the rural and inner city mental health satellite centers provide a wide range of social and preventive services in addition to traditional clinical treatment. At what point does it become necessary to examine the purposes served by such a chaotic and unintegrated system of human services? Will not the professions themselves be driven to examine the educational and practice philosophies that have brought about a situation that leaves people without service in most parts of the country, while even the best staffed services do not fully represent the capabilities of the health and mental health professions?

When asked to speak on community care in Great Britain in 1961, Richard M. Titmuss entitled his paper "Community Care: Fact or Fiction?" He described the bad fit between facilities, services, and patient and community needs. His recommendations were very much to the heart of the issue: first, an earmarked grant to expand local authority community care; and second, funds to increase social work training "irrespective of speciality," and a Royal Commission "on the recruitment and training of doctors with special reference to the need for education in social and psychological medicine."[21] He recognized the compelling need for adequate funding and staffing, and for moving the medical community in the direction of a social mission if proper care of the mentally ill and retarded were truly to be made a matter of national policy.

Social Work Education and Manpower Issues

The history of social work education reveals a close association with the preparation of skilled manpower for mental health services. Psychiatric social workers and medical social workers were involved in service delivery in the health and mental health systems in the United States from the first decade of this century. Specialized associations of members with high concern for standards in graduate education supported the development of master's level curricula staffed by qualified instructors. This preparation for practice involved a quantity and quality of field experience that would assure graduates competent in team diagnosis, treatment, care, and rehabilitation of the mentally ill. The rapid growth of numbers of social workers in medical, hospital, and other health services is reported in a recent study. Between 1960 and 1970, the numbers increased from 9,795 to 24,233. The author projects an 85 percent increase in all social service workers over the 217,000 social service workers reported in 1970, or a total of 402,000 by 1980.[22]

Social workers in mental health have participated in the increases. The most recent staffing study of mental health facilities reveals a 26 percent increase in numbers of positions for social workers between 1968 and 1972.[23] A health manpower report reveals that 70 percent of social workers in mental health in 1972 had masters or doctors degrees.[24] These growth data suggest the need to look closely at the capacity of educational resources to meet the anticipated need for increased numbers of qualified staff.

By 1955, the National Association of Social Workers included the American Association of Psychiatric Social Workers and five other specialized organizations. Elements of specialized content in mental health are now found distributed throughout the curriculum or are found in specialized emphasis in post-MSW programs.[25] The burden of special emphasis occurs mainly in the field experience of masters students. These occur in mental health centers, child guidance clinics, mental health clinics, mental hospitals, residential treatment centers, and institutions for the mentally retarded, as well as in mental health associations or state and local mental health programs.

The movement toward a generic masters level curriculum was accomplished in 1959. Instead of indoctrination in a single method, such as casework or group work, students now receive an orientation to all methods over the two-year course. Depending on the clinical (micro) or community (macro) career objectives of the student, the program is modified through electives to meet the special needs of students aiming at CMH careers. Some students with objectives in administration or middle management (mezzo) undertake field experiences in administration in mental health or in posts which deal with organizational analysis and evaluation. The leadership for these educational programs tends to come from social workers who have themselves served in mental health centers or in psychiatric social work positions. While there is as yet no agreement on the precise range of activities undertaken by social workers in entrance positions in mental health, it seems clear, from the manpower data we have just examined, that the two most frequently found levels of preparation are the BA and the MSW degrees. The National Association of Social Workers has published a short statement on standards for social service manpower, which describes in brief the types of functions carried by the social workers (BA) and graduate social workers (MSW).[26] Most of the functions outlined are activities of social work staff in mental health facilities. With the substantive move away from organization of the NASW to include specialized fields of practice, there is no focal point in prospect for the development of knowledge about social work in mental health (a major concern of the Council on Social Work in Mental Health and Psychiatric Services, which was eliminated in 1975). In recent years there has been a dearth of good practice studies dealing with social work in community mental health. The issue of defining boundaries of practice between levels of practitioners and among the several mental health professions has not yet been squarely addressed. Systematic studies on the division of labor are much needed to identify more clearly not only the knowledge base of such practice but also the possible economies which might result if some of the present duplication or overlapping in functions could be eliminated.

The social work profession is at an interesting point of transition. The rage of the late 1960s has subsided but has not been without important results. Social work education now has significantly more content on ethnic and racial minorities than before. A large increase in minority students and faculty in universities has not been without its impact on curricula. The introduction of content on paraprofessionals in the health, mental health, and human services delivery system is now part of social work education. Two task forces, one on practice and education and a second on structure and quality of education have returned highly important, and, in the latter case, controversial recommendations to the Council on Social Work Education.[27] The proposal to move toward a completely different pattern of professional education for social work set off a storm of protest that brought about revisions in the recommendations and left the present form of MSW and doctorate education still standing. The existence of three professional degrees—BSW, MSW and DSW—suggests that some difficulties may be encountered, considering the reality of personnel needs in the field. The existence of CMH centers and practice in CMH, with its wide range of competencies and its heavy demand for a combination of clinical and community service skill, together tend to force social work to move toward a resolution of the issues of generic and specialized education and practice. The fact that national health insurance is predicted before 1980 suggests the need to move in a timely manner. Reimbursement for service is clearly related to proof that the service can properly diagnose, treat, or prevent some health problem.

The skills of social work in the team situation are clearly related to all these purposes.

It is worth noting that at a major conference on social work education in community mental health, the consensus was "that social work has a key role to play in community mental health that stresses rehabilitation, health promotion and primary prevention." The same report stated, "There was considerable feeling that social work has too readily adopted the traditional medical-psychiatric treatment model and as a result has relegated itself to a secondary or auxiliary role in most mental health programs."[28]

Where in the Future?

This chapter has outlined the trends in the development of mental health services and has noted the movement of social work into clinical and community service functions in old (hospital based) and new (CMHC based) systems of service. New legislation and recent judicial decisions have resulted in great pressures on the service system (and social work). Deinstitutionalization has produced a perplexing state of affairs. The drive toward expansion of community based service has forced a movement toward integrated and consolidated human services. While community care has seemed to be a highly desirable alternative to institutional care, not all studies verify this impression. Lerman in his recent report on community treatment in delinquency postulates that community care cannot, in fact, be shown to be more effective than institutional care.[29]

The nation is confronted with a struggle to maintain quality social and health services in the face of an economic crisis that has forced economizing in operational costs and parsimony in planning for service expansion at a time when more is known about service delivery than ever before. The poor, minority, and other underserved populations have just had some suggestion of what it means to have increased social and health services based in their own communities, with staff drawn in some small part from people of their own ethnic and racial derivation. The result is a paradox for the consumers, the taxpayers, the planners, the professionals, and paraprofessionals who provide the service. The need is there, the means for helping are known, but the fiscal reach of the state and the nation falls short of proper provision for facilities and services. The major states have devoted arduous efforts to devising changes in structure and function. The programs described in "Where is My Home?" illustrate attempts being made to convert mental hospitals into community service as well as treatment organizations.[30] Changing the name of the hospital unfortunately does not always change the system. Too little has been done to prepare communities for the arrival of large numbers of mental patients in remission, or older persons who should not have been sent to a mental hospital in the first instance. The silting up of nursing homes and long-term care facilities has been one result.

Social policy requires that persons "at risk" receive a high priority service. Social workers have long experience in working with persons at risk and with socioeconomic institutions that place them in that position. Perhaps more attention to prevention modalities will have some effect on the presently unmanageable work load. The resources of practice and education in social work should be given some redirection with this goal in mind. The task for the future will be how to deal with existing social and health problems while maintaining some reserves of energy and wisdom to work on innovations and new theory to better use the slim resources assigned to social and health caring functions.

Notes

1. John F. Kennedy, "Mental Illness and Mental Retardation," Message from the President of the U.S. to the 88th Congress, Document 58, (U.S. Government Printing Office, 5 Feb. 1963).

2. Alan I. Levenson, "The Community Mental Health Centers Program," in *Handbook of Community Mental Health,* ed. by Stuart E. Golann and Carl Eisdorfer (New York City: Appleton-Century-Crofts, 1972).

3. U.S. Congress, "Community Mental Health Centers Amendments of 1975," Title III, Public Law 94-63 (Washington, D.C.: U.S. Government Printing Office, 29 July 1975).

4. See the discussion of the Johnson decision in "Staffing of State and County Mental Hospitals," HEW, *Statistical Note 122* (Sept. 1975); "State Agrees To Transfer 2,650 Out of Willowbrook," *New York Times,* 27 April 1975, p. 1; "High Court Upholds Donaldson," *Civil Liberties* 308 (Sept. 1975), pp. 1, 7.

5. "Change Ordered in Mental Care," *Washington Post,* 30 Dec. 1975, p. 1.

6. For a detailed review of the essential components of this act, see HEW, "Health Planning and Resources Development Act of 1974," Publication No. (HRA) 75-14015.

7. E. James Lieberman, ed., *Mental Health: The Public Health Challenge* (Washington, D.C.: American Public Health Association, 1975).

8. Michael M. Davis, the noted health economist, long wrote on this subject; see his final statement, written at age 91, "What Are We Heading for in Medical Care?" *American Journal of Public Health* 61 (1971): 651–53.

9. U.S. Congress, "Social Services Amendments Act of 1974" Public Law 93-647, 93rd Congress H.R. 17045 (Washington, D.C.: U.S. Government Printing Office, 4 Jan. 1975).

10. *The Washington Report* 2 (Jan. 1976): 5, wrote that Title XX for all its problems inspires "great excitement and hope among the social welfare constituency, in part because it might be the beginning of a free-standing social services system . . . coordinated as an equal partner with delivery systems for health, housing, income, education and manpower services."

11. Frank M. Ochberg, "Government Policies and Programs for Therapeutic Community in America," (Rockville, Md., National Institute of Mental Health, xeroxed, April 1975).

12. Two useful sources on the roles of the paraprofessional are F. Riessman, J. Cohen, and A. Pearl, eds., *Mental Health of the Poor* (New York City: Free Press, 1964), and F. Sobey, *The Nonprofessional Revolution in Mental Health* (New York City: Columbia University Press, 1970). It is clear that the paraprofessional in mental health is a permanent addition to the manpower pool.

13. Raymond M. Glasscote, James B. Raybin, Clifford B. Reifler, and Andrew W. Kane, *The Alternative Services* (Washington, D.C.: American Psychiatric Association, 1975).

14. Lawrence K. Berg, William J. Reid, and Stephen Z. Cohen, *Social Workers in Community Mental Health* (School of Social Service Administration, University of Chicago, 1972), pp. 63–64, 97.

15. Esther V. Muhlenberger, "Collaboration for Community Mental Health," *Social Work* 20 (Nov. 1975): 445–47; George W. Polley, Loring W. McAllister, Ted W. Olson, and Karen P. Wilson, "Mental Health Training for County Welfare Social Work Personnel: An Exercise in Education and Community Organization," *Community Mental Health Journal* 7 (March 1971): 29–38.

16. Rosalie A. Kane, *Interprofessional Teamwork* (Syracuse, N.Y.: Syracuse University School of Social Work, 1975).

17. Howard J. Parad and Lydia Rapoport, "Advanced Social Work Educational Programs in Community Mental Health," in *Handbook of Community Mental Health,* Golann and Eisdorfer, eds. (New York City: Appleton-Century-Crofts, 1972), pp. 873–88.

18. HEW, *Forward Plan for Health: FY 1977–81,* Public Health Service, Publication No. (OS) 76-50024 (Washington, D.C.: U.S. Government Printing Office, August 1975).

19. The Report of the Joint Commission on Mental Health of Children asserts, "We must face the fact that our best and most enlightened efforts at promotion of positive, vigorous health and competence in children will never be completely adequate"; in *Crisis in Child Mental Health* (New York City: Harper and Row, 1970), pp. 28–29.

20. C. C. Cleland and G. V. Sluyter, "The Alabama Decision: Unequivocal Blessing?" *Community Mental Health Journal* 10 (Winter 1974): 409–13; the Johnson decision required the State of Alabama to employ five social workers for every 250 beds in mental institutions. Of the 5, 2 were to be MSWs and three BA level social workers.

21. Richard M. Titmuss, "Community Care: Fact or Fiction?" in *Commitment to Welfare* (London: George Allen and Unwin, 1968), pp. 104–09.

22. Sheldon Siegel, *Social Service Manpower Needs: An Overview to 1980* (New York City: Council on Social Work Education, 1975), p. 14.

23. Carl A. Taube, "Staffing of Mental Health Facilities United States 1972," HEW Public Health Service Publication No. (ADM) 74-28, reprinted 1974.

24. HEW, "Social Work" (chap. 30), in *Health Resources Statistics,* Publication No. (HRA) 75-1509 (Washington, D.C.: U.S. Government Printing Office, 1975), pp. 283–89.

25. Parad and Rapoport, "Advanced Social Work Educational Programs," in *Handbook of Community Mental Health,* ed. by Golann and Eisdorfer.

26. National Association of Social Workers, "Standards for Social Service Manpower," Policy Statement 4 (Washington, D.C.: NASW, undated), pp. 16–17.

27. The Council on Social Work Education sponsored these two task forces during 1972-1974. The final reports (both available from the CSWE) outline a substantial series of recommendations. The Task Force on Practice and Education recommended closer communication between faculty and field agencies. The Task Force on Structure and Quality recommended a shift of the entrance degree to the BSW and the introduction of a three-year practice doctorate. It proposed the field consider phasing out the MSW degree after eight years. The latter report was not accepted, but modified by the subsequent actions of the governing bodies of the CSWE.

28. Harold L. McPheeters, "Implementation Issues," in *Community Mental Health in Social Work Education* (Atlanta: Southern Regional Education Board, 1975), pp. 87–91.

29. Paul Lerman, *Community Treatment and Social Control* (Chicago: University of Chicago Press, 1975). A recent report by Robert D. Vintner, George Downs, and John Hall, *Juvenile Corrections in the States: Residential Programs and Deinstitutionalization* (Ann Arbor, Mich.: Institute of Continuing Legal Education School of Social Work, 1975), raises similar questions about deinstitutionalization in delinquency. For several reasons, "The savings realized through development of the less costly community programs are . . . insufficient to result

in major reductions in . . . overall correctional costs" (page 57).
30. "Where is My Home?" Proceedings of a conference on the closing of State Hospitals, (The Stanford Research Institute, Menlo Park, Calif., 1974).

Bibliography

Berg, Lawrence K., William J. Reid, and Stephen Z. Cohen. *Social Workers in Community Mental Health* (School of Social Service Administration, University of Chicago, 1972), pp. 63–64, 97.

Cleland, C.C., and G.V. Sluyter. "The Alabama Decision: Unequivical Blessing?" *Community Mental Health Journal,* Winter, 1974, Vol. 10, No. 4, pp. 409–413.

"Change Ordered in Mental Care" Washington *Post,* December 30, 1975, p. 1.

"Community Mental Health Centers Amendments of 1975" Title III Public Law 94–63, July 29, 1975 (Washington, D.C., U.S. Gov't Printing Office, 1975).

Forward Plan for Health: FY 1977–81, Public Health Service, U.S. Dept. of HEW, DHEW Publication No (OS) 76–50024 (Washington, D.C.: U.S. Gov't Printing Office, August 1975).

Glasscote, Raymond M., James B. Raybin, Clifford B. Reifler, and Andrew W. Kane. *The Alternative Services* (Washington, D.C.: The American Psychiatric Association, 1975).

"Health Planning and Health Resources Development Act of 1974" 93rd Congress Public Law 93–641 (Washington, D.C.: U.S. Gov't Printing Office, 1975).

Kane, Rosalie A. *Interprofessional Teamwork,* Manpower Monograph Number Eight, (Syracuse, N.Y.: Syracuse University School of Social Work, 1975).

Lerman, Paul. *Community Treatment and Social Control,* (Chicago: Univ. of Chicago Press, 1975).

Levenson, Alan I. "The Community Mental Health Centers Program" in *Handbook of Community Mental Health,* Stuart E. Golann and Carl Eisdorfer, Eds. (New York: Appleton-Century-Crofts, 1972).

McPheeters, Harold L. "Implementation Issues" in *Community Mental Health in Social Work Education* (Atlanta, Georgia: Southern Regional Education Education Board, 1975), pp. 87–91.

Mental Health: The Public Health Challenge, E. James Lieberman, ed. (Washington, D.C., American Public Health Ass'n, 1975).

Mental Illness and Mental Retardation: Message from the President of the United States 88th Congress, Document No. 58, February 5, 1963 (Washington, D.C., U.S. Gov't Printing Office, 1963).

Muhlenberger, Esther V. "Collaboration for Community Mental Health" *Social Work,* Nov., 1975, Vol. 20, No. 6, pp. 445–447.

Ochberg, Frank M. "Government Policies and Programs for Therapeutic Community in America" April 7, 1975. Xeroxed, 26 pp. (Rockville, Md., National Institute of Mental Health).

Parad, Howard J., and Lydia Rapoport. "Advanced Sŏcial Work Educational Programs in Community Mental Health" in *Handbook of Community Mental Health,* Stuart E. Golann and Carl Eisdorfer, eds. (New York: Appleton-Century-Crofts, 1972), pp. 873–888.

Polley, George W., Loring W. McAllister, Ted W. Olson, and Karen P. Wilson. "Mental Health Training for County Welfare Social Work Personnel: An Exercise in Education and Community Organization," *Community Mental Health Journal.* Vol. 7, No. 1, March, 1971, pp. 29–38.

Siegel, Sheldon. *Social Service Manpower Needs: An Overview to 1980* (New York: Council on Social Work Education, 1975), p. 14.

"Social Services Amendments Act of 1974" Public Law 93–647, 93rd Congress H.R. 17045, January 4, 1975 (Washington, D.C.: U.S. Gov't Printing Office, 1975).

"Standards for Social Service Manpower" NASW Policy Statement No. 4 (Washington, D.C., National Association of Social Workers, undated), pp. 16–17.

"State Agrees to Transfer 2,650 Out of Willowbrook" New York *Times,* April 27, 1975, p. 1.

Titmuss, Richard M. "Community Care: Fact or Fiction" in *Commitment to Welfare,* (London: George Allen and Unwin, Ltd., 1968, pp. 104–109.

U.S. Dept. of Health, Education and Welfare *Health Resources Statistics, 1974,* Chapter 30, "Social Work" DHEW Publication No. (HRA) 75–1509, (Washington, D.C.: U.S. Gov't Printing Office, 1975) pp. 283–289.

U.S. Dept. of Health, Education and Welfare Public Health Service, *"Staffing of Mental Health Facilities United States, 1972"* Carl A. Taube, DHEW Publication No. (ADM) 74–28, reprinted 1974.

"Where is My Home?" Proceedings of a conference on the closing of State Hospitals, (The Stanford Research Institute, Menlo Park, Calif., 1974).

4

Innovations for Social Services in Health Care

BARBARA BERKMAN

Significant policy innovations in the delivery of health care services are presented in this chapter. New concepts in health care delivery, and structural changes inside and outside the hospital system, provide a much needed base for helping community citizens with their social health needs. The chapter highlights the expanded roles of social workers in the interdisciplinary health care team of newer programs.

Instruments are being developed to help the social work practitioner perceive those problems which require his intervention more selectively and to resolve them more effectively. The problem-oriented record, social need and outcome classifications, and audit questions are among the instruments that provide clear, concise, unified statements of what social workers do in their practice. Constructive use of these tools should lead workers to be truly accountable to consumers by improving interstaff communication as well as the practitioner's assessments and interventions on behalf of individuals and families.

OF the estimated 137,000 social workers in the United States, approximately 25,500 (19 percent) are working in health programs.[1] Traditionally, the majority of these social workers (over 15,000) have been employed by hospitals,[2] where there has been continuous growth of social work departments. For example, a 1961 survey found that only 669 hospitals (25 percent) had social work departments. In 1971, 2,722 hospitals (43 percent) had social service departments.[3] The increase in hospital social services is in response to the highly complex social and economic problems surrounding illness and the need of patients and their families for help in dealing with the impact of illness and hospitalization.[4] With continuous population growth, an estimated 275 million people by 1985, the need will increase for social services as a vital component in the delivery of medical care. And if a national health insurance program should emerge with medical social services perceived as an essential benefit, social service in the health field will inevitably become the largest field of practice in social work.

The same basic knowledge and practice is brought to the medical setting by the social worker as to any other, but the health setting has specific goals and demands that require adaptation of the social worker's skills.[5] In a medical setting, the services offered by the social worker are inevitably affected by the structure and program in which they are offered. The major objective of any health setting is the care of the patient. The medical based social worker is by necessity involved in a multidisciplinary approach to patient care, collaborating with doctors, nurses, and many other health service workers in sharing expertise and knowledge. Social service in the health setting has multiple goals: to assist patients in the optimum use of health care programs; to socialize the institutional program in the interest of patient need; to make programs available and accessible to all persons in need; and to provide direct therapeutic help for the many psychosocial and environmental needs which physically ill persons and their families may encounter.

The Needs of Physically Ill Persons and Their Families

The physically ill person and his family encounter innumerable problems engendered by the illness situation.[6] Some of these problems are directly related to the patient's illness or handicap and its effects on him: the patient may be experiencing discomfort, pain, or temporary or permanent limitations. There is often anxiety about the nature of the illness or the medical procedures involved. The patient may have to enter the hospital and so, in addition to worries about his physical condition, will be concerned about his family, his job, and his finances.[7] His absence from the home may bring difficulties for the family accustomed to his presence. The medical reality of his condition may force changes in the family's previous life pattern. The patient may have to alter his living arrangements, going from home to chronic hospital or nursing home. Household responsibilities may have to be transferred from the patient to a hired homemaker.

The social worker knows that the ability of the individual and his family to use medical care, follow medical recommendations, and decide between alternative courses, are closely interrelated to the many social and psychological factors they must cope with during illness and hospitalization. In the process of identifying the patient's and family's needs, the social worker assesses the family constellation and each member's role within it, the quality of the family relationships, the patient's past experiences in managing stressful or crisis situations, the patient's and family's attitudes toward the current illness, and the physical, emotional, family, and community resources available to meet the identified needs.[8]

Many of the patient's and family's needs are medical-social, generated by the impact of illness, hospitalization, and discharge of the patient. It is therefore important to clarify and classify these needs. The following medical-social need classification focuses on the two crucial areas of impact of illness needs and discharge oriented needs.

Illness and hospitalization needs

These needs often reflect the anxieties and fears precipitated by the illness and are compounded by the patient's separation from his usual environment.

1. Anxiety reactions:	Patient or family member depressed, angry, fearful, or particularly anxious about a range of possible factors (diagnostic procedures, treatment, surgery or hospital course).
2. Adverse home life:	Family relationships adversely affect the patient's physical condition or response to treatment.
3. Complaints:	Patient or family member complains about hospital and medical services (such as room, food, personnel, doctor).
4. High social risk:	Patient or family is considered high social risk (child abuse, drug abuse, alcoholism, lead poisoning, etc.) which precipitates need for medical care.

5. Multiple health problems:	Patient/family has multiple current health needs or complex history of various medical problems.
6. "Problem" patient:	Patient or family reactions (acting out behavior) cause problems for staff
7. Social problems deter use of medical care:	Social and psychological deterents to use of medical care (such as lack of child care arrangements).
8. Tensions in role relations:	Psychosocial problems as direct result of hospitalization (such as felt absence of patient at home; new social roles must be assumed by family members).

Discharge oriented social needs

Discharge oriented needs are those related to facilitating a patient's discharge from the hospital. Discharge oriented patient situations may reach social workers at any time during the patient's illness and should not be thought limited to a later phase of hospitalization.

1. Hindrances to discharge:	Patient or family member has psychological or social or legal deterents to use of medical care or posthospital planning.
2. Concrete aids:	Concrete aids have been medically recommended (such as appliances, transportation from hospital).
3. Fear of prognosis:	Patient or family member upset, fearful, or particularly anxious about prognosis, projected postdischarge therapeutic regimen, or death of patient.
4. Finances:	Patient's financial situation is inadequate for hospital or posthospital needs.
5. Home supports:	Patient's physical condition indicates need for assistance at home after hospitalization (such as homemaker, nursing services, home aide, domestic).

6. Housing:	Patient's previous housing facilities are unsuitable for continued needs.
7. Long term institutional care:	Patient's physical condition requires long term institutional care after discharge (such as nursing home, home for aged, chronic disease hospital).
8. Temporary institutional care:	Temporary institutional care away from home needed following discharge (such as convalescent care).

The delivery of social services to patients and their families requires full use of social work practice skills. If it is determined that social service help should involve direct clinical services to patients and families, this may be accomplished through individual casework treatment, family therapy involving a multiperson family interview approach, or a group therapy program, such as one in which mothers focus on the emotional and family living problems created by a child's chronic illness.

As a form of indirect service on behalf of patients and their families, medical social workers may give consultative service to other members of the medical team, to community agencies, and to other persons or groups seeking guidance in helping the patients.[9] This consultation may be either informal or formalized through patient-care conferences. The social worker in the medical care team conference must supply the most meaningful interpretations possible of the social situation of the patient to promote appropriate medical-social planning. By broadening the dimensions in which the patient is viewed in the health setting, social workers make an important contribution to improving the effectiveness of medical care. The social worker, therefore, in collaboration with other medical and health personnel, supports and furthers the objectives of the overall medical or health program. Collaboration is the *sine qua non* of social service delivery in health services.

Another role for medical social workers is emerging in their community activities—serving on health and welfare councils, on neighborhood councils, and on legislative committees. In this capacity the social worker can initiate as well as support community services for patients and families. At the same time the medical social worker can relate back to the health center the needs of community residents as well as conveying their attitudes toward health care and the providing institution.[10]

Unique perhaps to the university affiliated medical center is the social worker's role in teaching medical students. For example, at one medical school, social workers are involved in a course, Introduction to Medicine, in which first-year medical students are taught to evaluate the social and psychological implications of their cases to bring about better awareness of the relationship between the patient's life style and his feelings about his physical condition. It is the social worker's goal to include within the medical discussion of the disease entity a consideration of the needs of the patient and family as human beings and as essential components of patient care and treatment.[11] Also prevalent in the university medical center is the social worker's involvement in research studies related to the delivery of social services, in exploring the social components of illness and medical care, as well as in collaborating with other disciplines such as medicine and nursing in research endeavors.

"New" Concepts in Health Care Delivery

There is increased concern in the health field that traditional health care delivery systems are not optimally meeting the needs of all citizens in this affluent society. Today a proliferation of "new" interrelated concepts is appearing with increasing frequency in the health literature and in legislation for health care delivery. Some of these new concepts are comprehensive health care, continuity of care, family-centered care, accountability, and consumer participation. While some of these terms are new to social service, most can be perceived as conceptualizations of basic human values that have been integral to the principles of medical social service since its earliest conception. However, the embodiment of these new values in health programs *is* new and possibly reflects the important influence of social work in shaping medical care philosophy and practice.[12] This is evidenced in the increased recognition by authors in the field that health problems are not just physiological but represent a complex amalgam of genetic, social, and environmental influences.[13]

Medical technology has brought about remarkable changes in the nature and scope of available medical services. For example, renal dialysis, open heart surgery, and kidney transplantation either didn't exist or were very rare in 1950; many hospitals now provide specialized facilities and services for illnesses which were previously treatable with only limited success, such as intensive care units for victims of heart attacks, severe burns, and traumatic shock.[14] Technical delivery is not the major problem for health care today, rather the pressing need is for a more comprehensive health care system. Comprehensive care is not now a reality either in medicine or in social work. Although people can now receive high quality medical and social service care, they must be able to traverse the many fragmented and diverse systems available to them. Entrance to these systems is often limited by financial and other eligibility requirements. There are diverse programs directed to such groups as the aged, the blind, crippled children, veterans, and members of the armed forces. Some people with multiple health problems must now go to a variety of specialities in a number of different health centers because no one will look at the total social health situation of the patient or evaluate a total social-medical care regimen. For example, some health departments now give preventive care to mothers and infants but do not usually give acute care.[15] This is true not only for government and charitable medical care but also for private care as well. With the maze of eligibility categories, difficult for even the experts to comprehend, finding the entrance to these systems can be practically impossible for the poor, the uneducated, and those with language barriers.

Comprehensive-continuous health care

The principles of comprehensive patient care are compatible with the principles of social work. Comprehensive health care delivery envisions a single system in which a full range of services—from diagnostic service to outpatient treatment and, when necessary, full hospital and posthospital care—are available to the consumer. Interrelated with the concept of comprehensive care is that of continuity of care, ideally conceived as the coordination of outpatient and inpatient services as well as continuity between physician and patient. Continuity of care can be interpreted as the patient coming to the same familiar place and seeing the same familiar faces. Thus the patient in the outpatient service of a hospital can expect to see the same physician and same social worker at each visit and by appointment.

Emphasis in comprehensive-continuous health care is on prevention and early detection of disease, with curative and rehabilitative health services as needed. One of the most significant aspects of comprehensive care is its collaborative multidisciplinary health team model. Another aspect is to provide patients access to community resources as a vital component of the comprehensive care program. What is conceived is a full array of primary preventive health care for families. The traditional approach to delivery of medical care and social services in health settings is now almost entirely sickness oriented. There are very few primary health care prevention programs in operation outside of public health.

Family-centered care

Another closely related concept is that of family-centered care, in which the family is treated as the patient. The family-centered approach is a means to achieve comprehensive, continuous health care. The idea is to promote family health maintenance through the making available preventive, treatment, and rehabilitative services. In addition, the health care system is to assume responsibility for coordinating patient use of related community social agencies as required. Another component of family-centered care is the extension of hospital services into the home of the patient, not only to better evaluate the patient's environment but also to save hospital beds for the more acutely ill patient.[16] The family-centered approach would enable the physician, social worker, and other members of the health care team to appreciate the impact of the individual's illness on the rest of the family and to understand how family relationships affect the onset and course of the disease. If continuity of care and family-centered care is to be part of a comprehensive health program, visiting the patient at home is an important component. Hospital care is not always the most optimum care, and home care sometimes can be the most efficient and appropriate care for the sick person.

Accountability

Accountability has become a key word in our contemporary society. Particularly vulnerable to the demand for accountability is the health care industry, where rising costs are leading consumers to question whether services received are realistically worthwhile.[17] Because of mounting public disquietude about the quality of medical care and because of spiraling costs with little evidence of improved care, the Congress acted in 1972 to amend sections of the Social Security Act dealing with Medicare (Title XVIII), Medicaid (Title XIX), and Maternal and Newborn Services (Title V). Public Law 92-603 prescribed Professional Standard Review Organizations under the predetermination and aegis of physicians and including nonphysician health care professionals among the members.

Professional Standard Review at this time encompasses (1) a peer review of the performance of individual practitioners; (2) utilization review committees and plans to validate patient admissions, their predicted length of stay, and any extended stay beyond the prescribed projection; and (3) a medical care evaluation (MCE) of the delivery of care.[18] The implementation of any of these mechanisms requires the development and ongoing modification of criteria, norms, and standards. Criteria are defined as predetermined elements of care against which the quality of a medical service may be compared. Norms are defined as numerical or statistical measures of usual, observed performance. Standards are the professionally defined range of acceptable variation from a norm or criteria. The purpose of criteria, norms, and standards is to permit selection cases where there is a higher than normal expectation that services have been improperly utilized or that substandard care has been delivered. Medicine is not alone in its move in this direction; social workers and other health care professionals are also moving towards similar accountability systems.

In the hospital where social work is currently financed primarily out of general hospital funds, social service departments are particularly under pressure to be accountable. A recent study found that hospital administrators interested in the use of social services often say that they do not have available funds to implement the program.[19] The study suggests that social work services are not well understood, and that the social work profession may need to interpret its activities more adequately to the larger health community. The National Association of Social Workers has recently emphasized the need for vendor status for the delivery of social service care. Efforts are being made to prove to providers in public programs such as Medicare and Medicaid and private insurance companies such as Blue Shield that social workers have their own reimbursable professional worth.[20] If social workers are to receive direct financial support for their programs, they must account for their service contribution to the health care of patients. The burden is on social work to show that its contribution is economically worthwhile and professionally sound.

Traditionally, medical social workers work in institutions where statistics often have been gathered by hospital administrators for cost analyses rather than for assessment and evaluation of performance. Over and above the issue of financial accountability is the question of performance accountability.[21] Is social work reaching the needs of the people it serves by the treatments provided, and are the services provided comprehensive enough? Social work professionals have not been unaware of many of the problems currently facing the delivery of social services in the health field. Criticism from within the field of medical social service has suggested that the services provided are not comprehensive, that patients are not returning for treatment, that the doctor is served and not the patient, and that the work is geared toward a middle class clientele rather than toward the poor.[22] In resolving these issues, we must first document both to other professionals and to our clientele the types of social needs with which social work can help and the contribution that social workers can actually make to the management of the social component of health.[23]

Consumer control

Another concept increasingly evident in the literature is that of consumer control of health service facilities. Some authors see this as the method by which health service institutions will become publicly accountable and accessible. To many it means participation by users or potential users of service on the boards of private or public agencies concerned with either the organization, financing, provision, planning, coordination, or regulation of health care services.[24] The new consumerism in health not only applies to traditionally inarticulate groups such as Blacks, Indians, Puerto Ricans, or poor Whites, but also to middle-class

Americans. Increasing consumer involvement in financing and delivery of health care reflects a fundamental change in our economy and society as a whole.[25] Supporting community involvement represents an exercise in basic social work concepts, namely the client's right to participation, individualization, and self-determination.[26]

Industrialization, urbanization, rising incomes, better communications, and higher educational levels have led to an increasingly better informed public. As people become more knowledgeable about the health care they receive, their expectations also increase. The consumer is now demanding a more significant role in health policy making. Through unions, employee benefit plans, neighborhood health centers, welfare organizations, and other types of organizations, consumers have been finding ways to obtain a greater degree of responsibile representation in their own medical care.[27] And it is the belief of many authors that the upsurge of consumerism, leading to more meaningful relationships between people and their health services, will rehumanize medical care in an age of technology and super-specialization.[28]

The principles embodied in these "new" concepts are now being integrated in many innovative health care programs both in hospitals and in new types of health delivery systems. The remainder of this chapter will discuss the role of the social worker in some of these new programs.

Innovations in Hospital Social Service

The modern hospital has been the principle center for development of quality medical care delivery systems and is projected by many experts as the hub for future medical health delivery systems.[29] Within this one institution, with its complex of internal and external audits and standards, there is the potential for providing a full range of comprehensive health services. There are almost 1.7 million hospital beds in the United States in about 7,000 hospitals.[30] Half of these are voluntary (nonprofit), general, short-term hospitals with 27 percent of the beds and 70 percent of all annual hospital admissions.[31] In recent years there has been a leveling off in use of inpatient services and a concomitant increase in the use of hospital outpatient facilities.[32] There are an estimated 180 million patient visits each year to the outpatient and emergency room facilities of the voluntary and public general hospital.[33] Outpatient services have had low prestige in the hospital's organizational and financial hierarchy, however, and have been poorly recognized in most health insurance programs. With growing consumer dissatisfaction with traditional outpatient clinics, hospitals and their social service departments are now looking for acceptable means to improve delivery of patient care and to implement comprehensive services for both inpatients and outpatients.

The issue of accountability

Helen Rehr has written that social services in the health care field are accountable (1) to the specific health care system of which the social service department is a component part; (2) to the clientele served or to be served; (3) to those who pay for the service and those who license, regulate, or accredit the service on the public's behalf; and (4) to the profession of social work.[34] The accountability of social service in hospitals is currently the subject of many innovative approaches—among them peer review mechanisms, problem-oriented records, and social health care audits.

Peer review as a means of quality control can take on many forms. Usually it is carried out by a committee made up of a number of qualified social service staff members who assess closed cases and comment on them to the practitioners. Staff members may be asked to appear before the committee and their practice assessed in person. Guidelines for the assessment are usually formulated and agreed upon by the staff. One Boston hospital's social service department defines the purpose of peer review in this way: "to ensure that the patient's medical, psychiatric, or social service record gives specific objective accounting of the social worker's participation in helping the patient solve his or her problems."[35] Peer review is perceived as only one of several means to assure quality of service.

Many hospitals and their social service departments are developing standardized problem-oriented medical record systems to meet accountability needs. The problem-oriented record is an organized method of keeping clear and concise statements of problems and of the courses of action taken toward resolving them. There are usually four steps in the process: (1) recording the data base, or what might be called the psychosocial history; (2) the problem list, or social need inventory of the client (the patient or family); (3) noting the plan for treatment, the proposed approach to each problem on the problem list; and (4) entering progress notes for each listed problem, or what could be considered outcome. The advantages of a well thought out, structured, and consistent record system are numerous; it improves communications between the different professionals who use the medical record, avoids duplication in data gathering and recording, and facilitates information retrieval. In relation to accountability, the problem-oriented record is a means of facilitating medical and social service audit and provides a standardized approach that can be utilized in the peer review process.

Recent exciting approaches to meeting accountability demands are hospital social service department audits and regional audits.[36] The social health care audit recently completed at Mount Sinai Hospital in New York City served two equally important PSRO purposes: evaluating services and generating profiles on patients, practitioners, and the department as a whole. The first set of audit questions asked were:

1. How did the client get into the social service system of care? Who referred him?
2. What did the referrer request?
3. Did the social worker agree with the referrer's assessment of psycho-social problems? Does the social worker perceive any problems differently?
4. What social need "contracts" for social service were made between worker and client?
5. Do social worker "outcomes" vary according to types of psycho-social needs?
6. What interventive activities were utilized? Over what period of time?
7. Can one develop a technique to determine normative ranges of interventive patterns related to number of contracts or disease entities?

In a similar approach to audit, the Massachusetts Ad Hoc Committee for Social Service Professional Standards Review is conducting a regional audit of adult medical and surgical patients served by New England hospital social service departments. This large scale survey is supported by the contributions of the individual participating hospitals, NASW, and the Society for Hospital Social Service Directors. The data collection instrument covers five areas essential for profile information:

1. Patient social indicators;
2. The patient's condition and its effects;
3. Social Service intervention patterns;
4. Social needs or problems dealt with by social workers;
5. Outcome of intervention.

The aim of the instrument is to enable profiles of care to be generated including a statement about social needs dealt with and outcome.

The regional audit and the individual hospital audits have more similarities than differences. Both are efforts toward gathering uniform individual case record data for statistical maintenance as a necessary preliminary to audit. Both are aimed at collecting quantitative normative data on intervention patterns as a necessary step towards developing criteria and standards. Both have determined that essential components of an audit system are specific delineations of client social needs and outcome of intervention directly related to client needs.

The instruments used in the New England regional work and the Mt. Sinai Hospital audit both represent orderly systems which clearly set forth selected social factors dealt with by social workers, the social needs involved, and the nature and outcome of intervention. These types of information classification will make assessment easier by making it possible to review social need identification and treatment plans as well as outcome. In addition, they will enable professionals to discuss patient needs in a mutually understandable and systematic way.

This delineation of social needs and outcome can also function as an educational device. By exposing other hospital staff members to a concise listing of what social workers do and the implications of the services we provide for particular patients and their families, we can go a long way toward interpreting our function to medical personnel and alerting them to the kinds of social health problems with which social workers can help. What is more, it can help our staff think along lines of selective problem perception and problem solving. Finally, this approach permits a way of looking at those needs that cannot be solved. Thus it is possible to identify gaps in current services and provide data for developing new social work programs.

Independent screening

A major problem handicapping the delivery of comprehensive social services in the hospital setting has been the traditional casefinding system.[37] Unchanged since 1905, the initial identification of persons in need of social service help is primarily left to other professionals, with the majority of social service clients referred by doctors. Therefore, in order for the patient or a family member to reach a hospital social worker during the course of the patient's illness, somebody has to perceive the social need; social services have to be considered the appropriate means for assistance; and a referral to social work must be made. Because persons outside the profession may not be familiar with the range of services and skills offered by social service, the traditional casefinding system (1) may exclude people who could benefit from their use, (2) may limit social service help to concrete services and fail to utilize the social worker's ability to help with the emotional impact of illness and hospitalization, and (3) may call in the social worker late in the hospitalization, thus limiting the amount of service a patient and family will receive and possibly influencing the outcome of the situation.

In a move to grapple with these problems, social work in the hospital is beginning to search for means to make its services available without waiting for the physician's perception of social need or prescription for social work intervention. Independent screening mechanisms are one means to free social workers from primary reliance on referrals, which now determines who reaches social service for help and when this help is offered. For example, one social service department in a major medical center in New York City has been working on a procedure to identify those parents whose social and emotional stress may interfere with their ability to cope with the needs of their chronically ill children.[38] The majority of ill children and their parents are referred to social workers for help by other professionals, primarily physicians. Too often, social and emotional problems are overlooked or go unnoticed by other professionals who are deeply involved with the patient's physical care. The proposed screening system will lead to earlier identification of patients and families with social needs. With earlier intervention, social workers can provide comprehensive services to help the children achieve optimum social functioning while minimizing the negative effects of parental stress reactions. Such services could reduce parent anxiety, facilitate better use of the institution, and assist parents in following the medical regimen. Earlier social service entry will also allow more timely access to available community resources, which frequently require extensive time to secure.

What is being suggested in such independent screening programs is a move away from an acute crisis intervention approach, which is often episodic and fragmented, to a more comprehensive, continuous delivery of service to those in need of help.[39] Independent screening also can lead referrers to perceive the full scope of the services social workers can offer and to call upon them more appropriately.

New manpower

In many hospitals, as well as in other health settings, professional social workers are now engaged in the teaching and supervision of persons with general secondary school or college educations who have become part of the social service force. The "professional" social worker may now be a graduate of a recognized undergraduate social work program especially in parts of the country where there are few Master's Level Social workers. Although the use of workers with BA degrees varies considerably among social service departments, these social work assistants (formerly called Case Aides) were originally hired in lieu of professionally trained social workers to solve a manpower shortage, even though master's degree persons would have been preferred for most positions.[40] More recently, the definition of specific tasks appropriately assignable to social work assistants has been the object of much research.[41] Many hospitals have evolved training programs and job descriptions for social work assistants, assigning to them specific tasks not requiring sophisticated casework skills.[42] Assistants are usually given limited responsibilities within particular cases. The intent is to integrate the work of the assistant into social work treatment, with more highly-trained social workers retaining responsibility for cases. This view holds that there exists a level of significant helping which does not have to be performed by the customary Master's level social workers, although it has to be planned and supervised by them.[43] The tasks are generally to secure and dispense information and provide concrete services. Many of these assistants, especially endowed with mature life experience, have moved beyond the provision of routine services to tasks requiring substantial understanding of human behavior, such as helping a patient to use a rehabilitation service.

Within the past ten years a different type of nonprofessional worker has become part of the hospital's social service force—the indigenous worker. This individual is indigenous to the community (usually lower socioeconomic) serviced by the institution and is recruited specifically for the job of social health worker. Indigenous workers were not employed because of a shortage of professional manpower but rather because of their ability to perform special functions and roles. They were chosen for their capacity to understand medical subjects and their aptitude for communicating effectively with both community people and other personnel in the health center. For example, one hospital's training manual allots to the indigenous worker the task of meeting programmatic needs identified in the population of users or prospective users of the hospital's ambulatory care services.[44] This hospital considers its "social health advocates" (their title for this level of manpower) to be key components of social services in the health field. They receive an intraining program to orient them to the job as well as close supervision from professional social workers.

The employment of indigenous workers has been described as making the delivery of services more palatable to the poor and more readily available to them, as well as giving them new employment opportunities.[45] Neighborhood health centers and family planning clinics are frequently staffed by neighborhood residents, and it has been reported that their presence induces the poor people in the community to utilize the professional services more and to find them more attractive.[46] The indigenous health worker has also been described as the means by which the health facility and community can mutually adjust to further the goal of comprehensive care.[47]

The use of indigenous workers is not without its problems. Often their past experience with social workers has been through public assistance and has been negative. In addition, many indigenous workers lack writing, analyzing, and interviewing skills, making supervision a complex endeavor.[48] These problems can be resolved, and the "new careers" concept of involving the poor and disadvantaged in health care delivery to their own community seems to have real advantages.[49] Their employment provides more personalized services to residents of the community and helps to dispel the image of the noncaring agency. The new worker acts as a valuable bridge, interpreting his community's values and particular needs to the agency's professionals, and reaching out to the residents of the lower socioeconomic community so that they will utilize the available health program.[50]

Patient service representatives

Recognizing the problems patients have in finding their way through the maze of fragmented outpatient services, numerous programs have developed a variety of guides, giving the positions names such as patient service representatives, health care expeditors, ombudsmen, patient service coordinators, patient counselors, and community relations workers.[51] The aim of all these programs is to make the available system of hospital services more responsive to patient needs. The patient representatives are advocates for patients, dealing with all types of problems, requests, and complaints. In some institutions they also serve as liaison with the community people who use the facilities.[52] For example, one program created by a hospital social service department registers and processes tthe many special requests, questions, and complaints received concerning the hospital's services.[53] Called the Patient Service Representative Program, it offers direct consultation, referral, and advocacy on behalf of patients. The program has three major objectives: personalized service in solving patient's problems relating to delivery of hospital services; liaison between the hospital and community agencies on behalf of clients; and a system of feedback to appropriate staff members regarding some of the innumerable obstacles that develop within the institution, which can delay or block the delivery of comprehensive medical and social services to patients. The coordinator of the program has access to all levels of staff throughout the hospital and is able to provide feedback to the medical, paramedical, and administrative services so that procedural changes can be made. Referrals to the Patient Service Representative are made by the hospital staff and by community agencies. Patients and their families can refer themselves, or can have their needs identified by the patient representatives in daily clinic and emergency service rounds. Social workers make extensive use of this innovative program, perceiving it as a valuable source of casefinding, as a centralized resource for information about the hospital and community, and as a means to solve hospital organizational problems faced by their clients, such as coordinating multiple clinic appointments when more than one specialist is needed or locating lost medical records.[54]

Structural changes

While many innovative efforts are emerging, structural changes in traditional outpatient departments are not achieved without mastering a multitude of complex problems of organization and design.[55] In their report on one hospital's proposal for replacing a traditional outpatient care system, Rehr and Goodrich concentrate on the organizational problems in the establishment of a comprehensive family-centered outpatient program.[56] Their model for a multidisciplinary group practice, with comprehensive services coordinated and available round the clock, is noteworthy. The key members of the health unit, all available in one location, were to be physicians, nurses, social workers, indigenous social health advocates hired from the hospital's community, and administrative staff. Consultants from other medical subspecialties were to be available as needed. Included in the proposed system was a home care program with home support aides to assist patients with special needs at home and with day care rehabilitation services. Satellites, such as storefront walk-in clinics, and special liaison with the local health department services were projected, and a community worker was appointed to develop better liaison between the hospital and its neighborhood.

The social worker in the program was conceived of as a collaborator with the physician and nurse in the care of registered persons and as the recognized coordinator of the known medical, social, emotional and environmental factors, emphasizing a family-centered approach. While social workers were to have a major role in screening social needs and coordinating family-centered care, they were also to serve as social-environmental diagnosticians, social therapists in social-health maintenance, and social health care programmers and social-health advocates. This innovative plan for an outpatient delivery system made social work an essential and inseparable component in the practice of comprehensive care delivery. Unfortunately, the program's creators were not aware of the organizational pressures to maintain the "status quo" and while some aspects of the original design were implemented, the comprehensive family-centered philosophy was basically thwarted before it could become a reality.

This model shows how hospitals are beginning to respond to changing community needs and consumer demands with new and imaginative uses of the health care team. Medical social service departments, which often mirror the fragmented practices of their medical colleagues, have begun to examine their own delivery systems, striving for "creative use of the whole range of social work modalities in health care."[57] Many other new forms of medical social services in hospitals have been created to aid individuals and families with social and health related problems, such as family clinics, group treatment, home care services, and transfer services. These approaches, while still comparatively rare, raise the hope that social service, along with medicine and nursing, is moving to replace its traditional and often fragmented delivery systems with a comprehensive and continuing service approach to patients and families.[58]

Innovations Outside the Hospital

Some major domestic health issues in the 1960s and 1970s have been the need for adequate medical care, unfilled health needs, and rising costs. The National Commission on Community Health Services recommended community planning for comprehensive personal health care to make services available, accessible, and acceptable to all residents of a community.[59]

Neighborhood Health Centers and health maintenance organizations are examples of responses to these needs.

Neighborhood health centers

The Office of Economic Opportunity Neighborhood Health Center Program was established in 1966, with an emphasis on free standing, community controlled centers, entirely separated from the hospital. This development reflected a growing dissatisfaction with hospital performance in meeting the health needs of the poor. These health centers were planned to offer a full range of ambulatory services, to work in liaison with other community services, to have close working relationships with a hospital and, as far as possible, to involve the local population in planning, operating, and working in the center.

In 1970, federal funding was being made to 49 OEO Neighborhood Health Centers serving an estimated 500,000 people each year. In addition, the federal government was funding 115 Maternal and Child Health Centers and another 35 General Health Care Centers.[60] The objectives of these centers vary. The OEO Neighborhood Health Centers, in particular, are involved not only in delivery of medical care but also in job training and other aspects of community development.[61] Recent changes in federal health service funding policies, perhaps moving toward national health insurance, throw into question the future of the many services presently offered by Neighborhood Health Centers and Maternal and Child Health Centers.

The principle of comprehensive care is basic to the philosophy of the neighborhood health center, which is intended to provide a single access to a full array of primary health care for families. Although the literature on social work participation in neighborhood health centers is limited, we seem to find that many of the problems faced by hospital based social workers occur there as well. The role of the social worker is not always clear, and social service utilization is often left dependent on requests for service by other members of the health care team. Availability of social workers does not assure that their services will be used or their skills accepted by either patients or other members of the health care team. These problems are exemplified in some programs reported in the literature.

Yale University designed a neighborhood family health care

project to demonstrate and evaluate a system of comprehensive health care that would treat whole families as the patient.[62] Their philosophy was that contemporary patterns of disease and disability demand primary emphasis on health maintenance measures and a focus on the family as the basic service unit. In their experimental model of a neighborhood family health center, the principles of comprehensive health care were implemented through a broad spectrum of preventive, curative, and rehabilitative health services. The center also was able to coordinate patient use of related community agencies.

The health team concept replaced the solo physician. Their team consisted of a medical student (with pediatrician and internist as preceptors), a public health nurse, a neighborhood health aide, and readily available consultants. The social workers, who were part of the consultation services, came from agencies separate from the center and were not actually an integral part of the health team. As before, the social worker was forced to rely on other members of the basic health team to identify persons in need of their services. Evaluation of need was considered a special consultative service and was undertaken in individual family situations only on the basis of the evaluation of the nurse and the doctor. While the social worker was consulted at the time of the initial family health plan if social or emotional problems were perceived by the physician or the nurse, it was the physician and nurse who then discussed with the family their need for counseling. This discussion did not necessarily mean that a referral to social service would be made; in fact, in one case cited in the project's report, the doctor engaged in counseling sessions with the family. After a three-month involvement with this family, with no improvements noted in areas in which social service intervention might have been appropriately offered earlier, the social worker was finally consulted regarding suggestions for new approaches to the problems and the "possible" direct involvement of social service.

If the case reported is typical of those in the early stages of the family health care program, it raises serious questions about the feasibility of continued reliance on "professional others" for the identification of persons in need of early social service intervention. Interestingly enough, the authors note that the program in future should be able to provide a workshop for students of nursing, social work, and health education, as well as medicine, where all can learn to work effectively as a team. The implication is that in the future social work will be included as a direct member of the primary health care team, and that a conjoint interprofessional educational program will be instituted as a means to enhance a truly collaborative process.

The Columbia Point program in Boston gives examples of other problems inherent in the delivery of social services in the neighborhood health center, even when the social worker is an actual member of the health care team.[63] The Columbia Point program consisted of four family health teams, each involving an internist, a pediatrician, several public health nurses, a number of nursing aides, social workers, and indigenous health aides who served as liaison between the professionals and the community. The health center emphasized home care and was staffed by physicians and auxiliary personnel twenty-four hours a day. Many of the basic patterns established at Columbia Point have been generally followed by the neighborhood health centers established in other areas.

It was the intention of the health center to improve the quality of care given to residents who found their way to its doors, but it also was designed to reach those who, until that time, had not made use of health care facilities. The health care team of physicians, nurses, and social workers was formed to increase efficiency, sensitivity, and understanding in dealing with relationships among physical, emotional, and social pathology in an individual or family. The physician was not viewed as the central person or director of the team; the person with the greatest rapport with the family and the greatest knowledge of the situation was to be in charge of any specific case.[64]

The Columbia Point program proved stressful for everyone who worked there. There was a great deal of blurring and overlapping in the role definitions and role activities of physicians, nurses, social workers, and family health workers.[65] The social workers felt they were being used by doctors and nurses in very instrumental ways for the delivery of concrete services rather than as counselors or problem solvers. In addition, there was an indication that the social workers' traditional orientation to practice did not equip them to work in this neighborhood health center because they lacked the flexibility necessary to relate effectively to the clientele and to their health team members. The social workers were accustomed to the confidential confines of an office, taking clients only if they could offer some counseling help. They were not used to home visits nor did they engage in any group therapy approaches. The professional objectivity that seemed to the social workers necessary to gain emotional leverage and make possible more than indiscriminate patronizing care, may have made them less acceptable to their team members. The nurses particularly viewed them as very traditional and noninvolved, doing only individual casework with set problems and having no involvement with groups of community people.

Some of these problems are countered in an innovative social work program in a comprehensive health center reported by Ruth Cowen.[66] From the onset, social service was established as an integral part of the center and social workers were assigned to health teams along with other members of the interdisciplinary staff. At the beginning of the project, however, social workers were as usual dependent on other staff members or outside resources for the identification of need for their service, so that intervention was often crises oriented. To change this situation, several social service screening devices were developed in the hope of independently identifying conditions threatening the well-being of a family at an early point when sound service, preventive help, or at least limitation of difficulties might be a realistic goal. Early casefinding was also accomplished through chart review, through meetings with other social agencies, through team conferences, and through the traditional referrals from other staff members. The program's social workers employed all three methods of service delivery—casework, group work, and community planning—depending on the needs of the individual or the nature of the community problem which came to their attention. In addition to the generalist role, the social worker acted as consultant to the other members of the health team on the social and emotional implications of the patient's illness.

Of additional interest here is how social workers utilized the neighborhood aides who were incorporated into the center. These aides observed social conditions, provided concrete services, guided homemaking tasks, assisted with food and clothing shopping, and gave long-term continued support to enhance social functioning. Significantly, they were perceived as giving helpful consultation to the social work staff about the lifestyle of poor families.

It is Neil Bracht's thesis that social work can make a significant contribution to the neighborhood health center. He has presented preliminary findings of his study of the changing function of social workers within the OEO Neighborhood Health Center Demonstration Program.[67] His research indicates that foremost among the activities of social workers in the project were education, consultation, and in-service training with indigenous personnel. He also reports that social workers entering OEO centers have been delegated more administrative responsibilities in the organization's planning of health services, and that the ability to apply public health and preventive models to social work practice is increasingly sought. Another suggestion is that a social worker can be a most effective agent in assisting the lay person and the consumer to become more knowledgeable about health and welfare issues, enabling them to become more influential at the policy-making level.

Social workers in the neighborhood health center need increased flexibility in traditional practice delivery. This was evidenced in the Yale project, at Columbia Point, in the Cowen project, and in the Bracht study. There must be increased involvement in administrative and community organization work as well as greater emphasis on collaborative interdisciplinary relationships and on flexible approaches to outreach and prevention.

Health maintenance organizations

Although the health maintenance organization is comparatively new under that name, there have been a number of such organizations in existence to serve as organizational models. A health maintenance organization is one that provides or arranges for the provision of comprehensive health services to enrolled individuals under a prepaid group health or other fee-for-service plan. There are now approximately 130 of them in the United States. Basically these organizations are a form of medical group practice, and some well-known clinics in the United States, such as the Mayo Clinic in Rochester, Minnesota, Lahey Clinic in Boston, and the Ochsner Clinic in New Orleans, were originally created in this manner. The two best known of the prepaid group practice insurance plans are the Health Insurance Plan (HIP) in

New York and Kaiser-Permanente on the West Coast. The prepaid group insurance plans emphasize preventive medicine. The Kaiser plan, for example, has a vested interest in keeping the patient well so that the cost of unnecessary medical procedures can be cut down. The program emphasizes ambulatory care rather than inpatient care, which also avoids expense. A study has found that Kaiser subscribers have greater ambulatory contact with physicians and other health practitioners than do Blue Cross–Blue Shield subscribers, but they spend far less time in the hospital.[68]

To many experts in the health care field, the health maintenance organization is a natural substitute for the old omnicompetent general practitioner. This approach is viewed as a means to provide comprehensive care while controlling spending and costs in the health care industry.[69] One of the major programs outlined in the 1975 federal budget was the establishment of health maintenance organization demonstration projects to provide health care on a prepaid basis with emphasis on preventive services. In 1975, fifty such health maintenance organizations were funded. At full capacity the HMOs are expected to serve about one million people, and a total of 170 HMOs are planned during the authorized period of legislation.[70] The experience of independent health insurance plans built around group medical practices and offering a wide range of health services to a defined population has demonstrated the feasibility in the United States of the development of health services of good quality and reasonable cost.[71]

The HMO concept also involves consumers in planning for provision of services. While such consumer control has been more or less implemented in the OEO Neighborhood Health Center Projects, the early prepaid group practices usually came into existence by enrolling large groups of consumers to form the nucleus of their program. For example, HIP was stimulated almost entirely by enrollment of city employees in New York, and the Kaiser Foundation Health Plan of Oregon was dominated by its early relationship to Kaiser employees and the Longshoremen's Union.

There remains the question of the role of the social worker in the expanding health maintenance organization concept. One of the general requirements of the new legislation is that an HMO provide medical social service. The major piece of reported research on the role of social work in the prepaid group practice is Eliot Freidson's *Patient's Views of Medical Practice,* a report on the Montefiore Medical Group in New York City.[72] A major finding of this study resembled findings on the role of the social worker in the neighborhood health center: the number of patients who utilized the social worker was much less than the number who utilized the public health nurse, and the professional workers of the program believed that of the doctors, nurses, and social workers, the social worker alone was seriously under utilized.

While a rather large proportion of the families enrolled in the program seemed to manifest problems that required counseling or referral for needs which the social worker was professionally equipped to provide, many of the patients did not use social service help. They persisted in seeking help from the physician or public health nurse for emotional problems and resisted referrals to the social worker. One of the major obstacles to the patients' acceptance of social service seemed to be that patients perceived the worker as concentrating her efforts on office visits and did not perceive how the social worker could understand problems in the home or in the school if she did not make home visits or school visits, as the public health nurse did. In addition, the social worker was viewed as a pleasant person but one who was unconnected with the day-to-day course of problems with colds and feeding and worrying about the children. These problems were taken to the familiar authority of the family doctor, the pediatrician, or the nurse. The social worker was not perceived to deal with normal problems, and the patients did not want to be identified as having abnormal situations that would need a psychologist or a social worker. The social worker's place in everyday team practice contrasted strongly to that of the nurse, whose relatively informal and highly accessible services seemed compatible with patient's perceptions of their problems.

This limited perception of social service may reflect the patient's resistance, as Freidson suggests, but medical social workers have frequently dealt with the hard-to-reach client. It may be that in the medical setting the patient's primary concern is for his health needs and referrals to social workers are resisted because the patient and his family do not understand what the social worker can do to help. The problem is probably related to the social worker's position in the group's medical team where she functioned as a relatively late source of consultation for "social" problems. The social worker's services may have been under utilized because they were incompatible with prevailing patient conceptions of the nature of the problems for which professional social work could help. This problem was exacerbated by a traditional referral system in which doctors and nurses requested the social worker's help for crises situations. This did nothing to indicate to patients what valuable contributions the social worker could make. Thus, we find that mere availability of the social worker on the health team does not result in automatic acceptance of her services, even though the health team members themselves felt that her interviews provided valuable information to the team in developing attitudes not only towards the family but also towards their own professional roles.[73]

Conclusion: Implementing Comprehensive Care

Social workers subscribe to the principles and philosophy of comprehensive health care delivery. They have always believed that health and medical care should be available and accessible to all persons and have recognized the interrelatedness of the physical, emotional, and social well-being of individuals and their families. Medical social work, in delivery of services to patients and their families, works in collaboration with other health professionals in what has been called a "health triad."[74] However, these three health professional groups—along with other professionals, paraprofessionals, and service workers—often have vastly different perspectives in their efforts to achieve the patient's maximum benefit. Each group functions with a high degree of autonomy, and there is often a lack of role differentiation that leads to confusion and poor working relationships. It has been demonstrated that these confusions between health care professionals are obstacles to achieving common goals on behalf of people in need.

Of particular concern to social workers has been the dysfunctional aspects of the traditional casefinding system in which other members of the health care team determine who needs social service help and when. This system frequently results in social workers giving late, episodic, and fragmented help in acute crisis situations. This referral system has remained basically unchanged through the years in hospitals and appears to have been adopted in the newer "innovative" health settings, such as the neighborhood health center and the health maintenance organization, as well.

Although social work, along with medicine and nursing, is contributing to the design of more comprehensive and socially effective medical care delivery systems, the problems inherent in the delivery of traditional medical social services are being manifested in the new programs whose very creation is a protest against antiquated service delivery. Clarification of the role of the social worker and appropriate utilization of social work services will not be achieved so long as social workers must continue to rely on the perspectives of other professions to determine the timing of their intervention and the types of social needs with which they can help. It is not enough to make social workers available as members of the health care team, for this does not ensure understanding or acceptance of their services by either the other members of the health team or the prospective clientele.

The goal of comprehensive care is not yet a reality and will not become one until a truly collaborative health care team is achieved. The question is how to effect this necessary collaboration among health professionals. At present, neither social work, nursing, nor medicine educates for interprofessional demands.[75] It is now being suggested that there is a need to enrich medical education with psychosocial knowledge, and social work education with biomedical knowledge. One means to accomplish this effectively would be through conjoint interdisciplinary teaching and learning experiences.[76]

Of particular concern to social work is the question of how to demonstrate to other health professionals and to clients of new comprehensive approaches to medical care the full contribution that social workers can make. The answer does not lie in the continuing institutionalization of the traditional dependent casefinding system. If the social needs that the social worker is best equipped to help with are defined, and independent responsibility is taken to identify those persons who can be helped, an important step will have been taken toward clairfying the social worker's role. But it is not enough that social workers assign themselves the roles of interpreters and helpers in relation to the emotional and social components of health. Rather these roles must be coordinated and legitimatized within the organization, both in the perception of the other team members as well as with the clients.

Independent screening mechanisms are one approach to solving the problem; aggressive collaborative involvement in both formal and informal health team conferences is another. Active reaching out to prospective clientele sitting in the waiting rooms of clinics is another. A problem-oriented social service entry in the medical record, clearly delineating the problem areas that social work has dealt with, and Social Health Care Evaluations are other means to communicate the social worker's areas of competence to other professionals who use the same medical record and who subsequently refer patients for social services.

The means to legitimate and substantiate the social worker's contribution to comprehensive health care delivery may vary within different interdisciplinary organizational structures. But rather than accept the 1905 model referral system still current, it is now imperative that workers make aggressive professional moves toward implementing comprehensive social service delivery within the context of the collaborative health care team.

Notes

1. HEW, *Health Resources Statistics* (Rockville, Md.: National Center for Health Statistics, February 1972), p. 241.

2. Milton Wittman, "Social Work Manpower for the Health Services," *American Journal of Public Health* 64 (April 1974): 371.

3. John H. Knowles, "The Hospital," *Scientific American* 229 (Sept. 1973): 131.

4. Ibid., p. 133.

5. Doris Siegel, "Social Work in the Medical Setting: An Instrument for Health," *Social Work* 2 (April 1957): 70–77.

6. For an interesting classification of social needs for hospitalized patients, see Barbara Gordon Berkman and Helen Rehr, "Classification of Social Needs of the Hospitalized Elderly Referred to Social Service," *Social Work* 17 (July 1972): 80–88.

7. For further examples of how social needs of patients have been perceived, see: Alice Ullmann and Gene G. Kassebaum, "Referrals and Services in a Medical Social Work Department," *Social Service Review* 35 (Sept. 1961): 258–68; E. M. Goldberg, J. Neill, B. M. Speak, and H. C. Faulkner, "Social Work in General Practice," *The Lancet* 5 (7 Sept. 1968): 552–55; E. Matilda Goldberg and June E. Neill, *Social Work*

in General Practice (London: George Allen and Unwin, 1972); and M. C. Goldwyn, "The Social Needs of Hospital Patients," *Medical Social Worker,* London: Westminster Hospital, pp. 149–52 (personal communication, 1968).

8. Helen Lokshin, "Helping the Aged Person with Medical Decision at Point of Crisis," *Journal of Jewish Communal Service* 41 (Summer 1965): 393–401.

9. American Hospital Association, "Essentials of Social Work Programs in Hospitals," printed by Visual Images, Arlington Heights, Ill. (1971), p. 12.

10. Ibid., p. 15.

11. Personal communication, Mrs. Jean Bernhard, Social Service Department, Mount Sinai Medical Center, New York City, 28 February 1974.

12. Sidney Hirsch and Abraham Lurie, "Social Work Dimensions in Shaping Medical Care Philosophy and Practice," *Social Work* 14 (April 1969): 75–79.

13. Anne R. Somers, *Health Care in Transition: Directions for the Future* (Chicago: Hospital Research and Educational Trust, 1972), pp. 15–25.

14. HEW, *Medical Care Expenditures, Prices, and Costs: Background Book,* Social Security Administration, Office of Research and Statistics (Sept. 1973), p. 31.

15. Bonnie Bullough and Vern L. Bullough, *Poverty, Ethnic Identity, and Health Care* (New York City: Appleton-Century-Crofts, 1972), p. 190.

16. George G. Reader, "The Cornell Comprehensive Care and Teaching Program," in *The Student-Physician Introductory Studies in the Sociology of Medical Education,* ed. by Robert K. Merton, George G. Reader, and Patricia L. Kendall (Cambridge: Harvard University Press, 1957), p. 85.

17. Herbert E. Klarman, Dorothy P. Rice, Barbara S. Cooper, and H. Louis Stettler 3, "Accounting for the Rise in Selected Medical Care Expenditures, 1929–1969," *American Journal of Public Health* 60 (June 1970): 1023–39.

18. Gaylen L. Newmark, "PSRO Regulations Now In Effect," *Hospitals,* JAHA (Feb. 1975), p. 32.

19. John T. Gentry, James E. Veney, A. D. Kaluzny, and Jane Sprague, "Promoting the Adoption of Social Work Services by Hospitals and Health Departments," *American Journal of Public Health* 63 (Feb. 1973): 121.

20. "NASW Digs In: Battles for Vendor Status," *NASW News* 18 (Sept. 1973): 5–6.

21. Eveline M. Burns, "Health Insurance: Not If, or When, But What Kind?" *American Journal of Public Health* 61 (Nov. 1971): 2171.

22. Bess Dana, "Social Work in the University Medical Center," *Johns Hopkins Medical Journal* 124 (May 1969): 277–82; John Mayer and Noel Timms, "Clash in Perspective Between Worker and Client," *So-*

cial Casework 50 (Jan. 1969): 32–40: Archie Hanlon, "Casework Beyond Bureaucracy," *Social Casework* 52 (April 1971): 195–200.

23. For two recent studies of the social worker's contribution in delivery of health care, see: Deborah Blumberg et al., "A Hospital Study of the Social Needs of Clients and the Role of Social Workers as Perceived by Social Workers and Their Clients" (May 1973), and Natalie Dixon et al., "An Accountability Study of Delivery of Social Services to Patients and Their Families" (May 1974)—both unpublished masters degree research projects, Simmons College School of Social Work, Boston.

24. Samuel Wolfe, "Consumerism and Health Care," *Public Administration Review* 31 (Sept.–Oct. 1971): 528–36.

25. Walter McNerney, "Medicine Faces the Consumer Movement," *Prism,* the Socioeconomic Magazine of the American Medical Association, vol. 6 (Sept. 1973), pp. 13–15.

26. National Association of Social Workers, *Community Involvement and Control in Health Services: A Challenge to Social Workers,* First Health Action Forum, New York City 1971.

27. Somers, *Health Care in Transition,* p. 24.

28. Wolfe, "Consumerism and Health Care," p. 535.

29. Somers, *Health Care in Transition,* pp. 27–38; and Rosemary Stevens, *American Medicine and the Public Interest* (New Haven and London: Yale University Press, 1972), p. 538.

30. Herbert Klarman, *Background, Issues and Policies in Health Services for the Aged in New York City* (New York City: NYC Interdepartmental Health Council, May 1962), p. 6.

31. H. M. Somers and A. R. Somers, *Patients, Doctors, and Health Insurance* (New York City: Anchor Books, 1961), p. 51.

32. Somers, *Health Care in Transition,* p. 28.

33. Knowles, "The Hospital," p. 130.

34. Helen Rehr, *Accountability for Social Services in Medical Settings,* paper presented 29 November 1973, New York University Medical Center, Metropolitan New York Chapter, Society for Hospital Social Work Directors, American Hospital Association.

35. Janet Wein, Director Social Service, New England Medical Center Hospital, Boston, May 1974, personal communication.

36. Barbara Berkman, "Are Social Service Audit Systems Feasible? Experiences with a Hospital-Based and Regional Approach," paper presented to Society for Hospital Social Work Directors, PSRO-UR and Social Work Working Conference, Ft. Worth, 18–21 Jan. 1976.

37. See Barbara Gordon Berkman and Helen Rehr, "Unanticipated Consequences of the Casefinding System in Hospital Social Service," *Social Work* 15 (April 1970): 63–68; idem, "Early Social Service Case Finding for Hospitalized Patients: An Experiment," *Social Service Review* 47 (June 1973): 256–65; idem, "The 'Sick Role' Cycle and the Timing of Social Work Intervention," *Social Service Review* 46 (Dec. 1972): 567–80; and Helen Rehr and Barbara Gordon Berkman, "Social Service Casefinding in the Hospital: Its Influence on the Utilization of Social Services," *American Journal of Public Health* 63 (Oct. 1973): 857–62.

38. Alma Young, Helen Rehr, and Barbara Berkman, "Social Needs Screening of Chronically Ill Children," proposal pending, Mount Sinai School of Medicine of the City University of New York, Department of Community Medicine (Social Work), 1974.

39. See Ruth Cowin, "Some New Dimensions of Social Work Practice in a Health Setting," *American Journal of Public Health* 60 (May 1970): 860–69; and Alma T. Young, Barbara Berkman, and Helen Rehr, "Women Who Seek Abortions: A Study," *Social Work* 18 (May 1973): 60–65.

40. Frank M. Loewenberg, "Social Workers and Indigenous Non-professionals: Some Structural Dilemmas," *Social Work* 13 (July 1968): 65.

41. Margaret M. Heyman, "A Study of Effective Utilization of Social Workers in a Hospital Setting," *Social Work* 6 (April 1961): 36–43; and Jean Dockhorn, "The Veterans Administration Social Work Assistants Project," in "Proceedings of a conference for social workers in the health field, Pittsburg, Penn., 2–7 May 1965," Public Health Service, Division of Chronic Diseases, Gerontology Branch, June 1965, pp. 129–43.

42. Janice Paneth, Associate Director, Social Service Department, Mount Sinai Medical Center, New York City, personal communication, June 1974.

43. Dockhorn, "VA Social Work Assistants Project," p. 131.

44. Florence T. Stein, "Social Health Advocate Training Program Manual," Social Service Department, Mount Sinai Hospital, New York City, June 1969.

45. Loewenberg, "Social Workers and Indigenous Nonprofessionals," p. 66.

46. Alan Gartner and Frank Riessman, "New Training for New Services," *Social Work* 17 (Nov. 1972): 56.

47. James E. Bates, Harry H. Lieberman, and Rodney N. Powell, "Provisions for Health Care in the Ghetto: The Family Health Team," *American Journal of Public Health* 60 (July 1970): 1222.

48. Pearl R. Roberts, "The Etiology of a New Careers Program in Public Health," *American Journal of Public Health* 63 (July 1963): 636.

49. Ibid., p. 637.

50. Robert Reiff and Frank Riessman, *The Indigenous Nonprofessional,* Community Mental Health Journal Monograph Series 1 (1970), p. 3.

51. For example: Gerald Katz, "Volunteers: Ombudsmen for Emergency Care Patients," *Volunteer Leader* (Feb. 1973), pp. 13–17; and Dames G. Stolhanske, "Is a Patient Counselor Worth the Investment?" *Group Practice* 20 (June–July 1971): 20–23.

52. Ruth W. Ravich, Helen Rehr, and Charles H. Goodrich, "Ombudsman: A New Concept in Voluntary Hospital Services," in *Human Services and Social Work Responsibility,* ed. by Willard C. Richan (New York City: National Association of Social Workers, 1969), p. 313.

53. Ruth Ravich, Helen Rehr, and Charles H. Goodrich, "Hospital

Ombudsman Smooths Flow of Services and Communications," *Hospitals* 43 (1 March 1969): 56–61.

54. Helen Rehr and Ruth Ravich, "Ombudsman Program Provides Feedback," *Hospitals* 48 (16 Sept. 1974): 62-67.

55. Charles H. Goodrich, Margaret C. Olendzki, and Annemarie F. Crocetti, "Hospital-Based Comprehensive Care: Is It a Failure?" *Medical Care* 10 (July–Aug. 1972): 363–68.

56. Helen Rehr and Charles H. Goodrich, "Problems of Innovation in a Hospital Setting," in *Human Services and Social Work Responsibility,* ed. by Willard C. Richan (New York City: NASW, 1969), pp. 303–10.

57. Dana, "Social Work in the University Medical Center," p. 280.

58. Helen Rehr, "Developing Community Organization: Planning Functions in a Modern Hospital," unpublished monograph, Dec. 1965.

59. National Commission on Community Health Services, *Comprehensive Health Care,* Report of Task Force on Comprehensive Personal Health Services (Washington, D.C.: Public Affairs Press, 1967), p. 25.

60. Stevens, *American Medicine and the Public Interest,* p. 521.

61. Bullough and Bullough, *Poverty, Ethnic Identity, and Health Care,* p. 173.

62. Jerome S. Beloff and E. Richard Weinerman, "Yale Studies in Family Health Care," *Journal of the American Medical Association* 199 (Feb. 1967): 383–89.

63. Seymour Bellin and H. Jack Geiger, "The Impact of a Neighborhood Health Center on Patients' Behavior and Attitudes Relating to Health Care: A Study of a Low Income Housing Project," *Medical Care* 10 (May–June 1972): 224–39.

64. H. David Banta and Renee C. Fox, "Role Strains of a Health Care Team in a Poverty Community" (The Columbia Point Experience), *Social Science and Medicine* 6 (Great Britain: Pergamon Press, 1972), 697–722.

65. Ibid., p. 717.

66. Cowin, "Some New Dimensions"; and Ruth A. Cowin, Elizabeth P. Rice, and William M. Schmidt, "Social Work in a Child Health Clinic: A Report of a Demonstration," *American Journal of Public Health* 55 (June 1965): 821–31.

67. Neil F. Bracht, "The Expanding Field of Community Medicine: Educational Implications for Social Work," a paper delivered at the 96th Annual Meeting of the American Public Health Association, Detroit, 11–15 Nov. 1968.

68. Bullough and Bullough, *Poverty, Ethnic Identity, and Health Care,* p. 192.

69. Ibid., pp. 189–93; Stevens, *American Medicine and the Public Interest,* p. 522; and HEW, *The Size and Shape of the Medical Care Dollar,* Social Security Administration, Office of Research and Statistics, Chart Book 1972, pp. 34–35.

70. American Public Health Association, *The Nation's Health* 4 (March 1974): 4.

71. Stevens, *American Medicine and the Public Interest,* p. 522.

72. Eliot Freidson, *Patients' Views of Medical Practice* (New York City: Russell Sage Foundation, 1961).

73. Ibid.

74. Helen Rehr, "Comparison of Health Care Professions on Predicted Outlook of Patient Compliance, and in General Attitudes Regarding Collaboration and Health Care," DSW dissertation, Columbia University, 1970.

75. Bess Dana et al., "An Agenda for the Future of Interprofessionalism," *Medicine and Social Work: An Exploration in Interprofessionalism,* Report of a Colloquium on Interprofessional Education and Practice in the Health Field, 18–19 April 1973, Mount Sinai Medical Center, New York City (New York: Prodist Press, 1974).

76. Ibid., and Elaine M. Brody, "Social Work as an Integral Part of Health Institutions: A Viable Relationship," paper presented at 23rd Middle Atlantic Hospital Assembly, Atlantic City, N.J., 25 May 1971.

5

Changing Approaches to Social Work with Older Adults

MARGARET E. HARTFORD and MARY M. SEGUIN

Until recently, social work practice has not placed a major emphasis on people near the end of the life cycle. Since the concepts of social gerontology are just beginning to emerge, it is likely that the next decade will witness important developments in work with older adults in all of the human services and especially in social work programs.

This chapter deals with some of the problems and major advances in developing services to meet the needs of both frail and well elderly persons. The greatest progress in this field of practice is in the public sector. National legislation has set in motion a rich diversity of services. Social workers specializing in the field of aging can expect to take new and expanded roles, both in the design of research on aging, in-service training, and service delivery within the newly established geriatric programs. The new employment opportunities for social workers in the field of aging require new combinations of methods or modalities, and collaboration with many other human service professionals in recently designed service milieus.

PRACTICE in the field of social gerontology is one of the developing frontiers in social work. Research findings that emerged in the 1960s are now being translated into programs. Now and in the near future, services with a population that is growing older will be a rapidly expanding field of practice for all the human services and especially in programs and activities appropriate to social workers. Many of these programs are multidisciplinary and demand collaboration among many professions and services. In some instances social work will carry the central administrative responsibility. In other instances, social workers will work collaterally with several professions, and in still others social work services will be an adjunct to another service profession.

Historical Perspective

Social work practice with older adults or in programs for the aging has existed for many years. Older adults have been served both within existing general social work programs and also in special programs established primarily for the aged. Until recently, however, there has not been a major emphasis on aging in social work practice, in education for practice, nor in the coordination and development of services. Notable exceptions have been the work of a few counseling agencies established primarily to serve older adults and their families, such as the Benjamin Rose Institute of Cleveland. This organization was begun in the early 1900s to locate resources necessary for social, health, and economic support of older people. Another long standing organization is the Social Service Department of the Philadelphia Geriatric Center. The programs for the elderly of the Jewish Family Service Agency of New York also have long historical roots, but such services have not been widespread throughout the country. Senior centers, "Golden Age Clubs," and other programs geared primarily toward recreation, informal education, and social activities have existed from the 1930s and 1940s and have expanded into hundreds of centers in the past thirty years. Recently, some of these agencies have become senior multiservice centers offering health services, meals, counseling, transportation, and in some instances even housing.[1]

The Social Security Act of the 1930s has been the major economic innovation. Among its provisions, the act included Social Security often called insurance and Old Age Assistance, which is now shifted into the Supplementary Security Income. In addition, there are independent retirement and pension plans provided by organizations, unions, corporations, and employees' groups. Philanthropic homes for the aged have long existed to house elderly persons who have no family or financial resources. They now also provide extensive health care to their residents, many of whom are very old and frail. Many elderly well individuals, who before Social Security would have had to become residents of homes for the aged, now live independently in the community. Similarly, tax supported county homes, if they exist at all, tend to serve a very old and frail population in need of health care. Some philanthropic homes, some tax supported institutions, and some proprietary (profit making) nursing homes qualified as extended care facilities when the Medicare legislation was enacted in 1965. This law provided for social work consultation and for the designation of an employee to give social work services in extended care facilities. Historically and currently, social workers have served in institutions for the aged as administrators, as consultants and instructors for other staff on the social components of care, and as counselors for residents and their families using both individual and group modalities. Subsidized public housing for the elderly emerged in the 1950s with social workers involved in management and on-site service.

Retirement communities for well elderly who wish the security of potential protection while remaining independent have also developed extensively in the last decade, but the pioneer work began earlier. Coordination was tried as early as the 1940s when a few welfare planning bodies had divisions of services for the aged. In some instances, because of the lack of services to coordinate and the reluctance of many agencies to move into service for the elderly, the planning councils themselves established direct services such as camps for senior citizens, or "golden age" centers, or information and referral centers.

The newer thrust toward services in the field of aging grows out of the increasing numbers of the aged in the population and the beginning recognition that more people who are old and healthy require new and different kinds of social programs and human services. The old now comprise approximately 10 percent of the population. Demographers tell us that with the apparent decrease in the birth rate and increased longevity, the older population may increase proportionately to 15 to 30 percent of the total by the year 2000.[2]

Powerlessness of the aged

Among the increasing proportion of older people in the total population are former leaders from every walk of life, people possessing all the skills necessary for achievement, people who have headed households, managed families, taught the young, directed every kind of industry, business, or labor organization, and operated their own lives into maturity. It might therefore be assumed that they would form a strong directing force in the population. The fact is, however, that until now the older population has tended to be a powerless segment of society both as individuals and collectively. A look at the sources of power shows why the aged are neither a powerful force in society nor powerful as individuals.[3]

People frequently give up the management of their families as their children mature and move out on their own. The grandparenting role is not generally a central one in our society; it lacks esteem, acclaim, and power in the American culture because of the continued reverence for youth, progress, and the future. Family functions for older adults decrease and become ambiguous and peripheral. Within organizations, there is a tendency to ask the older leadership to move over and make room for young leaders with new ideas and new vigor. Except where associations stabilize in membership and grow older together, organizations tend to depose older leadership and leave the aged person without any major influence if in fact he continues to participate actively at all. This is true in community service groups, labor organizations, churches, local political associations and activities—not excluding those in the social welfare and social work arena!

Mandatory retirement removes employees from the major occupational structure and, even among personnel in professions where practice is self-motivated, there is pressure to retire and pass responsibility along to younger people. The older worker is relieved of his occupational role and loses access to positions of achievement that carry the highest esteem in a work and production oriented culture. The loss of status and position reduces the person's sense of power within himself and within society.

In politics and in the judicial system, there has been opportunity for leaders to retain their positions well past middle age. However, the aged politicians have tended to act in behalf of their younger constituencies and have not taken leadership in seeking power for the older population. They do not tend to see the elderly as their reference group. In the societal sense, then, there are social role losses—family, associational, occupational, and political—that reduce social power and access to power in the social system. In addition, retirement from the work force tends to cause a reduction of income for most people, giving less access to economic power.

Within the person there are generally physiological and psychological changes that affect social participation. Endocrine, cellular, circulatory, respiratory, and digestive modifications in the body tend to reduce physical vigor. While mental capacities may remain at their former levels barring illnesses, catastrophies, or psychological disengagement, mental stimulation may be reduced by lack of opportunity to be intellectually engaged. Work, social relationships, and study are no longer integral parts of the daily routine that brought continual mental exercise.

The achievement oriented culture has thus far based its value system on the future, youth, progress, change, material acquisition, vigor, and newness. The antique, the past, the traditional, and the old, receive only sentimental and patronizing acknowledgement. The older individual and the older population lose status, power, and function, as well as roles and personal vigor. These factors are inseparable and have prevented older adults from becoming a strong unified power group in their own behalf.

Increasing the Power of the Elderly

In recent years, there has been a growing recognition that one other source of power—numbers united through organization—may be used for political, social, and economic thrust. Advocacy and activist organizations have come into being—for example, the Gray Panthers, the United Senior Citizen's groups, and the National Council on the Aging—working in aggressive and militant ways to modify the social, economic, and political aspects of the society. Other organizations, such as the National Retired Teachers Association and the American Association of Retired Persons with over 9 million members in the mid-1970s, have moved to provide services for older people in their own behalf and have used traditional methods to work for legislative and structural changes. In all of this organization to seek recognition and collective power, social workers have had a significant part, especially those whose specialty is community organization, planning, and group leadership. There will be continued need for this type of social work leadership skill in assisting older people to organize and become a powerful force in their own behalf in society.

Some social workers have also organized older adults into supportive groups that encourage the individual older person to improve self-confidence and self-awareness. These groups give primary attention to the participant rather than to collective action for social change. One goes with the other, however; a person who feels better about himself can function better and be more assertive in acquiring his rights. Collective action that effects social changes, on the other hand, also brings recognition, produces a sense of adequacy, and gives power.[4] Social workers in the field of aging, therefore, are finding that they need a methodology that combines understanding of the dynamics of behavior, of the personality factors supporting ego functioning, of the effect of role functioning, and of the social and cultural factors that reinforce or diminish a person's sense of adequacy. Further, social workers must be knowledgeable about individual and group supports for individual older persons, task achievement aspects of interpersonal relationships, and social and community influence and power. Awareness of the relationship among alienation, achievement, isolation, and interpersonal functioning and the continuity of social attachments is crucial for the social worker who practices with older adults. This is true whether the work is with individuals or families, or with small groups organized for self-development, sustained functioning, or community action.

Social work functions in programs by and for elders

One social worker as catalyst, for example, can facilitate older volunteer and paid workers in developing services to meet the needs of both frail and well elderly persons where the community has a high density of people age 60 and over. Many older suburbs, city centers, and small towns have concentrations of retired persons whose talents can be adapted from previous occupations and put to new uses. Some can develop a battery of survival services—home delivered meals, telephone reassurance networks, handyman home repairs, shoppers, visitors, and other such programs. With these supports, some of their frail neighbors can remain in their own homes and avoid premature institutional care. Other senior volunteer and paid workers can, at the same time, develop adult education and related services—classes, forums, or task forces—for the enhancement of the older individual and for the effective exercise of civic responsibilities. Together, batteries of such services can result not only in improved quality of life for both the frail and the well older participant but have a visibility and vitality that will elicit positive support from the wider community. This recognition will attract senior adults both to operate the programs and to receive the services.

Public services and governmental stimuli for service

While social services for older adults were stimulated initially by voluntary associations, probably the greatest advancement in recent years has come within the public sector. The Social Security Act of the 1930s was of course a significant step toward supporting the economic well-being of older adults. Improvement in medicine, in health and nutrition, in care and protection have all interacted to provide healthier, more prolonged lives. The original Older Americans Act of 1965 was intended to provide federal assistance to the states to develop new and improved programs to help older persons through community planning and services, to support training of personnel to work with older adults, and to promote research for better services. The act established the Administration on Aging within the Department of Health, Education, and Welfare. This act and its subsequent amendments,[5] has had a far-reaching effect on public programs in the field of aging.

Through the provisions of the act, local communities and organizations may request financial support through local, state, regional, or federal governmental sources for establishing the programs and services for the elderly specified in the legislation. In addition to funds for research and training of personnel to work with the aged, the act also provided for a National Clearing House of information and resources and created the Federal Council on Aging. The Federal Council—composed of fifteen members representative of older Americans, national organizations with interest in aging, and the general public—includes several social workers. While a very small group, it is influential in guiding policy and in directing administrative positions on services for the elderly. The involvement of social workers in this group is therefore significant.

The Older Americans Act encourages state and local agencies to concentrate resources and to foster the development of comprehensive and coordinated service systems to provide programs for older persons. It also encourages local groups to provide for social services, to recognize and, where appropriate, reassign existing functions in order to maintain maximum independence and dignity in a home atmosphere for older people who are capable of self-care if they have appropriate support. It looks toward the removal of individual and social barriers to personal and economic independence for the older person. Thus the Act proceeds from a philosophical position of maximum independence for the elderly that is compatible with social worker ethics and values. The law interprets social services to include health, continuing education, welfare, information and referral, recreation, homemakers, counseling, transportation to facilitate the use of services, services to encourage use of facilities, adequate housing, and services such as home health care that help to avoid institutionalization.

The result of such provisions was the establishment of the State Offices on Aging throughout the nation and also Area Agencies on Aging. The Area Agencies sometimes serve a metropolitan area and sometimes a combination of several counties under the jurisdiction of the state agencies. The management of these services requires not only knowledge of gerontology but also skills in community organization, planning, and administrative management. Social workers who have such skills have found their way into these agencies, and have been involved not only in management but in developing the training materials and offering the training programs.

Knowledge of social gerontology must accompany organizational skills. For instance, in organizing a local citizens sponsoring body, the social worker needs to consider how something like loss of ability to drive a car can exclude many older persons who otherwise could make an excellent contribution to the advisory group. If meetings are set at times or places impossible for a person with some energy loss or visual impairment, his contribution will be lost. Time and place of meetings, transportation facilities, pacing of sessions, use of written communications—all need to be considered. Innovative means of engaging older adults in organizational and administrative functions may also need to be considered. The social worker who understands the aging phenomena will not only be attuned to the appropriate engagement of older adults but will be able to contribute specialized input to program design based on knowledge of need rather than hunches.

One of the main provisions of the Older Americans Act was the development of multipurpose centers—community facilities "for the organization and provision of health, social and educational services."[6] Following the model of the old settlement house or community center, many of the multiservice centers have been established in middle and lower income communities. Some are administered by social workers and staffed by a variety of professional personnel, including health specialists, recreation workers, and adult educators. Depending upon the host setting or the establishing organization, social workers may provide the major services or may collaborate with public administrators, nurses, nutritionists, adult educators, and psychologists. The social workers in these settings contribute their understanding of human behavior dynamics and their skills in working at various levels and in different modalities. The work in the multiservice center may include counseling of older adults and their families on such matters as the psychological, physical, and emotional needs of the elderly. Counseling may also deal with family problems resulting from the increasing incidence of three- to five-generation families with two generations of older adults. The social worker may assume responsibility for groups of older adults, helping them with socialization, recreational activity, adjustment to role losses, losses of peers or mates, lack of mobility, and adaptation to changing cultural patterns and lifestyles.

Work with groups in the multiservice center may involve establishing new services or organizing advocacy and citizen support groups. Thus the social worker in the multiservice center will find himself practicing a variety of modalities previously seen as casework, group work and community organization, and perhaps some administration. In addition, he will be expected to cooperate and collaborate in planning and providing services with medical doctors and dentists, public health nurses and nutritionists, public officials, psychologists, educators, lawyers, and financial advisers. The functions of the helping and healing professions may blur somewhat as they work together within the multiservice center, but the common binding factor for all these professionals is their concern with and knowledge about older adults. Social workers, who have worked at the neighborhood level and who believe in the capacity of people to be as independent as possible and to function in their own behalf, have a major synthesizing and leadership role to play in the multiservice center. The social worker needs to feel secure in his own expertise while accepting and supporting the other professionals whose skills interface with his.

The Older Americans Volunteer Programs, initially part of the Older Americans Act and later transferred to the Domestic Volunteer Services Act of 1973, is administered through ACTION. These programs provide opportunities for retired persons to perform volunteer services in private, nonprofit governmental organizations. Programs established in this title of the act include Retired Senior Volunteer Programs (RSVP), Foster Grandparents, and Older American Community Service Programs that provide senior health aides and senior companions. In the latter two programs, low income volunteers over age 60 receive a stipend. They offer person-to-person services in health, education, welfare, and related settings where children may have special needs, as in the case of Foster Grandparents, or in programs of adults with disabilities, as in the case of Senior Companions. All of the ACTION older volunteer programs,[7] the Senior Corps of Retired Executives (SCORE) of the Department of Labor, and Green Thumb of the Department of Agriculture enable retired persons to enact worker roles often no longer available to them in the labor force. Within these programs, social workers have been responsible for developing the curriculum for and training the paid personnel,[8] for serving as consultants in program development, and, in some instances, for acting as staff in local projects. Social workers in senior volunteer programs have recruited and trained volunteers for many kinds of services, have developed settings in which volunteers could work, and have matched volunteers with supervised settings.[9] Social work practice knowledge and skill with individuals and groups are important, as are community organization skills for determining the location of settings, for developing and managing advisory boards, and for raising the funds needed for local continuance of these programs.

Title VII of the Older Americans Act provides for nutrition

programs to enable low income older Americans to have low-cost, nutritionally sound meals served in strategically located settings. The Act also provides for rehabilitative services and activities in the same setting to reduce the social isolation of those receiving the meals. Within this latter purpose falls the responsibility of social workers, who must collaborate with health nutritionists and offer organization and interactional opportunities so that the older people who participate may connect with each other. As these programs have come into being, social relations has become a very strong component. Repeatedly older people who have participated in the program have indicated that they were coming to the program for more than the one balanced meal a day. They were coming to get out of the house, to have someone to talk with, to find new friends, to be with others. Thus the social work component of providing social and interpersonal activities (clubs, classes, recreational activities, health screening, information and referral, educational experiences, self-actualizing groups, and exercise programs) before and after the meals have become crucial to the program. In some instances the social worker is the manager and program developer, in others the direct service provider. Some programs have made a social worker available once a week who specializes in counseling older adults and their families. Other programs have used such a social worker for group counseling or supportive groups.

Another part of the nutrition program has been home delivered meals to isolated older persons, called Meals on Wheels in some communities. While meals are frequently delivered by volunteers who carry in food and leave, social workers recognized a social need and began to reorganize some programs so that a volunteer would go in to join the person for conversation along with the meal. "Have Lunch with a Friend" is the title of one such program. Volunteers, trained by social workers in a program managed by social workers, realize the importance of the social aspect of meals for both enjoyment and nutritional benefit.

The provisions of the Older Americans Act set in motion a myriad of potential services under governmental or voluntary auspices stimulated by public funds and sometimes supplemented or matched with private funds. These programs have helped social workers and others in the human service professions to become more sensitive to the needs of the elderly within the community. Services may be under the auspices of churches, schools, public housing estates, universities and community colleages, public recreation centers, and community mental health centers. Youth service organizations such as the Ys, the Scouts, and Boys and Girls Clubs have extended their services in some areas to offer special programs for senior adults or intergenerational programs for the elderly and children. Here again, the unique contribution of social workers is recognition of the social and interpersonal component for people who may easily become isolated, rejected, withdrawn, or disengaged. People who are capable of a great deal of independence also need systems in which they can make contributions or find enjoyment. Social workers have the knowledge, skill, and philosophy to provide such systems.

Stimulated by the medical assistance programs of the Social Security Act, social workers have also entered the health care field, either in home health care or nursing homes and extended care. While the frail elderly in institutions of all kinds number only about 5 percent of the aged population at any one time, they have an urgent need for the services that social workers in health services can give. Some programs include social workers as practitioners; others use social workers as consultants on the social problems of older adults in the institutional setting. Social workers educated primarily for direct service using individual or group methods can find themselves facilitating the work of others, including associates, paraprofessionals, or workers in other practices.[10] They offer in-service training to aides, attendants, and others who work directly with patients and residents. They also offer consultation on social needs to administrators, ward nurses, and others who manage the services. They serve as members of utilization review committees in extended care facilities. All these functions require skill in translating their knowledge and methods into concepts that others can use.[11] Private corporations of social workers, sometimes in collaboration with psychologists or medical doctors, are being established in some communities. They offer specialized services for the elderly within institutions and in home aftercare.

While only few of the elderly are in nursing homes at any one time, the area is one of considerable concern and one in which social workers have long been active. In some states licensure requires that a social worker be included in the staff either part or full time. The well-educated professional social worker keeps before nursing home administrators and functionary personnel important considerations such as the effect of the milieu on its residents and the role of privacy in maintaining personal integration. They uphold the need for self-determination in some aspects of the residents' lives, the need of everyone to have interpersonal connections including at least one confidant, and the need for activity and engagement. Utilizing the studies made by social workers of the precipitating factors in the institutionalization of older adults,[12] workers are aware that older people are institutionalized usually after all other resources have been exhausted in families or in the community, or when the person is very old, single, widowed, or otherwise without family support.

The opening of geriatric centers on an outpatient or short term care basis has introduced social workers as part of a service team. They work with specialists in occupational therapy, physical therapy, nursing, medicine, psychiatry, and psychology. The social worker may be a therapist, the manager of the social milieu in these settings, or do follow-up work on the social implications of the medical or psychiatric treatment.

In home health care services such as Visiting Nurses Associations or public health nursing services, social service departments are being established to provide supportive services, information and referral, location of other resources, financial assistance, location of homemakers services, and other needs frequently found when the visiting nurse enters the family. Here the social worker serves as a secondary service provider and collaborator with the health specialist, who is the central service deliverer.

As large numbers of Second World War veterans arrive at retirement age, the Veterans Administration is developing Centers on Aging to serve this population. Within the next decade, the VA will become one of the major service providers for the elderly. Already the federal government is beginning to put major support of aging programs within the Veterans Administration. Many social workers specializing in the field of aging can expect to take new and expanded roles within it, both in designing research on aging, in-service training, and service delivery.

Conservatorship is another area of services for older adults or in their behalf. Public guardian or probate court workers step in when people are no longer capable of making legal or financial decisions. The social workers are becoming knowledgeable of appropriate law, of financial institutions, and of taxes, and they are learning to collaborate with lawyers, doctors, psychiatrists, and bankers or other financial officers in working out plans for the protection and benefit of older persons or their relatives. Sometimes the social worker becomes the advocate for the older person when others are trying to exploit him.

Law centers and legal aid services for the elderly and programs of attorney generals' offices for investigating exploitation of the elderly have begun to emerge, using social workers as team members with lawyers. Social workers engage in investigation and help older people to understand their rights, especially in consumer concerns relating to things like medical devices, insurance plans, food plans, vitamins, and medicines. Social workers are also taking advocacy roles in offices of consumer affairs that are being opened to protect the aged from exploitation. A few programs have established a follow-up service with older adults who have been victims of street attacks, robberies, muggings, and con games. The social worker attempts to help older victims deal with their fear and the tendency toward isolation that may result.

New services in the field of aging being offered by traditional agencies and organizations include outreach programs and drop-in centers in areas of high concentration of older populations. Such centers offer counseling, sometimes food service, and chances for conversation and social relations. Frequently they are manned by well-trained senior volunteers, who can serve as peer counselors and work under the supervision of a social worker. Some retired social workers also staff these services, which have been established by Family Service agencies and community centers.

Preretirement education and planning is being offered by some community service agencies, colleges, unions, businesses, and industries. They help people to anticipate new roles or role changes, and meet them by developing new skills and interests, new health habits, and general conditioning for long life ahead. In some of these programs, social workers collaborate with personnel managers, financial planners, bankers, clergy, librarians, adult educators, and physical educators to meet the formerly neglected needs of middle aged and older workers.[13] These older individuals must make a social transition from labor force participation to retirement and usually a financial transition as well from full wages to a reduced income derived from other sources.

Other innovative services for older adults are being offered by boards of education, community colleges, and other educational institutions. These include classes for enhancement, continued education, and survival—courses in consumer education, health, nutrition, financial planning, and independent living. Classes are held on campuses and in day care centers for impaired older adults, nursing homes, senior centers in housing estates, parks, and churches. Some are held in conjunction with food and nutrition programs. Some educational institutions sponsor volunteer programs, counseling, activities centers, emeritus colleges, and other programs and services managed and operated largely by retired persons. Social workers are serving as instructors and community program directors, as well as providing the direct service with older adults and their families under these auspices. Many retired social workers are also participating in these educational programs as both teachers and students.

One of the most recent trends in social work practice is the development of the social gerontologist with a special degree or certificate in gerontology. This may be a dual degree combining an MSW with a Master of Science in Gerontology, or a Certificate in Gerontology in addition to the MSW or, in a few locations, a Master of Public Administration combined with a Master of Social Work with a specialty in Gerontology. The growing body of specialized knowledge in gerontology—encompassing biology, physiology, sociology, psychology, economics, politics, and philosophy of aging—forms a basis for the development of services and programs specifically geared to the needs of the elderly and their relatives. Although the ideal may be integration of services for older adults into general social welfare services for all people, it appears that so far the needs of the aged have been neglected in traditional settings. To some extent this neglect has been modified only by the availability of governmental funds for services for the elderly. Under these circumstances it may be necessary for services for senior adults to be segregated until services exist generally for elderly and until social attitudes change to include older adults in all services.

Of additional special concern for social workers are some of the minority elderly: Blacks, Mexican-Americans, Asians, and American Indians. Only limited health services and social services exist for these people. While all workers pay into Social Security, only a limited number of minority people live to benefit because of their shorter life expectancy. Social workers have pioneered in work for the benefit of minority peoples and can provide special knowledge in this area. As yet there are few community facilities and special programs, even though the Older Americans Act does give special mention to the needs of minority elderly. Less than a proportionate number of social workers specialized in aging are Black, Mexican-American or Asian. In a period of sensitivity to the development of minority leadership, the development and special recruitment of minorities for social work is a critical need.

Finally, there is the specialist in aging in professional education for social work. Several schools of social work have included a full sequence of courses in aging, and there are several gerontological institutes connected with schools of social work. Some have faculty members who combine skill in teaching social work with the specialty in gerontology. Doctoral programs at several schools of social work offer a specialty in gerontology for educators, administrators, policy planners, or therapists. The demographic predictions for the next twenty-five years indicate that, although there will be an increasing need for specialists in gerontology, all social workers will require some knowledge of aging and programs for older adults. Most practitioners being educated today will have within the next generation some of their practice in work with and in behalf of older adults.

Summary

While some social workers have been engaged in work with older adults for many years, emphasis in the field of aging is only beginning to gain momentum, opening many new areas of work and many new employment opportunities. It is clear, however, that most social workers functioning with older adults need more than the traditional single method specialized social work skills. Both the well elderly who primarily need socialization and survival services and the impaired elderly who need health care and social supports demand a new combination of methods or modalities. Social workers practicing in programs for the aged must be able to combine skills in direct work with individuals and families through individual and group methods, and must be able to follow through on the creation of new programs through planning, development, and administration. In addition they must have collaborative skills to work with other professionals and consultative skills to help others to develop and maintain programs. This demand for a range of social work skills in a variety of modalities may be due to the newness of the programs and the rapid emergence of new services, or it may be due to a recognition that when services are delivered on a population basis rather than a single problem basis, the modalities cannot be separated. In any event, the field of services for the aging has emerged as one of the most complex and exciting new frontiers within social work.

Notes

1. Elaine Brody, "Aging," *Encyclopedia of Social Work* 16th issue (New York City: National Association of Social Workers, 1971), Vol. 1, pp. 51–74.

2. Jacob Siegel and William O'Leary, "Some Demographic Aspects of Aging in the United States," *Current Population Reports: Special Report,* Series P23, No. 43 (Washington, D.C.: U.S. Government Printing Office, 1973), p. 6.

3. Frederick Eisele, "Political Consequences of Aging," *The Annals* (Sept. 1974).

4. Esther Twente, *Never Too Old: The Aged in Community Life* (San Francisco: Jossey-Bass, 1970).

5. U.S. Department of Health, Education and Welfare, Office of Human Development, Administration on Aging, *Older Americans Act of 1965, As Amended and Related Acts* (Washington, D.C.: U.S. Government Printing Office, 1976).

6. U.S. Congress, *Oversight Hearing on Older Americans Before the Select Committee on Education,* held in Los Angeles 14 May 1973 (Washington, D.C.: U.S. Government Printing Office, 1973).

7. HEW, *Older Americans Act of 1965.*

8. Mary M. Seguin, Margaret E. Hartford, et al., *Curriculum for Older Americans Volunteer Programs, ACTION* (Cleveland: Human Services Design Laboratory, School of Applied Social Sciences, Case Western Reserve University, 1973).

9. Mary M. Seguin, *Older Volunteer Training Program,* a position paper on issues and training models related to volunteerism and the older

volunteer (Los Angeles: Ethel Percy Andrus Gerontology Center, University of Southern California, 1972).

10. Arthur N. Schwartz and Ivan N. Mensh, *Professional Obligations and Approaches to the Aging* (Springfield, Ill.: Charles E. Thomas, Publisher, 1974).

11. Abraham Monk, "A Conceptual Base for Second Generation Programs in Gerontological Social Work," *Journal of Education for Social Work* 11 (Fall 1975).

12. Margaret Blenkner, "Environmental Changes and the Aging Individual," *The Gerontologist* 7 (No. 1, 1967): 101–05; Morton A. Lieberman, "Institutionalization of the Aged: Effects on Behavior," *Journal of Gerontology* 24 (No. 3, 1969): 330–40.

13. Robert Morris, "Aging and the Field of Social Work," in *Aging and Society,* vol. 2, ed. by Matilda W. Riley, John W. Riley, Jr., and Marilyn E. Johnson (New York City: Russell Sage Foundation, 1969), p. 16.

Bibliography

Blenkner, Margaret. "Environmental changes and the aging individual" *The Gerontologist,* Vol. 7, No. 1, 1967, pp. 101–105.

Brody, Elaine. "Aging" *Encyclopedia of Social Work,* Sixteenth Issue, New York: National Association of Social Workers, 1971. Vol. 1, pp. 51–74.

Eisele, Frederick, ed. "Political consequences of aging" *The Annals* (September, 1974).

Lieberman, Morton A. "Institutionalization of the aged: effects on behavior" *Journal of Gerontology* Vol. 24, No. 3, 1969, pp. 330–40.

Monk, Abraham. "A conceptual base for second generation programs in gerontological social work" *Journal of Education for Social Work,* Vol. 11, No. 3 (Fall 1975).

Morris, Robert. "Aging and the field of social work" In Matilda Riley, *et al. Aging and Society,* Vol. 2, New York: Russell Sage Foundation, 1969.

Riley, Matilda W., John W. Riley, Jr., and Marilyn E. Johnson. *Aging and Society* Vol. 2, New York: Russell Sage Foundation, 1969, p. 16.

Schwartz, Arthur N. and Ivan N. Mensh. *Professional Obligations and Approaches to the Aging,* Springfield Ill.: Charles E. Thomas, Publisher, 1974.

Seguin, Mary M. *Older Volunteer Training Program: a position paper on issues and training models related to volunteerism and the older volunteer.* Los Angeles: Ethel Percy Andrus Gerontology Center, University of Southern California, 1972.

Seguin, Mary M., Margaret E. Hartford, *et al. Curriculum for Older Americans Volunteer Programs, ACTION.* Cleveland: Human Services Design Laboratory, School of Applied Social Sciences, Case Western Reserve University, 1973.

Siegel, Jacob and William O'Leary. "Some demographic aspects of aging in the United States." *Current Population Reports: Special Report.* Washington, D.C.: U.S. Government Printing Office, 1973, (Series P23, No. 43), p. 6.

Twente, Esther. *Never Too Old: The Aged in Community Life.* San Francisco: Jossey-Bass, Inc., 1970.

U.S. Congress. 93rd. House Hearings. *Oversight Hearing On Older Americans before the Select Committee on Education.* Washington, D.C.: U.S. Government Printing Office, 1973 (Held in Los Angeles, California, May 14, 1973).

U.S. Department of Health, Education and Welfare. Office of Human Development. Administration on Aging. *Older Americans Act of 1965, As Amended and Related Acts.* Washington, D.C.: U.S. Government Printing Office, 1976.

Part II. Ecological Perspectives

6

Social Work in Industrial Social Welfare

SHIRLEY HELLENBRAND and ROSLYN YASSER

Social workers in the industrial social welfare field have an opportunity to offer social services to a large, underserved population in a setting that is central to their lives and familiar to them. The new "helping team" described here represents a functional alliance of social workers and crucial persons in the work world, linked in turn to many other human service workers.

The changing approach of this new helping team includes helping people to maintain work roles whenever possible, flexible intervention modes, a crisis orientation, and where indicated three-way interviewing on the work site. The chapter highlights social work practice at multiple levels—with individual employees, groups of employees, and organizations in the community—all within an ecological perspective.

The social work practitioner starts where the client is by making creative use of his work milieu for clinical as well as more broadly based social purposes—for example, consumer education, legal protection, or retirement planning. And the possibility now exists for working with potentially powerful allies to influence legislative policy for social benefit.

INDUSTRIAL social welfare offers social services to people within their work communities and in ways that enlist the powerful resources of the world of work. It is a fertile new frontier for social work practice. To call this new territory, however, is not wholly accurate. This social work specialization has long been established in continental Europe. Here in the United States, Bertha Reynolds experimented with social work services for members of the National Maritime Union during the Second

World War. Perhaps we should say that industrial social welfare is rediscovered territory that can now be better appreciated and explored.

The field of industrial social welfare is large, and its structure is complex. It is, in fact, a third welfare system with linkages to the public and voluntary sectors. This chapter will first briefly consider some industrial applications of new practice perspectives and theoretical tools and the relationship of the world of work to social work; second, it will describe some management-sponsored social work programs. The major focus will be on the development of a social service program within a union setting—with discussion of the unique resources of the setting, the issues in service delivery, and case material illustrating the distinctive characteristics of the setting. Finally, we will look at the application of the practice innovations to the broader field of social work.

New Practice Perspectives

During the past decade, the social work literature has abounded in suggestions for new models of social work practice and service delivery. Several themes have appeared frequently: (1) social services should be made available within the everyday environment of people; (2) practice should take an ecological perspective; (3) crisis intervention and other extremely useful planned short-term services should be widely available; and (4) social workers should enlist support for social welfare programs from influential sectors in the community.

Industrial social welfare offers remarkable opportunities for putting these ideas into operation and testing their validity. Let us examine each briefly.

1. Social services should be made available within the natural, everyday environments of people, in the places where they are engaged in important activities and relationships. What is a more natural environment for 80 million Americans than the world of work or a more natural locale for delivering social services? Entry into this world would connect social work more closely with the mainstream of American life.

2. An ecological perspective[1] for social work practice is highly congruent with the needs and lifestyles of working people. It

results in help matched to the problem as the client defines it, intervention that engages the strengths and growth potentials of individuals, and active utilization of the supports in their social network.

3. The development during recent years of a "life model" of helping, of crisis theory and crisis intervention, of task-centered and other forms of planned short-term treatment provides theoretical and technical tools for successful social work entry into the world of work.

4. Industrial social welfare would give social workers new opportunities to enlist the power of the world of work, particularly unions, to press for changes in aspects of the health, legal, and welfare systems that are dysfunctional for working class people.

The World of Work

Many members of the world of work are low and moderate income working people who have been neglected and poorly served with social services as well as with health care and legal services. Social work overtures to the working class are long overdue but will not necessarily be met by an immediate warm response.

Lower income working people, their unions, and industrial management view social workers with some wariness, distrust, and at times, dislike. Many working class people perceive social workers as busybodies who use their taxes to coddle "lazy chiselers" and who make jobs for themselves. Unions and their membership identify social work with private "charity" and bureaucratic red tape. Corporate management tends to see social work as wasteful and ineffective. Changes in these perceptions will not come easily.

In part this situation has arisen because social workers often have not been attuned to working class populations. We have concentrated on the nonworking poor, on disorganized families and their children, and on counseling services to middle class families. To offer social services in the world of work, we will need to be familiar with that world, its language and customs, its demands and strains, and its resources.[2] There is a lot to be learned by social workers about the world of work and by that world about the professional help social workers have to offer.

A number of successful programs indicate that many millions of people can be helped in their own environment. This area offers opportunities for new applications of social work knowledge and skills, for richer use of professionals and paraprofessionals, for the active engagement of the work system in the helping network. With the knowledge and experience gained from contact with working people in their world, social workers can sensitize community agencies to the problems and inform them of more effective ways to serve working class populations. Industry and labor may acquire new ideas about what social work can contribute to the individual and community and be more ready to support social services. And social workers may be able to enlist new and powerful allies in the world of work to press for changes in some institutions.

Management-sponsored social service projects

During the last few years, management has successfully undertaken a number of industrial social welfare projects, all of which have some common features. They all recognize the crucial role of work in people's lives and the importance of providing services that will enable people to continue to function on their jobs. All the programs offer social service to a new, hitherto underserved population. All try to involve the work network—supervisors, foremen, union representatives—at least in casefinding and referral and, to the extent possible, in supportive and follow-up activities. All programs, when successful, find their staff resources overwhelmed and must go beyond one-to-one contacts to develop other ways to meet employees' service needs: community resources, mutual aid self-help groups dealing with common problems (such as family life education and retirement), and so on. In all the industry-sponsored programs, there is some ambiguity in the role of the social worker, who needs to negotiate a delicately balanced professional tightrope to serve the individual client and management without being coopted by them.

One area of concern to management has been employees whose job performance is impaired by alcohol abuse. These employees, who are found in all occupations and industries and at all economic levels, are often excellent workers when sober. But how to keep them sober? The Hughes Bill of 1970 induced industry and the civil service to develop alcoholism programs stressing early case discovery through the worker's supervisor and communication with the worker that his job was in jeopardy. In most of the programs, the medical or personnel office referred the employee to a community facility for treatment as is done with other diseases. Insurance generally covers part or all of the treatment. The most serious flaw in this approach has been the lack of follow-up. The worker-patient may not pursue referral, may get lost in the maze of community agencies, or may make partial use of resources while his job performance continues to deteriorate. One demonstration project (of the Industrial Unit of the Addiction Research Foundation of Ontario), where the worker's supervisor was involved during the period of treatment and, as necessary, afterwards as well, achieved an 85 percent rate of success in the first year.[3] Continued involvement of the work community thus emerges as a basic concept in industrial social service.

In the 1960s many large industrial corporations were induced to train and hire inexperienced, long-term unemployed persons, including many from minority groups. It quickly became evident that entry into the world of work created new tensions (changes in family role assignments, debt problems) which often hindered work performance. Social agencies and large companies began joint planning based on collaborative study.[4] One example of a management-contracted social service program to deal with this problem is furnished by the Xerox Corporation and the Family Service of Rochester, New York.[5]

Xerox purchases the service of one agency professional as a Family Relations Counselor. This social worker has familiarized himself with the work environment and language, the plant set-up, jobs, and their stresses. Referrals come from the employee relations advisor, supervisors, foremen, and fellow workers. For job-related problems, the employee is helped to utilize regular company channels. Communications are facilitated and company resources are identified for particular employee needs. In addition, management's official position encourages employees to seek agency help for a variety of personal and family situations. Interviewing and follow-through is available three days a week at the work site (on company time), while other time is available at the agency office for employees who prefer it. Xerox discovered that family and personal problems were not unique to the poor and to minority groups but were also of serious concern to supervisory, administrative, and technical personnel.

Financial counseling has a high priority at Xerox, as at most work community programs. This program generated an independent Consumer Credit Counseling Service which works closely with the Family Service. It has become a basic precept in industrial social service that social workers must be attuned to recurring financial crises and their highly-charged relationship to family problems.

Other patterns of industry-financed social service programs are described by Francis M. Moynihan[6] and by Skidmore, Balsam, and Jones.[7] In the first, the Family Agency of Metropolitan Detroit planned and gave leadership for two eight-week workshops for supervisors of the Michigan Bell Telephone Company. Workshop focus was on providing knowledge of simple interviewing techniques and interactional processes to help the supervisory personnel understand and deal with new, high-risk employees.

Skidmore and colleagues discuss the provision of social services to the employees of Kennecott Copper Corporation by INSIGHT, a service staffed by Otto Jones, his assistant, and three second-year students from the graduate school of social work, University of Utah. While the specific details vary, there are several generally similar programs in various parts of the country, namely company-financed social work resources where employees with job or other difficulties can be helped. INSIGHT's statistics indicate that absenteeism, costs of weekly indemnity, and hospital and medical costs were significantly reduced.[8]

The major innovations in these programs are related to the new populations served and to the new integration of social work in industry. Material available thus far indicates little change in practice technology itself nor has there been much discussion of possible ambiguities and conflicts for the social worker. How does his being in the plant by management's authority affect his interventions in job-related difficulties? How does he resolve conflicting pulls and loyalties? These questions await answers.

We turn now to the major focus of this chapter.

Social Service Programs in Unions

The first union-based program was developed by Bertha Reynolds within the National Maritime Union during the Second

World War. Reynolds[9] perceived that program as a move in a fresh direction to link social work more clearly and closely to working people and to social living. However, the program was discontinued after the end of the war. The next major pioneering venture was a mental health care project organized in the Sidney Hillman Health Center. The center was an out-patient medical clinic under the auspices of the New York Joint Board of the Amalgamated Clothing Workers of America and the New York Clothing Manufacturers Association. The project was financed by the National Institute of Mental Health and the Rehabilitation Services Administration. This project, under the leadership of Hyman Weiner, Sheila Akabas, and John Sommer of the Industrial Social Welfare Center of the Columbia University School of Social Work, was a landmark in industrial social welfare and is described in *Mental Health Care in the World of Work*.[10] The project and the book have great import for social work practice as a vivid example of an ecological systems approach. Weiner, Akabas, and Sommer, fresh from their work in the mental health clinic project, were also the designers and consultants for the Personal Service Unit program which will be discussed later. The practice innovations developed in the mental health care project greatly influenced the direction of the Personal Service Unit.

In approaching the world of work as an arena for the delivery of mental health care, Weiner and his colleagues decided against emphasizing the problems of the work organization as a contributing factor in the emotional disorder of the labor force, but they decided also against simply offering ''the existing psychotherapeutic technology'' to a new group, the underserved blue collar population. They did not wish to create another overcrowded clinic, as isolated from the world of work as other community mental health clinics. They accepted the idea that work is one of the basic activities in a person's life, a source of purchasing power and social status and the traditional test of participation in American society.

Weiner and his colleagues saw workers' ''participation in the world of work as oxygen, sustaining them in the face of emotional disorder.''[11] At any point in time, however, many workers in the labor force have trouble maintaining themselves on their jobs because of emotional difficulties. The goal of the clinic would be to maintain workers on their jobs or return them to work after recuperation whenever possible. Rather than being peripheral, mental health care would move the "world of work to front and center in the treatment process." In order for "the clinic to implement such an objective and for professionals to be accepted in the world of work, substantial changes in clinical technology and service delivery systems are needed."[12]

Two conditions had to be met for such a project to succeed: management and labor had to see mental health services as relevant to their own organizational interests, and workers had to see therapeutic help as a desirable way to deal with emotional illness. The attitude of union leadership—representatives and shop stewards and the like—was crucial, since they could identify emotionally ill workers and legitimate help-seeking behavior. Participation in clinical activities could meet the union's needs since a union is always in the market for new personal services to help maintain the loyalty of its membership. In addition, a union is under pressure to maintain an experienced labor force for the industry.

The authors developed a new professional technology which took as its point of departure the notion that the milieu of the industrial institution contributes in many specific ways to the treatment process.

Once a person's emotional problem is visualized in terms of its impact on the functioning of the individual within the environment in which he works, the range of actors in the treatment process is potentially broadened. It extends past the usual dyad of therapist and patient to include all those in the institutional network who are significant to the functioning of the individual or the work community. Industrial representatives possess the knowledge to comprehend the work situation and the power to influence it. There proved to be at least five ways in which representatives of the functional community of work can make significant clinical imputs.

1. Case finding—the world of work is able to identify the emotional problem as it is evidenced in deviation from expected performance in terms of task, relationships and routines.

2. Diagnostic process—the world of work is able to contribute valuable information about the way in which the emotional problem expresses itself in terms of dysfunctional behavior as well as help identify what in the work environment may "tip the scale."

3. Referral—the world of work is able to help in engaging the worker in the treatment process by transferring trust or invoking potential sanctions.

4. Treatment—the world of work is able to participate in deciding what environmental modification in the realm of task, routine or relationship is necessary and to seek its implementation including enlisting the support of co-workers. When employment cannot be maintained, the industrial representative also has the power to safeguard a job.

5. Follow up—the world of work is able to serve as the "eyes and ears" of the treatment team directly at the work site.[13]

This staffing principle, encouraging the participation of many people in the system, resulted in:

—change (dilution) in the relationship of patient and therapist and consequently less dependence on the part of the patient;

—prevention of the isolation of the clinic by removing the magic of the treatment process;

—development of a structure which transcends the individual patient and his problem to become a system of providing help in which people are able to contribute based on their own roles;

—clarification of a useful backup role for community facilities.[14]

The Sidney Hillman Health Center experience suggested several guiding principles for the development of a social service delivery system within a union setting:

1. The importance of institutional commitment; that is, leadership sanction and accessibility, resource allocation (physical facilities, clerical help, access to information).

2. Service geared to functional objectives: job maintenance or return to work.
3. Service delivery adapted to low-income working people: their needs, pace, lifestyle and culture.
4. Enlistment and utilization of people within the world of work as helpers in the treatment process, from case finding through follow-up. This creates significant changes in practice methodology.
5. Development of linkages between the world of work and community health and social services.

These principles were the foundation stones for the Personal Service Unit of District Council 37.

The Personal Service Unit of District Council 37

In spring 1971, the Personal Service Unit of District Council 37 was established at the offices of the Union's Health and Security Plan. It is responsible to the administrator of the Health and Security Plan and to the leadership of the union.* The Industrial Social Welfare Center of Columbia University School of Social Work provided ongoing, onsite, technical assistance for program development. The program is union-financed, union-housed and integrated into the fabric of the union system by utilizing the union hierarchy and its network in the helping process.

District Council 37, American Federation of State, County and Municipal Employees, is the parent body of more than sixty locals whose membership represents most of New York's civil service employees, except for teachers and uniformed personnel. The political stance of District Council 37 and its national union is progressive, giving leadership in areas of social and economic welfare, political reform, and civil rights. This public sector union represents one of the youngest and fastest growing unions in this country. Its membership is heterogeneous in its ethnic, racial, and income level makeup. The membership includes blue collar motor vehicle operators, engineers, architects, social workers, hospital nurses' aides, and clerical workers.

In order for a union-based social service program to exist, it

* The Executive Director, Victor Gotbaum and his Associates, Lillian Roberts and Edward Maher.

must get through the gate guarded by the union hierarchy.[15] Only when union staff pronounce the social worker trustworthy can direct access to membership be secured. The union officialdom—executive director, union president—must give the service the necessary sanction—and support verbal, written, and financial. To maintain this support, the social worker needs to demonstrate through his practice that union members in need can be helped. The key to that success is the involvement of the union representative in the process of securing help whenever possible.

To offer social services within the union setting, the social worker needs to know and understand the complex union world. Let us look at some of the key topographical features of that world.

The union hierarchy and job protection processes

At each work site, unionized workers elect shop stewards from within their own ranks to represent them in their dealings with management. Where the work site is very large and requires several stewards, a chapter chairman or chief shop steward may also be elected and given time from his regular job to carry out union business. These men and women are key front line figures in enforcing the union contract with management and the work rules and safety regulations on the job. They must look after the general well being and protection of the members.[16] Three other members of the union hierarchy are commonly involved in protection of employees' rights: (1) a union grievance representative, paid for by management and usually released on a full-time basis to the union to cover a designated number of employees; (2) a union representative or business agent, paid for and on the staff of the union; and (3) a union designated lawyer. What the representative is called (shop steward, chapter chairman, business agent, grievance representative, or union representative) varies from union to union. In this chapter we will use the title union representative.

Unions generally attempt in their collective bargaining with management to institutionalize a formal hearing procedure to handle disputes arising from either worker or management initiative. In addition, there are informal mechanisms. More powerful unions are able to obtain hearing procedures that afford the worker greater protection. Opportunities for social service intervention exist in such hearing processes. A union representative may be approached by an employee with a grievance that is really not a work issue but reflects a worker's personal problem. Management may take disciplinary action against an emotionally ill union member because his functioning has deteriorated.

New professional alliance

Union shop stewards and representatives perform many roles beyond their specified union duties of job protection. They are involved on a day-to-day basis with their fellow workers' lives and are often the first person a worker goes to with a family, emotional, or financial problem. They are also the first to notice erratic, changed behavior in a formerly competent, productive worker. The representative's formal and informal roles make him a powerful and influential potential ally for the social work practioner. When and in what ways would a union steward or representative work with a social worker? A paranoid member may approach the representative with his fantasy of persecution. Utilizing grievance procedures in such instances is clearly unproductive; the social worker may provide more effective answers. If a union member is facing the possibility of job loss because of a personal problem such as alcoholism, the social worker may be able to handle the member's resistance and move him into rehabilitation. The union representative can negotiate with management and guarantee the job if the member cooperates.

In these collaborative efforts, both social worker and union representative gain benefits in addition to helping an individual member. The union rep has found an alternative to transferring the worker to a new job location, a holding action until the next occurrence of inappropriate behavior. The social worker has gained access to job power, a resource not commonly available in nonindustrial settings. He has been able to modify the union representative's perception of social work. And most important, when social workers help maintain workers on the job, the service is congruent with the union's primary charge of economic security for its workers.[17]

Beyond his role in referral and job protection, the union representative can participate in diagnostic assessment and intervention. He can supply the social worker with information from the job site about the member's job situation, behavior, and relationships that helps the clinician make technical decisions. This is similar to collaboration with parents to determine the interventive plan most likely to succeed for a child showing behavior problems in school. With the union representative's help, decisions can be made regarding changes in the member's job. Transfer to new location, assignment to a different job utilizing different skills, creating supportive alliances on the work site—all may be implemented with the union's assistance and members' cooperation.

The most exciting development has been these new alliances created between the social work staff and union personnel. Just as the treatment of a patient in a hospital requires the cooperation and participation of the doctor, social worker, nurse, nurse's aide, and orderly, the treatment of a person in job jeopardy requires the participation of social worker, union representative, and management.

When this service started, the union representative saw the Personal Service Unit as a place to drop off difficult cases, men and women who had been transferred from job site to job site, who were on their way out of the work force. On the other hand, unions reps often felt threatened by the social worker. The representatives had been doing personal services for a long time—who were these professionals to tell them how to do their business?

A crucial alliance was formed between the union representative, whose function is job protection, and the Personal Service Unit worker who can help him with this function. The members knew and trusted the union officer. The helping process was made much simpler when the unit staff were designated as union people—also to be trusted.

The new alliance was enhanced when a mental health training program for union representatives was developed jointly by the Industrial Center and District Council 37. Training sessions focused on how to identify a worker in personal difficulties, how to talk to him and refer him to Personal Service. Union representatives began to understand that there were no easy answers to many workers' problems and that they had an important part to play in the member's entering and staying with the treatment.

The Personal Service Unit Center has within its reach a broad range of human, technical, and financial resources. District Council 37, through its Health and Security Plan, offers extensive benefits which include life insurance, disability, major medical, dental, optical, drug, pension counseling, health insurance information, presurgical consultation, and work health hazard investigation.

The Personal Service Unit and Service Delivery

Over two hundred members come to the Personal Service Unit each month for help with a variety of problems—financial, mental health (including job related), housing, legal, and medical rehabilitation. Different problems demand different kinds of services. Physical health problems generate requests for concrete services—financial help and/or linkage to a community resource. Mental health problems require counseling primarily. The service picture that emerges reflects a creative mix of in person interviewing, extensive phone work, and activity with union personnel, family members, and community agencies. One Personal Service Unit worker, although based in the union office, spends up to 50 percent of his time visiting union offices, community agencies, day care facilities, homes, schools, courts, and work sites.

Within the union structure, a social worker's previously held ideas about privacy, appointment schedules, and even the principal of confidentiality may become somewhat altered. Interviewing is done in small, glassed cubicles. While at union headquarters, union representatives and members who want to see one of the social workers will walk right into the worker's office. Union members share their work problems freely with union representatives and often wish them included in interviews. However, the social worker must maintain his responsibility to keep information confidential and, in this instance, not adopt to the norm of the union.[18] When the member does want the union representative or even his supervisor to understand from the professional his depression or anxiety, a joint talk is arranged for this purpose.

Early dilemmas, possible solutions

The unit, early in its development, had to make decisions on its function, what it could do most effectively, and how best to carry out is responsibilities. Questions continually raised were: Should the service primarily provide linkage and referral to community resources? Should the Personal Service Unit become involved in long-term service? How would an ever-increasing demand for service, including members requiring long-term help, affect the unit's ability to respond quickly? What kind of a mix between brief and longer term treatment would be sound and viable? What divisions of labor should exist within the unit staff?

Both the union and the Personal Service staff wished to offer as much in-house service as possible. Given the strain of an increasing case load, the unit recognized after its first year that service must emphasize short-term crisis intervention and effective community referrals.

In many instances the alliances cultivated in the community were utilized not only for referral purposes but also to provide the staff with a continuing supply of resources that would also aid in in-house treatment. The employment of many union members in city service agencies offers the unit unique opportunities to develop alliances in the city courts—criminal, small claims, civil courts—and in welfare agencies, consumer affairs offices, and the Housing Authority.

Finding medical and mental health community services to meet members' needs has not been easy. In the area of emergency hospitalization, linkages were established with several hospitals in the community where employees' insurance benefits provided financial coverage. Here, the limitations of the benefits became critical. New York City employees' Blue Cross policies will not cover psychiatric care in a city hospital, often a place where union members might be employed. Contact with the community hospitals and with the family service agencies highlighted their professionals' frequent disregard of the patient as a worker. This was evident when appointment times were offered that were incompatible with the job schedule, when the hospital and agency workers showed no interest in work-related problems, and when fee schedules were far out-of-line with earnings.

In an attempt to deal with some of the problems presented by the community medical and psychiatric services, the Industrial Center initiated a seminar with a large voluntary hospital. Participating were some of its professional social work and psychiatric staff, the various unions' Personal Service staffs, and the Industrial Center staff. Over a period of six months, this group reviewed some of the work-related problems of patients receiving psychiatric treatment in the hospital. Relationships developed, and both union and hospital workers began to make better use of each other. Treatment began to focus more on problems relating to return to work, and the hospital social worker began to use the union person as a supportive ally in getting the patient back to work. Union representatives began to develop a greater trust in the professional arrangement of the hospital. Not all problems were solved, but an honest dialogue between the union and the mental health community was begun.

Service priorities

Inevitably the case load increased, and the Personal Service Unit could not expand sufficiently to give rapid service to all cases. Priorities were established: first, members requiring emergency hospitalization, then cases of severe financial crisis and situations of serious job jeopardy.

Most service is short-term. Longer term service is given under certain special conditions: (1) in job jeopardy situations where the member is not sufficiently motivated to follow through on a community referral but will maintain contact with the Personal Service Unit; (2) in situations where no community services exists (as in the south Bronx area of New York City); and (3) when social work staff, and particularly students doing field work, need some opportunities for the learning experiences and gratifications offered by longer periods of worker-client contact. It is very difficult to make definite statements about the length of involvement, although the unit attempts to keep the long-term cases to a minimum.

Staffing patterns

The Personal Service Unit staff consists of four MSW social workers, two nonprofessional social workers long familiar with union structure and benefits, and MSW students. Thus far there has been little formal differentiation in case or task allocation. All staff members take initial calls and do first interviews so that business can be carried on and service offered at all times. Staff meetings twice a week, chaired by the director, provide opportunities for staff to get an overall perspective on problems brought to the unit, for case distribution and for pooling resources. As might be expected, individual staff members have developed expertise in different areas, such as alcoholism, housing, and garnishee problems. These specializations were supported with staff using each other's special knowledge to achieve maximum effectiveness. The small size of the unit and the staff's excitement about the development of the service and of their own work permitted informality, intimacy, and tolerance of individual styles.

Case activity generates new programs

Experience revealed some problems that concerned many members. This led to formation of groups, such as those for alcoholic members in job jeopardy, parents of children with behavior problems and school difficulties, single adults frustrated by their jobs and their social lives, and workers approaching retirement. One widespread concern was consumer problems. A members' group was organized with the aid of a Personal Service staff worker and has been active now for two years. One particular consumer problem that emerged was the difficulty experienced by low- and middle-income workers in obtaining necessary legal services. The Personal Service Unit, with the Social Welfare Industrial Center, brought to the union officials' attention the need for legal services for their workers. The union is now embarked on a prepaid civil legal service program for its members that combines the skills of the lawyer, paralegal persons, and the social worker.

Personal Service identified areas of financial crisis (loss of job, forced retirement, inadequate pension and social security benefits) that often resulted in workers having to apply for public assistance. These problems were brought to the attention of union leadership, who established a delegates committee made up of union members representing city health agencies, welfare centers, retirees' association, and Personal Service staff. They were to study the problems and make recommendations to the council for action. As a result, a group of union retirees was mobilized to visit and apply pressure to existing SSI centers, and the union's legislative component has lobbied for the enactment of more responsible measures regarding emergency needs in SSI and welfare.

Workers in job jeopardy because of alcoholism preferred a union rather than a management program. When the City of New York Health Services Administration received a grant for alcoholism treatment, their recognition of the importance of union cooperation resulted in the Personal Service Unit's participation in negotiating a joint union-management collaboration on policy and program. What was achieved through these negotiations was assignment of two counselors, paid for by the city, to the Personal Service Unit. Some cooperation and liaison with Health Services' treatment program has been initiated.

As a next step, the Personal Service Unit will further explore new divisions of labor and new roles for the professional social worker, the union representative, and union members in the delivery of social services. More decentralized service is essential for this union, whose membership works and lives in all five boroughs of New York City. Shop stewards at the different work sites can be given information about various resources—for example, for consumer problems. Decentralization may serve to stimulate demands by union members that local community agencies take more responsibility for giving service. Continuing active involvement of leadership and membership with service delivery is essential.

Practice in a Union Setting

It is clear that there are many special features which give social work practice here not only a union label but also a distinctive shape and style. The Personal Service Unit is housed in union headquarters where members are accustomed to come for many purposes—meetings, classes, inquiries about benefits, and so forth. The building is familiar, almost home territory. To some extent, members feel it belongs to them. Their dues pay for it and for union staff salaries. Union services are a right. Generally members of District Council 37 perceive the union as benign, as being on their side. There is a feeling of union brotherhood, in which the Personal Service Unit is included. These features, as well as the informality of the setting, serve to lessen some of the sense of strangeness and social distance often felt by working class people in social agency waiting rooms and offices. Users of services are referred to as "members in need" rather than as clients. The rather cramped quarters, lack of private offices, and constant friendly chatter are not necessarily the most comfortable or efficient working arrangements for professional staff, but the benefits may outweigh the drawbacks.

Social work intervention is strongly focused on enhancing members' coping capabilities, adaptive skills, knowledge, and use of resources. The Personal Service Unit, in keeping with union philosophy, is committed to helping members to continue as workers wherever possible. Maintaining a link through a work role with the larger community, the ability to be self-supporting, these are seen as having important positive effects on a person's perception of himself and on his general physical, mental, and social functioning.

Several of the following case illustrations demonstrate social work intervention in job jeopardy situations. Many other kinds of problems are brought in by members. Low-income workers in particular are subject to multiple stresses which threaten their functioning. A nurse's aide, recently separated from her husband, calls to ask about summer planning or a possible summer job for her 14-year-old son. A 56-year-old library employee comes in concerned that her own functioning is suffering from her worry about her husband's health and job difficulties. A young clerk wants help because the family finances and stability have been upset by the return home of a disturbed older sister and her children. Personal Service functions in such cases to clarify the help sought and needed, and to find, recommend, and facilitate access to services that can alleviate these threats to members' functioning. This may be done largely through telephone contacts, or may involve one or more office interviews with members and possibly with other family members.

The following is an example of a job jeopardy situation.

Miss Atkins, chapter chairwoman in a large city hospital, referred Mr. E., an ambulance technician on the job for fifteen years, whose frequent lateness and absence over the past eighteen months put him in serious job jeopardy. A job hearing date was being set. At this crisis point Mr. E. accepted referral for that afternoon.

The initial interview revealed that Mr. E., a well-groomed black man in his 30s, was troubled about his wife's drug use and frequent overnight absence from home. Although he had helped her get treatment and she was now drug-free, she had lost her former interest in home and children (four, ages 18 to 7). His feelings of shock and subsequent depression resulted in difficulty in getting to work and, when there, in completing a day's work. His frequent absences had run him into debt. Mr. E. described symptoms of depression, among them fear of losing his job, and asked for psychiatric treatment. The initial interview ended with three task assignments for the following week: (1) Mr. E. would get in to work; (2) Personal Service would arrange for psychiatric referral; and (3) both would inform the chairwoman and ask for postponement of the hearing until they could bring in a definite treatment plan.

In the next twenty-five days the worker arranged referral to a mental health clinic and kept contact with Mr. E., to help contain his anxiety until he could start treatment, as well as with the chairwoman, who followed Mr. E.'s work pattern. When the chairwoman reported Mr. E. absent again, the worker followed up and found that Mr. E. was too depressed and upset to work. Clinic and chairwoman cooperated with Personal Service in arranging a one-month leave of absence on psychiatric grounds. Through similar cooperation, disability benefits plus salary were arranged. Although Mr. E. kept contact with the chairwoman and worker, he was unwilling to involve his wife at that time. Mr. E. began clinic treatment and returned to work after the month's leave.

Contacts with the chairwoman two and four months later revealed that Mr. E. was working regularly; and the job hearing was indefinitely postponed. The clinic found Mr. E. to be a motivated patient. When the clinic assigned him to a midafternoon therapy group, time off was arranged by the chairwoman. The clinic was to make efforts to involve Mrs. E.

Some of the diagnostic thinking, theoretical underpinnings, and interventive skills in this case are common to sound social work practice in any setting, but there are some distinctive practice features.

First, initial and major case focus is on helping this depressed, troubled man retain his long-term role as a self-supporting work-er—a role important to him and his family and to his image of himself. Had Mr. E. first approached a mental health clinic or a family agency, the problem for attention would have been his symptomatology or the marital relationship and involvement of Mrs. E. in treatment. While these are crucial elements, Mr. E.'s immediate concern was the threat to his job. The time that would have been needed to shift his perception of the problem and to involve Mrs. E. might have created additional work difficulties. That would further have diminished his self-esteem and compounded the marital and financial tensions. Thus social work intervention is geared to a functional objective—helping Mr. E. maintain his work role. From this steady base he will be in a better position to reach out for other help.

Second is the close team work with the chapter chairwoman, the hub of Mr. E.'s work world, who, together with the Personal Service, worked to safeguard Mr. E.'s job. The information from Miss Atkins that Mr. E. did not get into work alerted the social worker to his depression and the need to reach out actively. As it became clear that Mr. E. was temporarily unable to work, Personal Service and the chairwoman shared tasks to facilitate his medical leave.

The third distinctive feature is the availability and utilization of union benefits which provide breathing space and support for Mr. E.—a leave of absence and additional financial benefits.

Securing a medical leave and linkage to a mental health clinic do not provide a full solution, in the sense that very serious, potentially disabling problems of concern to Mr. E. and Mrs. E. (and probably their children) remain and need attention. What interventive modality or combination of modalities will be most effective for the E.'s requires further exploration with them and is undoubtedly a longer term therapeutic task.

The Personal Service Unit provided access to help in a world reasonably familiar to Mr. E. The experience was successful and strengthening in both concrete and emotional ways. Furthermore, Mr. E.'s ability to retain his worker role provides social, psychological and economic supports. He and the family can work on their intrafamilial problems from a position of some successful coping.

Job related difficulties may take many forms.

Mr. L., a 62-year-old orthodox Jewish man, a Parks Department employee for over thirty years, was referred to

Personal Services by a union representative. He complained of nervous tension, weight loss, depression, and anxiety, all related to his recent promotion to a supervising job. Unable to cope with his administrative responsibilities, he felt persecuted by his boss and by the black employees he supervised. Medical reports were negative.

At Mr. L.'s suggestion, three months medical leave with disability benefits and referral to psychiatric treatment were explored and arranged. Efforts to contact Mrs. L. revealed that she was angry and unsympathetic, refusing to be involved.

During the treatment period, the Personal Service worker continued seeing Mr. L. While not working, he was bored and resentful but still feared his recent job responsibilities. His sense of failure, reinforced by his wife, was intensified by his idleness. Frequent visits to the union office served as a link to his work world, which he feared losing.

Personal Service explored returning Mr. L. to his former job status, the solution of Mr. L.'s choice with the concurrence of the therapist. The union representative initiated the lengthy procedures for reinstatement to his old job line at a site closer to home. Personal Service helped him remain in therapy and, with the union representative, secured an extension of sick leave benefits until he was able to return to his old job line. He still has some symptoms but is functioning.

Again, some features in this case are steady, unromantic bread and butter aspects of social work practice—clinical symptoms like depression, anxiety and persecutory ideas, the need for psychiatric referral, attempting to involve a client's wife, and so on. What is different is the social worker's attention to the new job responsibilities as the factor that precipitated or, more likely, exacerbated Mr. L.'s symptoms. While a constricted personality and life style, marital difficulties, Mr. L.'s age, and negative attitudes of younger minority group workers all affected Mr. L.'s "problem," the Personal Service Unit worker did not focus on these aspects but on the member's wish to retain his all-important work role. The union representative was an important and powerful ally; the union machinery—sick leave and disability benefits—were crucial tools.

In view of Mr. L.'s definition of his problem and the help he was ready to use, the most feasible goal was reduction of symptoms and restoration of the previous level of functioning. The work role, a heavy emotional and social investment to Mr. L., is the one most amenable to intervention. The L. case also suggests the need for preretirement programs to help members cope with this maturational crisis.

Here is still another variation (indeed there are many) on the job jeopardy theme.

> A 22-year-old pretty black nurse's aide, Miss G., was referred by Mrs. Draper, the chapter chairwoman, because of frequent lateness and absence.
>
> Miss G. was in conflict about her work and about her home life. Indication of shallow personality, an unsatisfactory relationship with the young man with whom she lived, and separation from her family were revealed in Personal Service interviews (not kept regularly). Discussion with the chairwoman confirmed a pattern of disorganization and lack of focus. With a tentative diagnosis of ambulatory schizophrenia, Miss G. was referred to a psychiatric clinic, but she attended only once.
>
> When Miss G.'s continued behavior was leading to a job hearing, both the chairwoman and Miss G.'s supervisor intervened to initiate re-referral at Personal Service.
>
> Further interviews explored her ambivalence about work; she mentioned the attraction of applying for welfare, like "some of my friends," as opposed to her desire to earn money. The setting of a job hearing date precipitated a crisis which revealed Miss G.'s ability to improve her attendance and punctuality. The result of the hearing was that Miss G. continued to work, contingent on continuing treatment at the Personal Service Unit.

In this kind of situation, the member in need was not sufficiently motivated to use a community resource. The union, in the person of the chapter chairwoman, offered much help to keep this young woman in the labor force. No other treatment resource will have the work allies that Personal Service Unit has. Information supplied by Mrs. Draper regarding Miss G.'s job performance and work relationships contributed significantly to the clinical impression. In addition, Mrs. Draper played an active part in the therapeutic process; she provided structure and reality pressures. Whether the Personal Service Unit worker can find some way to reduce Miss G's ambivalence and self-defeating behavior evident in other areas as well as on the job or whether management will refuse to maintain an irresponsible employee, are still in questions.

The union setting opens up many possibilities for helping low- and middle-income working people. Such people are highly vulnerable to various forms of consumer fraud and other exploitation. The union's knowledge and clout can be used on their behalf. The following two situations illustrate these kinds of problems.

Two years ago, Mr. J., a 59-year-old laborer in the Parks Department, had cosigned a loan of $700 for a friend who skipped town. On a judgment, his salary was garnished and the loan was repaid in full. Mr. J. now badly needed a loan for himself but, in a year of trying to restore his credit rating, could not get the financial company to state in writing that he had fulfilled his obligation.

Unable to make any headway with the finance company official by explaining Mr. J.'s difficulties, the Personal Service worker suggested he would publicize the company's uncooperativeness to the union's 100,000 members. The letter restoring the member's credit rating was received ten days later.

Mrs. M., a 58-year-old dietary aide at a county hospital, had made a verbal contract with a home repair company for a minor porch remodeling job for "under $300." She accepted their offer to help her get a loan to pay for the job and, after three days of work, signed what she believed to be a statement that the job was satisfactorily completed.

A savings bank later asserted they had paid the repair company and were holding Mrs. M. for a $4000 loan they claimed she had signed for. The repair company disappeared and the bank has not produced either the contract or copies of the terms of repayment which they claim to have sent to

Mrs. M. A Personal Service worker helped Mrs. M. file a complaint with the attorney general's office and will continue efforts to get them to move on the case.

These kinds of cases indicate the varied problems brought to the Personal Service Unit and how the union's strength can be used on members' behalf. They highlight the more general need for consumer education for union members and for legal assistance programs to serve members' nonjob related legal problems. We have already mentioned the successful efforts of Personal Service Unit to stimulate the creation of these kinds of services.

Conclusion: Implications for Practice

Industrial social welfare offers new means to reach and serve neglected populations in a setting that is central to their lives and in ways that are congruent with their life styles. This field of practice, more particularly when it is union based, offers opportunities to enlist powerful allies from the world of work in the interventive network, both for the individual case and for large groups of working people with common needs and concerns.

This field of practice like others, especially those in host settings, has its constraints. The provision of social services is a secondary concern to labor and management, both of whom have primarily economic and political objectives. Social workers must find ways to fit into the industrial setting, to meet its demands, and to respect the organization's needs and priorities.

Two final observations have implications for social work practice and education. Knowledge about the world of work is not for specialists only, for social workers employed in industrial social welfare settings. It is difficult to predict how many social workers will actually be employed in the near future in union or industry sponsored programs, but new patterns of social work activity in relation to industry are emerging and will probably proliferate. An extensive network of benefits and services are available to people working for particular companies or who are members of a particular union. The social agency based or hospital based social worker who is informed about the financial and service resources within the occupational welfare system may be able to secure prompt, low-cost or free services for clients who need them but cannot afford them. Furthermore, a social worker who is aware of the human resources within the work setting can seek these out for his worker-clients.

In another approach, a union or a corporation might use its welfare funds to purchase services in the community for its workers or members on a prepaid or reimbursement basis. Those agencies—and social workers—who understand the special needs of workers and their families, the nature of work settings, and the need to reach out and make linkages with the work world will be the professional sources to which industry and unions will turn.[19] Knowledge about the work world, working class people, and the occupational social welfare system should be standard equipment for all social workers.

The final comment is related to the development of social work theory. For some time now, theoreticians have suggested general systems theory as a framework for more broadly-based and effective social work practice. William Gordon's formulation,[20] that practice should be located "at the interface or the meeting place of person and environment," is often invoked. Thus far, however, there have been few translations into practice. Building bridges between systems theory and practice remains a difficult, delicate task. Industrial social welfare offers unusually suitable terrain for such attempts.

For example, there has been considerable discussion in the literature of extended action systems. Hartman writes, "The extended action system stance guides the worker in following the need or the problem presented by the client system wherever it leads, utilizing a variety of interventive methods and mobilizing whatever action systems appear to be appropriate."[21] The extended action system is a core component of industrial social welfare. Particularly in a union setting, a key aspect of service delivery is the active enlistment of the world of work system—union rep, chapter chairman, and foreman or supervisor—as resources and helpers for the worker member who is having difficulty. This may be done in various ways—telephone communication, three-way interview, on-site visits—and at various points in the helping process.

Another common example of the extended action system is the involvement of other union members or community resources on a member's behalf. A supervisor in a Department of Social Service welfare center can help the union social worker and the member understand some of the intricacies of eligibility for various services; Hospital supervisory personnel can clarify the steps in admission to a detoxification program.

Similarly, Hartman defines the "extended client system" as "a group of people sharing a common problem or status or limited geographical locale. The guide for action is the same as in the extended action system stance: to follow the problems wherever they lead and to devise and utilize whatever action system, roles or stategies appear useful and appropriate."[22] A work site naturally groups many people who share common concerns and problems—such as child care needs, consumer concerns, retirement planning, job jeopardy because of substance abuse, and many others. But on a work site, people also share a wider world of satisfying as well as difficult experiences. Thus helping workers to join together in mutual aid ventures would be a natural function for a social worker in industrial settings.

In conclusion, we suggest that, in addition to the other new opportunities offered by industrial social welfare, this field of practice, particularly in union settings, provides natural laboratories to develop and test an ecological systems model of social work practice.

Notes

1. Carel Germain, "An Ecological Perspective in Casework Practice," *Social Casework* 54 (June 1973).

2. There is considerable literature on working class people and their world and perceptions. A few references are: Marc Fried, *The World of the Urban Working Class* (Cambridge: Harvard University Press, 1973); Sar Levitan, ed., *Blue Collar Workers: A Symposium on Middle America* (New York City: McGraw Hill, 1971); P. and B. Sexton, *Blue Collars and Hard Hats: The Working Classes and the Future of American Politics* (New York City: Random House, 1972); and Arthur Shastak, *Blue Collar Life* (New York City, Random House, 1969).

3. Margaret Heyman, "Employer Sponsored Programs for Problem Drinkers," *Social Casework* 52 (Nov. 1971).

4. Hanlon and Jacobs, "Social Work and Private Industry," *Social Casework* 50 (March 1969).

5. Elizabeth Mills, "Family Counseling in an Industrial Job Support Program," *Social Casework* 53 (Dec. 1972).

6. Francis Moynihan, "Closing the Gap Between Family Service and Private Industry," *Social Casework* 52 (Feb. 1971).

7. Skidmore, Balsam, and Jones, "Social Work Practice in Industry," *Social Work* 19 (May 1974).

8. Ibid., p. 283.

9. Bertha Reynolds, *Social Work and Social Living* (New York City: Citadel Press, 1951).

10. Weiner, Akabas, and Sommer, *Mental Health Care in the World of Work* (New York City: Associated Press, 1973).

11. Ibid., p. 143.

12. Ibid.

13. Ibid., p. 74.

14. Ibid., pp. 147–48.

15. R. Yasser and J. Sommer, "A Union Finds a Way to Provide Social Services for Its Members," *Social Welfare Forum* (New York: Columbia University Press, 1974).

16. AFSCME, *Steward Handbook* (Washington, D.C.: AFSCME Publications Department, undated).

17. Yasser and Sommer, "A Union Finds a Way," pp. 8–9.

18. Weiner, Akabas, and Sommer, *Mental Health Care,* p. 65.

19. Paul Kurzman, "Industrial Social Welfare Casebook" (unpublished), Industrial Social Welfare Center, Columbia University, New York City, 1974.

20. William Gordon, "Basic Constructs for an Integrative and Generative Conception of Social Work," in *The General Systems Approach: Contributions Toward an Holistic Conception of Social Work,* ed. by Gordon Hearn (New York City: CSWE, 1969).

21. Ann Hartman, "The Generic Stance and the Family Agency," *Social Casework* 55 (April 1974): 203.

22. Ibid., p. 205.

7

A Developmental-Educational
Approach to Child Treatment

JAMES K. WHITTAKER

*This chapter describes a responsive and comprehensive
social work ecological system for treating troubled
children in residential group care. A perceived
change—that child populations in the programs now
appear to be more disturbed—leads to discussion of
commonly observed problem-clusters and appropriate
modern therapeutic interventions.*

*The proposed ecological model involves parents as full
and equal partners in the helping process. It develops
linkages with school, peer group, juvenile justice systems,
and other systems that form a service net to insure
continuity of care from pre-care to aftercare. Within the
therapeutic milieu, learning skill for daily living is
stressed. A richly eclectic array of behavioral
modification, psychotherapy, and educational program
activities for child, peer group, and family is presented.
Expanded roles and knowledge areas are required for
social work staff.*

> ecology: the totality or pattern of relations between organisms and their environment
> —Webster's New Collegiate Dictionary

THE current fabric of group care services for troubled children is more crazy quilt than tapestry. All manner of programs—residential treatment centers, group homes, day treatment programs, crisis shelters—exist in the community and reflect a growing heterodoxy of treatment philosophy, use of professional staff, and program goals. One potentially unifying idea—that of a therapeutic milieu—has been so liberally interpreted that it has lost much of its descriptive power. Who, after all, would admit to having an untherapeutic milieu? Group child care is in the midst of a great experiment—or, perhaps, many experiments—to test the validity of that inviolate principle enunciated at the First White House Conference on Children in 1909 and echoed by planners and practitioners ever since: "The home is the highest and finest product of civilization" and, by implication, the first choice for placement.

It is perhaps a paradox that while the field of child welfare and juvenile corrections is moving away from a reliance on institutions in favor of community based programs, "mainstreaming," and "normalization," parents in ever greater numbers are asserting that they alone are not sufficient to meet all of the developmental needs of their normal children, let alone of their troubled offspring. In fact, what has happened is that the distinction between family and agency is blurring a bit as parents become increasingly involved at all levels of the helping process for their own children. The age of the consumer in child welfare is upon us.

All of these forces create problems and opportunities for the traditionally trained caseworker with troubled children in a group care setting who suddenly finds her authority as the expert challenged by the child care staff, her clinical wisdom openly scorned in the professional literature, and her judgment called into question by parents who want to be full and equal partners in the helping process. To consider the future role for social work practice in group care settings, we must first try to understand where the field appears to be heading.

Many residential and community treatment programs have experienced only limited success because they could not affect the disturbed or delinquent child's total life sphere—family, peer group, school, and neighborhood. Indeed, the child's posttreatment environment looms ever larger as the crucial variable in determining success.[1] At the same time, professionals and planners are currently in the midst of a debate over institutional versus community treatment which conveniently sidesteps the issue of how one goes about designing a therapeutic milieu for troubled children—either institutional or community based—which takes into account all the key elements in the child's life web and uses every possible teaching format for growth and change. As a beginning step in this direction, this chapter will attempt to do three things:

1. To identify the major assumptions on which any future model of residential or day treatment for children should be based.
2. To identify the distinguishing characteristics of the child population at risk.
3. To briefly identify the essential features of a developmental/educational paradigm of a therapeutic milieu.

Assumptions of Treatment

The current move towards deinstitutionalization in child mental health and juvenile corrections is to some extent based on a false dichotomy between residential and community based programs.

Since Aichorn's pioneering effort, a sizable literature has developed on residential treatment for the child who is disturbed or delinquent or both.[2] This literature—largely grounded in ego psychology concepts—has recently been supplemented by a growing number of studies which describe the application of behavioral principles to the therapeutic milieu.[3] At the same time that we are amassing knowledge on how to construct ameliorative environments for children, residential treatment programs are increasingly coming under fire for being both too costly and ineffective in meeting the needs of the troubled child. Community treatment, one hears, is to be the wave of the future and indeed the most recent census figures tend to support the picture of a diminishing institutional population.

Clearly, the central rationale for community based treatment—to bring the treatment closer to the child's natural environment—is sound. But if the locus of treatment is important, so is the focus: buying a home in the community and staffing it with a largely untrained set of houseparents does not make for a sophisticated or effective treatment program. Further, if it is true that some children can remain at home while they and their families receive help, others—for a variety of reasons—continue to require total or partial care away from home. In sum, the real issue is not the relative merits of residential or community treatment; rather, it is how best to translate the most useful knowledge from clinical research and practice to a whole range of smaller, community based residential and day programs for children.

Support systems for the family

The basic purpose of residential and day programs for troubled children should be to function as a family support system, rather than to treat children in isolation from their families and home communities.

The nuclear family—natural or foster—continues to be seen as the optimal environment for child rearing in American society. Partly because they were physically isolated from their client's communities and partly because parents were presumed to be causative agents in the child's problems, many residential treatment centers developed a stance which separated parents from the treatment of their child. Since few programs had the resources to maintain children through emancipation, the problem of continuity of care became readily apparent at the time of discharge. Rather than being seen as substitutes for family living, child treatment programs should be seen as helping natural parents or foster parents develop models of quality child rearing with children who have special life adjustment problems. What literature exists on the permanence of therapeutic change in children suggests the importance of involving parents—particularly mothers—in the child's treatment. In those programs that have involved parents as full and equal partners in the helping process, the results have been impressive.[4]

The ecological view

Successful treatment programs will be those that actively seek to develop linkages with the other major systems in which the child participates—school, peer group, juvenile justice system, recreation, and occupational systems.

A truly ecological view of child treatment requires intervention in a number of different supporting systems to insure continuity of care. In providing children's services, the goal should be to develop a service net rather than an aggregate of isolated services. What happens to the child once he leaves the treatment program will probably be more important than anything that happened to him while in residence. This explains the discrepancy between in-program and follow-up adjustment of some juvenile offenders from sophisticated treatment programs.

Child treatment programs should focus on growth and development in the child's total life sphere, rather than on the amelioration of psychiatrically defined syndromes or the extinction of certain problematical behaviors.

The basic purpose of child helping should be to teach skills for living. Residential or day programs should offer first and foremost a model of quality child rearing, which begins not by emphasizing the differences of "special" children, but by recognizing the competence and mastery that all children need to develop in basic life skills. By definition, such an orientation would include a variety of formats for teaching—behavioral modification programs, games and activities, psychotherapy, special education, group life—no one of which constitutes a total living-learning culture. Neither insight therapy nor behavior modification of itself provides education for living. An orientation to total child growth and development requires three additional steps.

1. De-mystifying the helping process. Parents and child care workers are most often the best experts on the children in their care. Both should be involved as central actors in the helping process, and this means having access to all information possessed by the clinicians. Too often parents and parenting persons have been kept in the dark regarding clinical assessments, which themselves are often couched in jargon designed more to obfuscate than elucidate. Assessment should include a look at the child's total range of functioning; it should not start with clinical presuppositions but with the areas that are causing parents and child the most pain and strain. Finally, taking the mystery out of child treatment means saying honestly, "I don't know," when the situation warrants.

2. Relabeling program elements. Much has been written of the dangers of labeling individual children. Similarly, program labels go a long way in helping the child define himself. The basic elements of the child treatment program require relabeling to reflect a living-learning, rather than an illness-treatment orientation. For example:

Campus	not	*Grounds*
Student	not	*Patient*
Dormitory	not	*Cottage*
Graduation	not	*Discharge*
Residential School	not	*Treatment Center*

The reason for this semantic change is partly political—*education* is more positively received in the society than is *treatment*—but also because it provides a much better set of descriptions of what the program is all about—teaching the child something about the reasonable limits of his own behavior and at the same time providing him with the opportunity to acquire competence in a whole range of life skills. The illness-treatment terminology suggests that the children have some identifiable psychic disease—a view which is not supported by the available evidence.

3. Designing learning experiences with an eye toward maximum portability. Adjustment within the program should be seen as the means and not the end of the helping process. Developing "marketable peer skills" should mean just that: how to make a friend, join a game, or negotiate with someone who is bigger and tougher than you. The ultimate proving ground should be the child's own home, school, and community.

The goal of evaluation

Children's residential and day programs should be able to demonstrate what it is they do in terms that can be understood by the general public.

Simply stated, sound evaluative procedures should be built into all child helping programs. The choice is not whether to evaluate, but who do we want doing the evaluation and what will be the criteria? In many studies, "success" has been very narrowly defined and often in ways not warranted by the treatment effort. The goal for evaluation should be as broad a set of measures as possible rather than a single criteria like "recidivism," "grades in school," or "absence of police contact." In order not to be stampeded in the rush for cost effectiveness and accountability, clinicians and administrators should be involved in the measurement themselves, in determining a wide range of "hard" and "soft" outcome criteria and in tailoring evaluation to individual programs.

Fortunately, research methodology has advanced to the point that we can overcome with controls some of the practical limitations in the traditional group design. The previously cited work of Browning and Stover and Johnson is particularly promising in this regard.[5] Evaluation need not be esoteric or highly complex;

we are a problem-focused group and so our research should be action research.

Finally, the impetus for evaluation is not simply political. We need to learn more about what works and what doesn't in children's programs and to build knowledge in an area of practice sorely in need of hard data.

Characteristics of the Child Population at Risk

Excluding the physically handicapped, there were approximately 220,000 children under age 18 in institutional care in 1970. They were housed in some 2,400 child caring institutions. In addition, over one million cases are handled in our juvenile courts yearly, and these figures may not accurately reflect the need for services or the number of children who may be improperly placed.[6]

Clinically, the population of children coming into residential and day treatment programs seems more disturbed than that of just a few years ago.[7] Most present a multiplicity of problems—interpersonal, emotional, learning, familial, physiological. This population encompasses a wide range of presenting problems and diagnostic labels—infantile autism, childhood schizophrenia, character disorder, minimal brain dysfunction, depressed, hyperkinetic, socially maladjusted, delinquent, and developmentally disordered. Without attempting to minimize real etiological and behavioral differences between these various subpopulations, there do seem to be some commonly observed problem clusters exhibited by these children which, taken together, comprise the Empty Bucket Syndrome. (This condition was identified by one child care worker who told me, "Picture a bucket whose bottom is full of holes. No matter how much water you pour in the top, the bucket always stays empty. That's what many of these kids are like.")

Figure 1. Some Commonly Observed Problem Clusters

Intrapersonal
{
Poorly developed impulse control
Low self image
Poorly developed modulation of emotion
}

Interpersonal ⎰Relationship deficits
⎱Family pain and strain

External ⎰Special Learning disabilities
⎱Limited play skills

The intrapersonal cluster

Poorly developed impulse control. Numerous clinicians have noted the low frustration tolerance and limited ability to postpone gratification characteristic of many of the children who come into residential or day treatment. Disruptive outbursts at home and in school are often part of the initial reason for referral. Trieschman has noted the faulty connection between thought, feeling, and action which many children exhibit in the course of a temper tantrum.[8] Lashing out at other persons, at objects, or at self becomes the characteristic way of dealing with frustration, strain, or anxiety. In purely behavioral terms, the "aggressive child" possesses only a limited repertoire of responses for dealing with frustration or provocation. A related characteristic is the apparent inability of many of these children to screen out peripheral stimuli; they are easily "contaged" by the misbehavior of other children and are especially prone to group excitement.

Low self image. "Bad," "evil," "stupid," "troublemaker" characterized the ways in which the "empty-bucket" child is likely to see himself. A fatalistic view of the potential for change ("I've always been this way") is supported by a string of unsuccessful experiences in school, at home, and with friends. In the Eriksonian sense, we see the antithesis of "I am what I will be" in the hollowness of the delinquent adolescent on whose forearm is etched, "Born to Lose," and in the impenetrability of the autistic child whose "fortress" is indeed "empty."

Poorly developed modulation of emotion. Many of the aforementioned children also lack skills in dealing appropriately and effectively with the normal range of human emotions—anger, fear, elation, and sadness. In addition to the problem of expressing emotion congruently, children have difficulty sorting out mixed emotions (particularly anger and sadness), or are emotionally labile.

The interpersonal cluster

Relationship deficits. The range of relationship deficits extends from the isolating autistic child who avoids even eye contact to the clinging, overpowering child who seems ready to submerge (or be submerged in) another. Some children are fearful of closeness and leery of adult relationships, while others react stereotypically to male or female authority figures. Often, these are children who have few friends because of their unpredictability, or their proclivity to "con" and manipulate, or their tendency to overload an individual relationship with too many demands. Such children may have difficulty in joining and leaving peer groups and in handling particular as opposed to universal relationships—for example, with a teacher. Some children simply lack the social skills that facilitate new relationships (such as small talk) and thus turn to disruptive, silly, or bizarre behavior as a way of handling their discomfort. In short, and for a variety of reasons, these are children who often relate to adults, if at all, in stereotypic ways.

Family pain and strain. It is safe to say that having a child with problems upsets the family equilibrium. Beyond that, these are three possible ways that the parents and child can be involved in problem causation: (1) parents to child, (2) child to parents, and (3) parents to child and child to parents. Typically, we have assumed condition (1), and indeed this hypothesis has been borne out by the scores of children who have suffered physical and emotional neglect and abuse, inconsistent parenting, and marital discord. Strain and pain in the family, however, may also be caused by an unpredictable, unrewarding, and nonresponsive child who would tax even the best of parents beyond the limits of their endurance. Research by Scopler and Loftin and Waxler and Mishler tends to support this point of view vis-à-vis psychotic children and their parents and raises serious questions about the family etiology hypothesis advanced by Bettelheim and others to explain these disturbances.[9] Similarly, some MBD research would appear to suggest that at least some of the "character disordered," acting-out children whose behavioral problems were previously thought to be the result of bad parenting could in fact have some genetic or physiological base to their difficulty.[10]

If the question of etiology remains an open one, the need for the restabilization of the family unit does not. For the family whose child is entering residential or day treatment, the critical issues include guilt over causation, divided loyalties of the child between parents and child care staff, stereotyping (parents and staff as "we" and "they"), and termination and after care.

The external cluster

Special learning disabilities. As a group, children coming into residential or day treatment present some combination of learning difficulties whose etiology is often unclear. For many, public school has been an essentially negative experience. In addition to specific learning difficulties, many of these children lack the interpersonal skills necessary to negotiate the bureaucracy of the public school. They are thus deprived of this important medium for competency acquisition and the high degree of positive social sanction that accompanies success in school.

Perhaps because of a presumed dichotomy between emotional and learning problems—and a helping approach that stressed resolving the former before addressing the latter—the school component of many residential and day programs for troubled children remains underdeveloped. Often, the clinical aura extends to the classroom even to the point of seeing personal analysis as an important, supporting part of teacher training.[11] Sustaining this line of thinking is the view that most learning problems are more psychogenic than physiological in origin.

Limited play skills. Play is assumed by many to have an important role in social and cognitive development.[12] It is noteworthy that in this area, the "empty bucket" is often most obvious. Many children have a limited repertoire of play skills and tend to overload one or two activities, in the same way that relationships get overloaded. Other children have difficulty in joining and participating in group activities as well as in playing alone. Others have behavioral problems—short attention span, low frustration tolerance—that get in the way of sustained enjoyment of activities. Often a child's bedroom, devoid of colorful decoration, artifacts, and projects, gives a clue to the deficits in this area. Again, in the Eriksonian sense, the child is deprived of an important medium for self-definition and "I am what I learn" connotes more "inferiority" than "industry."

In sum, examining these problem clusters gives a general picture of a child who, in Robert White's conceptual scheme, lacks "competence" and "confidence" in a wide variety of life spheres.[13] Using White's framework for competency as a base for assessment, such a child may be diagnosed as having failed to develop emotional, social, and physical competence for internal psychological reasons (faulty and incomplete ego development); physiological reasons (MBD, speech or hearing deficits, developmental disability); environmental reasons (unstable, inconsistent, threatening environment); or some combination of the above. In this sense, the acting out of the hyperkinetic or delinquent child as well as the repetitive activity of the autistic or learning disordered child may indicate crude attempts to master an environment, or a portion of an environment, that is perceived as threatening, confusing, and unpredictable. The acquisition of competence and mastery, therefore, becomes the primary goal of intervention.

Granting differences between individual children and differences between subpopulations of troubled children—delinquent, psychotic, learning disordered—an ideal therapeutic environment can be suggested, and will be discussed in the next section.

A Developmental-Educational Paradigm of the Therapeutic Milieu

Just as we lack a definitive explanation for the etiology of many childhood disorders, we lack a completed theory on how to change children's behavior. Thus, much of our intervention will be experimental and pragmatic and will derive from a problem orientation rather than a theoretical one. Basically, a therapeutic milieu should provide a multidimensional context for competency acquisition, where the events of daily living—the rules, the routines, the games and activities, the psychotherapy, and the classroom edcuation—become the context not just for helping a child to manage his behavior, but a medium for helping him to expand his competence to the full limit of his developmental potential. The entire milieu becomes both means and context for growth and change, informed by a culture that stresses learning through living. Competency acquisition occurs on three levels:

1. Intrapersonal, by helping the child to deal effectively and appropriately with impulses and emotions—anger, sadness, fear, elation, and excitement. Children learn through insight

to link feelings, thoughts, and actions and, in essence, to gain control over their internal environment.

2. Interpersonal, by helping the child to interact effectively with peers and adults. How do you let someone know that you really like them? How do you enter an established clique? What can you say or do when another child is bugging you? How do you get out of the scapegoat role?

3. Environmental, by helping the child to master the multiple worlds he inhabits. This involves academic skills and physical skills, as well as acquisition of competence in new social situations.

In this paradigm all areas are equal in importance. For a given child, learning how to swim may be as important as learning how to read a book or learning a new way of mastering an angry feeling. "Competence" is closely related to "confidence"—one's self-appraisal of competence—and often the development of mastery in one area has a generalizing effect to others. For example, the child who learns how to deal with the frustration of not always having the teacher at his beck and call increases the likelihood that he will stay in the classroom long enough to pick up some reading skills. One doesn't have to believe in the concept "ego" to see that mastery enhances self-image and increases the likelihood that new and more difficult challenges will be attempted—joining the activity, testing out the new foster home, trying out the new school. Finally, the development of a broad range of competencies means that any single area—home, school, peer group—assumes less crucial importance.

The teaching context

Competency acquisition occurs in a variety of teaching formats, linked with several different learning processes—insight learning, reward and punishment learning, imitation-identification learning, and motor learning. Table 2 indicates how these teaching formats articulate with the previously identified problem clusters and processes of learning. What is important is that no one educational format will answer all of a child's learning problems. Overreliance on a single format—whether behavior modification, psychotherapy, or program activities—ignores the fact that children learn in a variety of ways and have a mixed bag of problems that do not neatly accommodate a single method of intervention. The particular mix of teaching formats will vary according to the overall program purpose, geographical area and special characteristics of the population served.[14]

Figure 2 represents an overview of the therapeutic milieu by means of the various formats available for teaching alternative behavior, their relationship to the problem clusters outlined in this chapter, and the mediating processes of learning involved. The categories "Hi," "Med," and "Min" are meant only to give a rough approximation of the power of each of the formats for addressing a specific problem area. The chart may be read horizontally or vertically. For example, "Rules" provide an effective teaching format for helping children master impulsive behavior but are less helpful in addressing familial or educational relationships, or problems related to self-image. Similarly, "Relationship Deficits" are most effectively helped through program activities, group meetings, life space interviews, and conjoint family treatment.

Obviously the ratings are open to differential interpretation and can only be a general guide for approaching the design of a therapuetic milieu, particularly in those settings that may be overemphasizing certain change formats to the exclusion of others. At the level of individual case planning, additional procedural specificity is needed which may, at times, contradict the general ratings. For example, one could conceive of a quite effective individual behavioral modification program specifically designed to teach relationship skills.

Organization and staffing

Basically, the therapeutic milieu requires two teaching roles, the life space educator and the classroom educator. At present, the latter is better defined than the former, although many have suggested the need for a new profession to expand and elaborate on what was previously subsumed under the child care role. In any event, the program should be child centered—as opposed to profession centered—with all staff members involved in at least a piece of the total action. This would prevent the creation of one group of professionals working solely with parents or with children and would eliminate a great deal of the potential rivalry and presumptiveness contained in such an arrangement. The basic

Figure 2. Paradigm of a Therapeutic Milieu

Teaching formats	Mediating processes of learning	Problem Clusters						
		Poor impulse control	Low self image	Poorly dev. mod. of emot.	Relat. deficits	Family pain & strain	Spec. learn. disabil.	Lim. play skills
Rules	1,2,3	Hi	Min	Mod	Min	Min	Min	Mod
Routines	1,2,3,4	Hi	Mod	Hi	Mod	Min	Min	Mod
Program activities	2,3,4	Hi	Hi	Min	Hi	Min	Min	Hi
Group mtgs.	1,2,3	Hi	Hi	Hi	Hi	Min	Min	Min
Individual Psychotherapy	1,3	Hi	Hi	Hi	Mod	Mod	Min	Min
Life space interviews	1,3	Hi	Hi	Hi	Hi	Min	Min	Mod
Token economy	2	Hi	Hi	Min	Min	Min	Hi	Mod
Special ed. class	1,2,3	Hi	Hi	Min	Min	Min	Hi	Min
Conjoint family treatment	1,3	Hi	Hi	Hi	Hi	Hi	Min	Min
Parent education group	1,3	Mod	Hi	Min	Min	Hi	Min	Mod
Parent involvement in life space	1,3	Hi	Hi	Mod	Mod	Hi	Min	Hi
Individual behavior mod. program	2,3	Hi	Hi	Hi	Mod	Mod	Hi	Mod

Key: 1—Insight; 2—Reward and punishment; 3—Imitation-identification; 4—Motoric; Hi—Highly applicable; Mod—Moderately applicable; Min—Minimally applicable.

child care professional—whether called "life space educator" or "educateur"—should play a pivotal role not only in the children's education but in the work with parents as well. The child caring person, with an intimate and specific knowledge of each child, possesses the kind of information that will be most helpful to parents in meeting the nitty gritty problems of everyday living. Hobbs, Barnes and Kelman, Phillips, Resnik, and Schopler and Reichler each suggest creative programmatic ways of combining child helping and parent helping.[15]

Social work, as the profession that has made the most significant contribution to child welfare services, is in a unique position to provide leadership in the development of future programs. But two traps must be avoided.

First, while there is clearly a proper place for individual oriented therapy in a group care program, it should no longer determine agency structure and organization. The idea of a psychiatric casework department, removed from the life space and operating in the relative safety of the fifty-minute hour, is as out of touch with the reality of the time as is traditional psychodiagnostic nomenclature.

Second, individual oriented casework training is simply insufficient to meet the demands of the emerging social work role in group child care. In addition to clinical skills, the social worker should be throughly grounded in basic child care work practice. This means some kind of boot training as a child care worker and the continued ability to work in the life space as consultant, supervisor, and crisis manager. Additional knowledge areas include program management, clinical research, program evaluation, family life education, group supervision, behavioral management, and program activities. MSW programs should take leadership in providing such a concentration, which would be particularly attractive to the child care worker who desires further education but wishes to remain in the field of group child care. AA and AB programs could offer sequences in direct child care work practice as an entry point for those who wish to work directly in the life space. There is currently a great deal of interest in educational programs for child care workers, particularly those based on the European "educateur" model, and several schools of social work have already established pilot programs in child care education.

Conclusion: A Note on the Problem of Transitions

As stated earlier, in-program adjustment must be seen as the means and not the end of child helping. The transition from a residential or day program to the child's home, school, and neighborhood represents a critical intervening variable in the ultimate prognosis. This suggests a much closer interface between home, school, and therapeutic milieu. Frequent home visits, multilevel parental contacts, and personal contact with schools, courts, and recreational agencies are all mechanisms for insuring that change achieved in the program is maintained. This again points up the folly of seeing residential and community based programs as mutually exclusive entities; both are needed to insure a continuum of services to the child and family facing the problem of reentry.

Finally, we need to think less rigidly and categorically about what "being in the program" means. Some children and their families may need only a piece of what we have to offer, or need booster shots of service in periods of high vulnerability. One of the great benefits of community treatment may be that it really makes the child's problems the community's problems and moves us away from the myopia of "out of sight, out of mind."

Notes

1. For examples of such evaluative studies, see: Melvin E. Allerhand, Ruth E. Weber, and Marie Haug, *Adaptation and Adaptability* (New York City: Child Welfare League of America, 1966); W. C. Berleman, J. R. Seaberg, and T. W. Steinburn, "The Delinquency Prevention Experiment of the Seattle Atlantic Street Center: A Final Evaluation," *Social Service Review* 46 (Sept. 1972): 323–47; E. C. Cavior, A. Schmidt, and L. Karacki, "An Evaluation of the Kennedy Youth Center Differential Treatment Program: In-Program and Twelve-Month Post-Release Outcome for Kennedy Youth Center, Ashland, and Englewood," Research Office, U.S. Bureau of Prisons, October 1972: H. Meyer, E. Borgatta, and W. Hones, *Girls at Vocational High* (New York City: Russell Sage Foundation, 1965); and Delores A. Taylor and Stuart W. Alpert, *Continuity and Support Following Residential Treatment* (New York City: Child Welfare League of America, 1973).

2. For a basic introduction to residential treatment, see: A. Aichorn, *Wayward Youth* (New York City: Viking Press, 1935); B. Bettelheim, *Truants from Life* (Glencoe, Ill.: Free Press, 1955); Child Welfare League of America, *From Chaos to Order: A Collective View of the Residential Treatment of Children* (New York City: CWLA, 1972); Hyman Grossbard, "Ego Deficiency in Delinquents," *Social Casework* 43 (1962): 171–78; Morris F. Mayer and Arthur Blum, eds., *Healing Through Living: A Symposium on Residential Treatment* (Springfield, Ill.: Charles C. Thomas, Publisher, 1971); J. D. Noshpitz, "Notes on the

Theory of Residential Treatment," *Journal of American Academy of Child Psychiatry* 1 (April 1962): 284–96; Howard Polsky and Daniel S. Claster, *The Dynamics of Residential Treatment: A Social Systems Analysis* (Chapel Hill: University of North Carolina Press, 1968); Fritz Redl, *When We Deal with Children* (New York City: Free Press, 1966); Fritz Redl and D. Wineman, *The Aggressive Child* (New York City: Free Press, 1958); A. E. Trieschman, J. K. Whittaker, and L. K. Brendtro, *The Other Twenty-three Hours: Child Care Work in a Therapeutic Milieu* (Chicago: Aldine, 1969); J. K. Whittaker, "Developing a Unified Theory of Residential Treatment," *Mental Hygiene* 54 (Jan. 1970): 166–69; and idem, "The Child Care Continuum: New Directions for Children's Residential Centers," *Child Care Quarterly* 2 (No. 2, 1973): 124–35.

3. For an introduction to the use of behavioral methods in residential treatment, see: R. M. Browning and D. O. Stover, *Behavior Modification in Child Treatment* (Chicago: Aldine-Atherton, 1971); O. I. Lovaas, "A Behavior Therapy Approach to the Treatment of Childhood Schizophrenia," in *Minnesota Symposium on Child Psychology,* vol. 1, ed. by J. P. Hill (Minneapolis: University of Minnesota Press, 1967), pp. 108–59; E. L. Phillips, E. A. Phillips, D. L. Fixsen, and M. M. Wolf, "Achievement Place: Behavior Shaping Works for Delinquents," *Psychology Today* 7 (June 1973): 74–80; and Roland G. Tharp and Ralph J. Wetzel, *Behavior Modification in the Natural Environment* (New York City: Academic Press, 1969).

4. See, for example, E. Levitt, "Research on Psychotherapy with Children," in *Handbook of Psychotherapy and Behavior Change,* ed. by A. E. Bergin and S. L. Garfield (New York City: John Wiley and Sons, 1971), pp. 474–95; and E. Schopler and R. Reichler, "Parents as Co-Therapists in the Treatment of Psychotic Children," *Journal of Autism and Child Schizophrenia* 1 (no. 1, 1971): 87–102.

5. See H. Johnson, "Demonstration of Goal Planning and Evaluative Research in a Residential Treatment Center," Mapleridge Residential Treatment Center, Edmonton, Alberta, May 1973.

6. See: A. Kadushin, *Child Welfare Services* (New York City: Macmillan Co., 1974), and D. M. Pappenfort, D. M. Kilpatrick, and R. W. Roberts, *Child Caring: Social Policy and the Institution* (Chicago: Aldine, 1973); see also the articles in *Encyclopedia of Social Work* (New York City: NASW, 1971) by H. Polsky, "Residential Treatment Homes," pp. 139–42, and H. Maier, "Child Care Workers," pp. 111–14.

7. For some clinical impressions, see: A. N. Maluccio and W. D. Marlow, "Residential Treatment of Emotionally Disturbed Children: A Review of the Literature," *Social Service* 46 (June 1972): 230–51; and A. Weintrob, "Changing Population in Adolescent Residential Treatment: New Problems for Program and Staff," *American Journal of Orthopsychiatry* 44 (July 1974): 604–11.

8. See Trieschman, Whittaker, and Brendtro, *The Other Twenty-Three Hours,* pp. 170–98.

9. See: B. Bettelheim, *The Empty Fortress* (New York City: Free Press, 1967); E. Schopler and J. Loftin, "Thought Disorders in Parents

of Psychotic Children: A Function of Test Anxiety," *Archives of General Psychiatry* 20 (Feb. 1969) 174–81; and N. E. Waxler and E. G. Mishler, "Parental Interaction with Schizophrenic Children and with Siblings: An Experimental Test of Some Etiology Theories," in *Annual Progress in Child Psychiatry and Child Development,* ed. by S. Chess and A. Thomas (New York City: Brunner/Mazel, 1972), pp. 568–89.

10. See: H. R. Huessy, "Study of the Prevalence and Therapy of the Choreiform Syndrome or Hyperkinesis in Rural Vermont," *Acta Paedopsychiat* 34 (1967): 130–35; J. R. Morrison and M. A. Stewart, "The Psychiatric Status of the Legal Families of Adopted Hyperactive Children," *Archives of General Psychiatry* 28 (June 1973); S. Walzer and P. H. Wolff, *Minimal Cerebral Dysfunction in Children* (New York City: Grune and Stratton, 1973); and J. K. Whittaker, "Causes of Childhood Disorders: New Findings," *Social Work* 21 (March 1976): 91–96.

11. See R. Ekstein, "The Educator's Task in a Residential Treatment Center: Coping with Conflicts of Growth or Growth of Conflicts," in *Healing Through Living,* ed. by Mayer and Blum.

12. For a beginning literature on the importance of play, see: E. H. Erikson, *Childhood and Society,* 2nd ed. (New York City: Norton, 1963); idem, "Toys and Reasons," in *Child Psychotherapy,* ed. by M. R. Haworth (New York City: Basic Books, 1964), pp. 3–11; R. Herron and Sutton-Smith, *Child's Play* (New York City: John Wiley and Sons, 1971); and J. L. Singer, *The Child's World of Make Believe* (New York City: Academic Press, 1973).

13. See R. W. White, "Competence and the Psychosexual Stages of Development," in *Nebraska Symposium on Motivation,* ed. by M. R. Jones (Lincoln: University of Nebraska Press, 1960).

14. There is no space here to elaborate on these teaching formats or to discuss how to blend them into a program that makes sense for the dilinquent adolescent, the autistic child, or the latency aged child with multiple learning handicaps. I am currently working on a larger treatment—*The Ecology of Child Treatment: Therapeutic Environments for Troubled Children* (Chicago: Aldine, manuscript in preparation)—giving more detailed explanations. For an introduction to the various teaching formats, see Trieschman, Whittaker, and Brendtro, *The Other Twenty-Three Hours,* pp. 24–37.

15. See, for example, F. H. Barnes and S. M. Kelman, "From Slogans to Concepts: A Basis for Change in Child Care Work," *Child Care Quarterly* 3 (Spring 1974): 7–24; John F. Kennedy Center for Research on Education and Human Development, *Project Re-Ed* (Nashville, Tenn.: George Peabody College for Teachers, 1969); David Resnik, "The Social Worker as Co-ordinator in Residential Treatment," *Social Casework* 48 (1967): 293–98; Phillips, Phillips, Fixsen and Wolf, "Achievement Place"; and Schopler and Reichler, "Parents as Co-Therapists."

Bibliography

Aichorn, A. *Wayward Youth*. New York: Viking Press, 1935.

Allerhand, Melvin E., Ruth E. Weber, Marie Haug. *Adaptation & Adaptability,* Child Welfare League of America, Inc., New York, New York, 1966.

Barnes, F.H., and S.M. Kelman. "From Slogans to Concepts: A Basis For Change In Child Care Work," *Child Care Quarterly,* 3, 1 (Spring, 1974), 7–24.

Berleman, W.C., J.R. Seaberg, and T.W. Steinburn. "The delinquency prevention experiment of the Seattle Atlantic Street Center: a final evaluation," *Social Service Review,* 46, 3, (September, 1972), 323–347.

Bettelheim, B. *Love is not enough*. New York: Free Press, 1950.

Bettelheim, B. *Truants From Life*. Glencoe: Free Press, 1955.

Browning, R.M., and D.O. Stover. *Behavior Modification In Child Treatment*. Chicago: Aldine-Atherton, 1971.

Cavior, E.C., A. Schmidt, L. Karacki. "An Evaluation of the Kennedy Youth Center Differential Treatment Program: In Program and 12 Month Post-Release Outcome for Kennedy Youth Center, Ashland and Englewood," Research Office: *U.S. Bureau of Prisons,* October, 1972.

Encyclopedia of Social Work. New York: NASW, 1971. 2 volumes. See: Polsky, H. "Residential Treatment Homes," 139–142; Maier, H. "Child Care Workers," 111–114.

Erikson, E.H. *Childhood and society*. New York: Norton, 1963, 2nd edition.

Erikson, E.H. Toys and reasons. In M.R. Haworth (ed.), *Child Psychotherapy*. New York: Basic Books, 1964, 3–11.

Foster, G.W., K.D. Vanderven, E. Kroner, and N.T. Carbonara. *Child Care Work with Emotionally Disturbed Children*. Pittsburgh: University of Pittsburgh Press, 1972.

From Chaos to Order. A Collective View of the Residential Treatment of Children, Child Welfare League of America, 1972.

Garland, J., H. Jones, and R.L. Kolodny. "A model for stages of development in social work groups." In S. Bernstein (ed.) *Explorations in Group Work*. Boston University School of Social Work, 1965, 12–53.

Grossbard, Hyman. "Ego Deficiency in Delinquents," *Social Casework,* Vol. 43, 1962, pp. 171–178.

Herron, R. and Sutton-Smith. *Child's Play*. New York: Wiley, 1971.

Hobbs, N., et al. *The Futures of Children: Categories, Labels and Their Consequences*. San Francisco: Jossey-Bass, 1974.

Johnson, H. "Demonstration of Goal Planning and Evaluative Research in a Residential Treatment Center." Edmonton, Alberta: Mapleridge

Residential Treatment Center, May, 1973.

Kadushin, A. *Child Welfare Services.* New York: Macmillan, 1974.

Langer, J. *Theories of Development.* New York: Holt, Rinehart & Winston, 1969.

Levitt, E. "Research on Psychotherapy with Children" in Bergin, A.E., and Garfield, S.L. *Handbook of Psychotherapy and Behavior Change.* New York: John Wiley & Sons, 1971, 474–495.

Lovaas, O.I. "A Behavior Therapy Approach to the Treatment of Childhood Schizophrenia." In J.P. Hill (ed.) *Minnesota Symposium on Child Psychology.* Vol. I, Minneapolis: University of Minnesota Press, 1967, 108–159.

Maluccio, A.N., and W.D. Marlow. "Residential Treatment of Emotionally Disturbed Children: A Review of the Literature." *Social Service Review.* 46, 2, (June, 1972), 230–251.

Matsushima, John. "Some Aspects of Defining 'success' in Residential Treatment." *Child Welfare.* Vol. 44, May 1965, 272–277.

Mayer, Morris F., and Arthur Blum, eds. *Healing Through Living. A Symposium on Residential Treatment,* Charles C. Thomas, Publisher, Illinois, 1971.

Meyer, H., E. Borgatta, and W. Hones. *Girls at Vocational High.* New York: Russell Sage, 1965.

Noshpitz, J.D. "Notes on the Theory of Residential Treatment," *Journal of American Academy of Child Psychiatry.* 1, 2, (April, 1962), 284–296.

Pappenfort, D.M., D.M. Kilpatrick, and R.W. Roberts. *Child Caring: Social Policy and The Institution.* Chicago: Aldine, 1973.

Phillips, E.L., E.A. Phillips, D.L. Fixsen, and M.M. Wolf. "Achievement Place: Behavior Shaping Works for Delinquents," *Psychology Today,* 7, 1, June 1973, 74–80.

Polsky, H.W. *Cottage six.* New York: Russell Sage, 1962.

Polsky, Howard, and Daniel S. Claster. *The Dynamics of Residential Treatment: A Social System Analysis,* University of North Carolina Press, Chapel Hill, North Carolina, 1968.

Project Re-Ed. John F. Kennedy Center for Research on Education and Human Development, George Peabody College for Teachers, Nashville Tennessee, 1969.

Redl, Fritz. *When We Deal with Children,* The Free Press, New York, 1966.

Redl, F. and D. Wineman. *The Aggressive Child.* New York: Free Press, 1958.

Resnik, David. "The Social Worker as Co-ordinator in Residential Treatment, *Social Casework,* Vol. 48, 1967, 293–98.

Robinson, H.B., and N.M. Robinson. *The Mentally Retarded Child.* New York: McGraw Hill, 1965.

Schopler, E. "Parents of Psychotic Children as Scapegoats," *Journal of Contemporary Psych.,* 4, 1, (Winter, 1971), 17–22.

Schopler, E., and J. Loftin. "Thought Disorders in Parents of Psychotic Children: a Function of Test Anxiety." *Arch. Gen. Psych.* 20, (February, 1969), 174–181.

Schopler, E., and R. Reichler, "Parents as Co-Therapists in the Treatment of Psychotic Children," *Jnl. Autism and Child. Schiz.,* 1, 1 (1971), 87–102.

Singer, J.L. *The Child's World of Make Believe.* New York: Academic Press, 1973.

Taylor, Delores A., and Stuart W. Alpert. *Continuity and Support Following Residential Treatment.* Child Welfare League of America, 1973.

Tharp, Roland G., and Ralph J. Wetzel. *Behavior Modification in the Natural Environment.* New York, Academic Press, 1969.

Trieschman, A.E., J.K. Whittaker, and L.K. Brendtro. *The Other 23 Hours: Child Care Work in a Therapeutic Milieu.* Chicago: Aldine, 1969.

Waxler, N.E., and E.G. Mishler. "Parental Interaction With Schizophrenic Children and With Siblings: an Experimental Test of Some Etiological Theories," in Chess, S. and Thomas, A., eds. *Annual Progress in Child Psychiatry and Child Development.* New York: Brunner/Mazel, 1972, 568–589.

Weintrob, A. "Changing Population in Adolescent Residential Treatment: New Problems For Program and Staff." *American Journal of Orthopsych.,* 44, 4, (July, 1974), 604–611.

White, R.W. "Competence and the Psychosexual Stages of Development," in M.R. Jones (ed.) *Nebraska Symposium on Motivation.* Lincoln: University of Nebraska Press, 1960.

Whittaker, J.K. "Developing A Unified Theory of Residential Treatment," *Mental Hygiene,* 54, 1, (Jan. 1970), 166–169.

Whittaker, J.K. "Training Child Care Staff: Pitfalls and Promises." *Mental Hygiene.* 54, 4, (October, 1970b), 516–519.

Whittaker, J.K. "Group Care For Children: Guidelines For Planning," *Social Work.* 17, 1 (January, 1972a), 51–61.

Whittaker, J.K. "The child care continuum: new directions for children's residential centers." *Child Care Quarterly.* 2(2), (1973), 124–135.

Whittaker, J.K., and A.E. Trieschman, eds. *Children away from home: A sourcebook in residential treatment.* Chicago: Aldine-Atherton, 1972.

Wolins, M., ed. *Successful Group Care: Explorations in the Powerful Environment.* Chicago: Aldine, 1974.

Part III. Individual and Small Group Services

8

An Adolescent Walk-in
Mental Health Center

MORRIS BLACK

*Social work practice with an adolescent population is
presented within the relatively new structural milieu of the
storefront, or walk-in, mental health center. Staffing
patterns also constitute a major change. Staff members
work with adolescents in their own milieus to help them
perceive the implications of their real life behavior and its
impact on their peers and on adults.*

*Examples of experiences at the center give the flavor of
a milieu session, the diversity of the youngsters served,
and the range of interventions performed by practitioners.*

*Two central themes of this chapter are that, first, sound
clinical understanding of human behavior and
development within a systemic, situational context is
essential for work in the storefront mental health
structure, and, second, the milieu itself is the primary
therapeutic modality responsible for helping many
youngsters and parents previously considered
hard-to-reach.*

IN recent years we have seen a proliferation of efforts to
make mental health resources available to youngsters and their
families. In part, these efforts arise from the profession's recognition of unmet needs in society and gaps in knowledge and practice. In addition, community criticism of established services has
led to a search for more effective methods of delivering mental
health care.

Recent developments have taken place within the growth of the
Community Mental Health Center movement (CMHC) of the
1960s. Following the public health model of outreach by early
detection and prevention, federal legislation provided for staffing
and building grants to establish a complex of services within a

community or circumscribed geographical area (catchment area).

Implicit in this legislation was a perceptible shift away from the approach of most psychiatric and child guidance clinics, whose focus was generally on the intrapsychic life of the youngster. The new approach was to consider his life in the broader context of community, school, peer group, and extended family, relating these to his inner life and the life of his immediate family. This shift was dictated in part by the painful realization that large segments of the population, mainly the poor, had no useful contact with the growing knowledge and skills of the mental health profession. There were state hospitals for the seriously disturbed and there were children's clinics patronized by the more motivated middle and working class families. There was a functioning system of available inpatient and outpatient services, but early detection and prevention approaches were not widely utilized.

The CMHC movement developed during a time when new knowledge, new resources, and new technology were leading to new conceptual frameworks in a number of disciplines. One concept, that of ecological systems, has proved useful in the understanding of mental health services. It has helped us to recognize that mental health services are created and provided within a network of systems and subsystems that include not just the client but the provider as well. Thus, effective and workable delivery of mental health services to children, adolescents, and their families within the CMHC movement requires a systematic recognition of:

1. The total life of the youngster and the various subsystems (family, school, peers, community) in which he lives.
2. The specificity of the street or neighborhood where the youngster lives and plays, including the location of available services.
3. The system of the service agency, its functions and goals, funding and mandating bodies, its own board, the subsystem of the particular unit or service which is part of a larger service or parent service or organization, and the practitioner-team unit operation.
4. The youngster's needs, untainted by preconceptions of the form and content of services required.

In the effort to respond creatively to the communities served and to use new conceptual frameworks for service, we tended for a time to reject as outdated clinical knowledge as well as any traditional service structure. And the appropriateness of new forms of outreach in the lifespace was amply demonstrated in dealing with many community mental health problems. But it became apparent that traditional psychotherapeutic approaches and methodology, with some appropriate changes, remained in other instances the treatment of choice and a viable framework for studying problems. The new approaches and concepts in community mental health revitalized rather than replaced existing forms of treatment. Sound clinical understanding of human behavior and development within a situational context remain essential for work in all mental health structures. The newer developments pertain more to changes in staff and in knowledge of the social and cultural milieu than to basic methodology.

In order to gain an appreciation of some of the recent structural and conceptual changes, as well as of problems in the delivery of mental health services, let us concentrate in this chapter on a specific program: the development of a storefront (or walk-in) program for adolescents from low income families.

The Storefront Outreach Program

The West Side Mental Health Services for Children and Youth of the Jewish Board of Guardians was set up in 1968 to provide a range of outpatient mental health services to youngsters and their families in a circumscribed geographical area in New York City. Programs of the West Side Office include an extensive individual, group, and family treatment program; consultation and mental health services in six local public schools; a community based parent education guidance program; a walk-in storefront crisis unit; and the Adolescent Storefront Walk-in Clinic that will be described here. The West Side Office is, in turn, one of twenty-two divisions of the parent agency that provides childrens' mental health services throughout New York City, including therapeutic nurseries, halfway houses, day and residential treatment facilities, and outpatient clinics. It is a private, voluntary agency that operates most of its units on a matching funds basis. The parent agency secures private or philanthropic funds and these are matched by the state through the local city mental health agency. This arrangement is distinct from those of many agencies which operate on total grants from the federal, state or city governments.

The area served by the West Side Office contains a wide range of ethnic and economic groups. Of the 110,000 people in the area, approximately 65 percent are White, 20 percent Hispanic, and 15 percent Black. The area attracts individuals arriving from Puerto Rico, Cuba, Costa Rica, Haiti, Santo Domingo, and Ecuador. The Black population includes Dominicans, Haitians, and Africans, as well as American Blacks from both the north and south. Economically, the area includes wealthy and middle class persons from all ethnic groups as well as those with very low incomes. A small but highly visible part of the population lives in dire poverty. The area is also characterized by an unusually large number of agencies and organizations in welfare, housing, and health care, although childrens' mental health services are less plentiful. In 1968, during the initiation of the West Side Office's programs, many of these neighborhood organizations were very actively involved in attempts to change the community. All were highly politicized and some were extremely militant. Thus, the West Side Office was dealing with a complex, sophisticated, and vocal community.

Development of the storefront concept

Respect for the community's legitimate interest in and concern about the proposed services led a staff task force of the West Side Office to undertake a survey of mental health needs of the youngsters in the community. Leaders in the community from both formal and informal institutions and agencies were contacted— not only representatives of schools, churches, and recreational centers, but also the more informal gatekeepers—the proprietor of the candy store where young people congregated, the owner of the pool parlor, and the neighborhood policeman. A recognized community interest in services for adolescents, particularly those who were not being reached through existing agencies and settings, was uncovered by the survey. The West Side Office accordingly gave top priority to an outreach program for this population. The problem of providing mental health services to these young people, who are both economically deprived as well as being Black and Hispanic, is compounded by the traditional resistance of adolescents to psychotherapeutic work. Lack of facilities for this age group is conspicuous in the mental health field generally. It is well known that these youngsters and their parents share a pervasive distrust and fear of most health and mental health facilities and tend to use them only when an emergency or crisis occurs. Clearly a hospital-based or formal clinic setting was not indicated.

Therefore a walk-in facility was established where the milieu itself became the primary therapeutic method. The storefront would not be a screen or funnel to move the youngsters into individual or group treatment apart from their contacts with staff in the milieu, but rather would provide a setting in which the youngsters' interactions with the staff and peers would be the basis for role modeling, identification, reality testing, and attaining socialization skills. Thus, staff would work with behavior in the milieu to help adolescents perceive the implications of their real life behavior and its impact on their peers and adults. Setting concrete achieveable vocational goals for the future became paramount among the real life concerns. Clinically, the milieu program was to provide an ego enhancing experience for adolescents at a crucial time of their development. Their ability to move in and out of the setting at their own pace and to choose a staff member or members with whom to relate (or not) was seen as appropriate for helping youngsters of this age group achieve greater ego autonomy.

The walk-in clinic was situated very close to a junior high school where consultation and mental health services were already being provided. This reflected the assumption that the schools were the most available institution for reaching the ethnic and economic diversity of the community. Whether they would be the most appropriate place to begin in other communities is moot; it made sense on the West Side of New York City because otherwise it would have been necessary to relate to literally hundreds of "communities"—streets, areas, ethnic groups—in order to make contact.

In inaugurating the storefront program, the West Side Office staff also made extensive contacts with many community groups and organizations, including the community psychiatry, child psychiatry, pediatrics, and youth divisions of the Roosevelt Hospital (the delegated CMHC for this area), units of the Mid–West Side Community Corporation (OEO), neighborhood health councils, the district school board and parent associations, and councils in individual schools. These contacts enabled staff to be in close touch with the community, to educate and be educated.

The program in operation

The storefront is open every afternoon for three hours, and one evening a week. Signs at the entrance list names of staff members on duty and state the sponsorship and service purpose. This introduces to concepts of contract-setting and accountability at the outset. A highly informal, relatively unstructured situation has been deliberately set up in which the youngsters themselves help shape the program and the format of the services. It is clearly stated to the youngsters in their initial contact, however, that the clinic is there to help them with their problems rather than to serve as a club house or recreation center. Those seeking recreational programs are directed to the appropriate facilities in the area.

The first youngsters seen in the storefront were invited there by the clinic consultants in the course of their work at the nearby school. In time, the clinic's target population learned of the program by way of the peer group grapevine, by seeing the storefront as they passed on the street, and through contacts with staff in the schools.

At present the walk-in clinic serves a completely self-referred population of approximately seventy-five youngsters. They come in after school either individually or in groups. They may appear every day or once or twice a week and may stay for five minutes or a few hours. There are usually about fifteen youngsters present each afternoon with three staff members on duty. Most relate to all staff members present, although some search for a particular person.

The youngsters initiate most of the discussions, taking up subjects like a fight with a friend, difficulty with a teacher, troubles at home, dating problems, sports, and current events. Those youngsters who continue to come do call on the clinic for help when a serious problem emerges or when they are ready to talk about an existing one. Depending on the situation, the staff may respond by standing by a youngster in court or in a police station, taking him to a hospital, or making home visits and talking with parents. Staff members have also become advocates for the adolescents by helping parents secure a Family Court Person In Need of Supervision (PINS) petition and placements in residential treatment centers. The latter was done in the case of a blatantly self-destructive psychotoic boy who was able to accept the help of the storefront director and use the more intensive and appropriate help secured for him. Those youngsters needing and accessible to a structured individual relationship can be assigned to individual storefront staff for regularly scheduled interviews, although this practice is the exception. The total environment (milieu) is designed to be the primary therapeutic agent, and informal, on-the-spot, individual meetings when indicated are the rule.

Most participants have no desire for the storefront to have any contact with their parents. As a mental health facility, however, it is legally responsible to obtain parental sanction for professional involvement with their youngsters. Thus, when a specific need is identified that requires community referral, counseling, testing, evaluation, or other outside services, parental approval is required and a fee for service is charged based on ability to pay. As the youngsters explore with staff what they are seeking, a decision is made with them about what services the clinic can offer, and an informal, verbal, but definite contract is made.

During its existence, the storefront has served youngsters ranging in age from 11 to 18 years, the majority of whom are Black and Hispanic, many of whom are economically deprived. They have had a wide variety of social and psychological disabilities cutting across all diagnostic categories, including psychosis. All of the expected adolescent maturational problems of physical and sexual development and identity and self-image confusion are seen. In addition, youngsters bring in problems specifically related to this inner-city community—such as racial identity and conflict, alcohol and drug use, and school and work decisions.

Initially, there was a lot of stereotyping of the youngsters by the staff, pervasive expectations that all Black and Hispanic children would be similar—nonverbal, nonintrospective, and resistant to forming relationships with adults. This personal and professional bias was challenged as many of the young people were actually very articulate, aware of their difficulties, and eager to enter relationships when they could define the boundaries of dependency and autonomy.

Differences in class, value orientation, and culture both within and between the groups quickly became apparent. Many Haitians were political refugees and came from intact and middle class oriented families; the Cuban youngsters were very similar. Dispelling these myths and stereotypes caused the staff to reexamine some of the myths surrounding treatment of this population—that they are inaccessible and untreatable; that all minority group youngsters require special settings and techniques; that they are essentially nonverbal and require a "here and now" approach; that they need activity; that all professionals are constricted, overly analytic, and dependent on a particular structure to function effectively.

These assumptions were found to be questionable in their sweeping generality, as many youngsters have been reached and helped who would ordinarily be considered too disturbed for outpatient treatment or would be seen as inaccessible to a relationship with an adult in a traditional framework. The storefront has dealt with youngsters who were exhibiting psychotic symptoms, both diagnosed and undiagnosed; drug abusers and pushers; and those unable to function in educational and recreational settings. Interestingly, in some cases when alternative treatment modalities or referral to other parts of the office were indicated and discussed with the youngsters, strong resistance emerged, even when staff offered to see them at the storefront.

The Importance of Staff

Staff design from the beginning has called for male and female professionals and paraprofessionals. There has been a concerted effort to maintain an ethnically integrated staff on all levels, some of whom are bilingual. A clinically sophisticated, experienced social worker with an MSW coordinates and supervises the program and the staff working there. Her continued presence has provided the vital factor of continuity. Presently three full-time paraprofessionals, three part-time social workers, a part-time psychiatrist, and two social work students work at the storefront. A minimum of three staff members are on duty during a session, which runs from two to five o'clock in the afternoon and from five to eight o'clock one evening a week.

This open-ended, informal group setting places demands on staff far beyond those made by other more structured "fifty-minute hour" forms of help. The success of such a program is completely dependent on the environment created, which in effect means the staff. Being on the firing line, staff members experience directly and continually the needs, pains, and achievements of the youngsters. While concern and commitment are prerequisites for the staff working in such a setting, it is their sensitivity, willingness, and capacity for honest self-reflection that really determines the quality of care given. The program also demands of staff that they deal with the realities of the youngster's lives, recognize psychopathology but focus on ego strengths, and be mature enough in their own emotional growth to set limits and resist overidentifying with the youngsters in their rebellion against authority.

In outreach programs particularly, since the children are frequently the products of crisis-prone families, they tend to re-create crises situations in the storefront setting. Therefore, staff in such programs need to have good impulse control and a repertoire of emotional responses available to them. They must be able to differentiate between crisis and noncrisis situations and to intervene effectively in both.

Initially staff were sought among persons who could understand the lifestyle and language of the youngsters to be served, on the assumption that similarity in background and lifestyle would enable them to reach the youngsters most effectively. It was soon learned that the personality and strengths of the worker, whether professional or paraprofessional, were much more important than their ethnic and economic background or professional discipline. Or, perhaps even more to the point, it was the ability to cope with real-life social behavior which transcended other variables. While some task differentiation in the storefront was originally intended, based on the differences in professional and paraprofessional training and experience, the pattern has evolved differently. Since the goal of milieu treatment is to provide a broad social learning and ego supportive experience in relation to peers and adults, the issue of who should do the treatment has not developed as a primary concern. Therefore, there has been relatively little splitting of staff along professional versus paraprofessional lines. As the goals and philosophy of the program became clearer, new staff were better screened and it was possible to predict more accurately their potential success or failure. Thus the tasks assigned to them were based on their individual talents as well as their skills.

As would be expected, staff success in dealing with the adolescents' provocations, emotional lability, sexuality, and aggression appears to be related to the workers' resolution of their own adolescent crises. Although this phenomenon was expected to be more apparent in the paraprofessionals, it has seemed to be equally operative among the professional staff, who may mask these difficulties by the use of professional jargon and maintenance of professional stance, which may serve as a distancing mechanism.

Professionals and paraprofessionals have been hired from diversified backgrounds, with the expectation that each would have a special contribution to make. Previous experience in hiring for community based outreach programs has shown that many individuals attracted by the excitement of these programs are eventually disappointed and upset by the apparent unresponsiveness on the part of some of the youngsters, the difficulties encountered in the day-to-day work, and the lack of immediate gratification for themselves. An enormous amount of strength is needed by staff members to cope with the intensity of the youngsters' sexual and aggressive behavior, their hostility, and their apparent lack of gratitude. It is quite common to see staff feel let down or betrayed by the youngsters.

Because of these inherent stresses in the work, it has been useful to include a brief contact in the storefront as part of the hiring process. This allows the applicant to make a much more realistic assessment of the job requirements, and for the staff and youngsters to interact with him or her. Frequently, the reaction of the applicant in the setting is more informative than either the individual interviews or the resume.

Staff members experience an intense emotional onslaught in their work with the youngsters. In such situations, they frequently counter with distancing mechanisms or allow themselves to be inducted into supporting the youngsters' efforts to maintain their maladaptive behavior patterns. Some staff members tend to respond more to the youngsters' hostility, provocativeness, and seductiveness than to the quieter, less dramatic aspects of their behavior.

Other youngsters do not come on strong; they lack individuation and present themselves as emotionally deprived. For some, literal and symbolic "parenting" is very much indicated, as a means of making up for profound unmet needs. For others parenting was not what was required, but because of their own anxieties, workers sometimes have failed to perceive that parenting alone was not the treatment of choice.

In the beginning, staff anxiety was sometimes expressed by converting it into hostility toward colleagues, supervisors, administrators, or members of other units within the parent agency. While it is important for operations like storefront programs to develop a cohesive staff with a sense of group identity, frequently there is a corresponding feeling of estrangement from the more structured units and a tendency to derogate them. Conversely, it appeared that the staff of the more structured units were made anxious by the lifestyles and behavior of youngsters being dealt with as well as the openness of the setting.

Therefore, a support system for staff was developed that provided an opportunity to share both positive and negative reactions to the adolescents, problems, successes, expectations, and goals. It also served to drain off anxiety and to free staff to focus their energy on their work. In the storefront, all staff now attend weekly in-service seminars at the office of the parent agency, weekly clinical and disposition staff meetings, a weekly rap session for communicating with other staff about milieu happenings, and a group process workshop conducted by our group therapy consultant to deal with intrastaff problems and issues of working in a milieu. All staff are closely supervised in groups that include both professionals and paraprofessionals. The kind of training and support system described are essential to providing and maintaining a high level of care.

In relation to support systems, the director or administrator of a childrens' mental health service needs to have both clinical and administrative skills. Some degree of free floating anxiety is always present in any mental health facility. This is particularly apparent in the development of new programs, especially non-traditional ones, where anxieties, tensions, and resistances are omnipresent and should be anticipated. The director needs to have an appreciation of the various systems within which he or she is operating and making decisions, such as the relation of the particular unit to the rest of that particular service, the relationship with the parent agency, with the mandating and funding agencies, with the community or "communities," and to the socioeconomic and political climate. The director, who is making judgments and decisions, has to take these factors into account as well as the internal problems of a particular unit so that programs and relationships can be facilitated both within and outside the service. While many of these factors cannot be changed, some others can—such as the level of staff anxiety—so that the director can help establish or provide constructive input into staff support systems. What is most critical, however, is a conscious understanding that multiple tensions and conflicts are part of the normal developmental process of any organization.

Quality of care should be of particular concern to all mental health practitioners, particularly those in outreach programs. Their "innovative" and "community action" components tend to put a special aura around these programs, a sense of excitement and activity. Frequently this very activity masks the lack of a thoughtful and professional approach. In studying the literature it is very important to sort out those elements that are public relations and political and those that are addressed to the real work that is going on.

To illustrate the flavor and atmosphere of the work in the storefront, a partial account of a milieu session follows. The material was presented at one of a series of staff meetings early in the life of the storefront when it appeared that the staff was placing too much stress on individual youngsters and their individual "problems" rather than relating to their behavior with peers and staff within the milieu in the here and now. The intention here is to demonstrate the natural flow of staff–youngster communication and the process involved. Typically, other regular recording in the storefront includes a daily log highlighting the group process or a particular crisis and information to be communicated to other staff not on duty that day.

Milieu Session, 3-29-74

On a snowy day in early spring a number of regularly attending adolescents arrive at the storefront and exchange greetings and small talk with each other and with staff members. Music is heard on the radio, a storefront worker, Harvey, demonstrates the use of a camera, and the youngstors choose for themselves whether to be involved in what is going on. Jane, who first sat apart staring, accepts the invitation of peers to join the camera group—an action initiated by a staff member. Harriet, a storefront staff director, comments that she likes a folk song just heard on the radio. A flurry of kids move to change the station and Harriet comments on the phenomenon. Jose, who had been working with the camera, aggressively pushes his way into the conversation on musical preferences. For a few minutes he responds to group pressure to tone down his characteristic boisterous, teasing manner, but not for long. . . . Jose begins to tease the others, disturbing them with behaviors he has exhibited on numerous occasions with peers and staff. Staff gradually move Jose into a conversation about the meaning of friendship, since the week before he had interpreted a worker's comment about liking him as a homosexual overture and expressed his feelings that males must fight or be considered homosexual. The attempt is to help Jose see that there is a wide spectrum of possible male–male relationships between the extremes of fighting and having sexual contact.

When later Jose has a private discussion with Harvey, it becomes apparent that about twenty minutes of closeness is all that he can tolerate, and he becomes more physical, taking karate stances, striking out with his hands, and blocking the door. The discussion is immediately terminated, and both the worker and Jose come back to the front of the clinic where a number of youngsters have spilled outside to play in the snow.

When the activity begins to drift back inside the storefront, the youngsters are reminded of the rules against snowballing inside, and the activity ends. George reminisces about happy summer experiences, and this stimulates talk about the youngsters' plans (or lack of plans) for the coming summer. Bruce announces that he is off to have his knee X-rayed. This elicits discussion among both staff and the group about how going to a doctor elicits anxiety in people.

As other youngsters eat or talk, Jose once again becomes excited and physically provocative. The staff decides that he has been with Harvey too much and Harvey separates from Jose. When the physical acting-out continues with Carlos and other peers, Jose is warned that he will have to leave. At this point, Carlos, whose meal was disrupted by Jose's pulling a string across the room, becomes angry at staff, first verbally, then physically, blocking the workers, pushing, and apparently beginning to lose control. He then succeeds in distracting Jose, who meanwhile had become seriously engaged in learning the basics of photography in Victor's office. Both boys fool around with the telephones. Carlos is asked to leave when he fails to accept warnings and staff efforts to point out the irrationality and provocativeness of his behavior. He is told that he cannot come back next week and warned of possible expulsion since he has not been able to respond to the limits set up and the storefront apparently is not being helpful to him. He seems contrite and Harriet, the storefront director, agrees to see him in school on Monday but not at the storefront. Carlos at first assents but ultimately expresses rage at being excluded from the storefront. Jose, taking all this in, agrees to leave also as the reality of his own possible expulsion comes a little closer to him. In contrast, the other girls and boys stay on, affected by the tension of this exchange but able to continue their activities with enthusiasm and appropriate restraint.

Comments

This session can be analyzed from a number of different perspectives—individual, group, staff, the setting itself, and so forth. To truly understand this interchange, it is necessary to know on some level what spill over from home, school, or community the individual child feeds into the situation. Also, the emotional climate of the storefront milieu over a period of time should be determined, as well as what affects or behavior are currently the central focus of the staff and youngsters. Has a youngster struggling to deal with a particular conflict set off staff reactions? Additionally, what is staff bringing to this particular session? Is there pressure from an external source to control behavior of youngsters (from the switchboard operator, the neighboring storekeepers, or others)?

Sessions exhibit in microcosm the youngster's world and how he or she is coping with or adapting to it. The crucial difference is that this is taking place in a therapeutic milieu where distance-closeness boundaries, reality-testing, and maladaptive patterns of behavior are viewed with a clinical eye, where staff can intervene at a critical time in the youngster's development. Adolescence is a phase in which there is normally a certain fluidity within the psychic structure and where the processes of ego differentiation and integration are actively going on. Thus, there is an opportunity for shifts in identification and for different role models. The therapeutic milieu becomes clearly a modality of treatment that makes possible clinical intervention for certain youngsters otherwise considered inaccessible.

This vignette also demonstrates that, although the youth are encouraged to interact spontaneously in this everyday setting, there are some common assumptions about their purposes and tasks and about the role of the staff in relation to them. Some of these assumptions* are:

1. All of the teenagers have common problems to work on, problems characteristic of their age group, and problems of ethnic, personal, and familial identity.
2. The nature and the intensity of the problems of the more deviant members of the group interfere with the group's ability to work together on their common problems—for instance, homosexual problems, acting-out by fighting, drug-taking, and so forth.
3. The central task for the social worker is to detect and challenge obstacles that impede the efforts of the group members to benefit from each other as they pursue their common concerns.
4. The milieu provides flexible, informal contact needed with stable, respectful, caring adults who can serve as role and learning models, and peers for mutual support. Its basic operating principle is that, along with mutual respect, consistent limits and discipline are openly communicated in an environment that tolerates no fighting or substance abuse or other behaviors defined as interfering with agreed-upon helping objectives.

The strengths of the milieu—its informality and unstructured quality—create many problems, such as difficulties of group management related to the serious pathology and group social stresses increasingly found among its adolescent population.

The setting has not only an impact on the youngsters but on the staff. The most obvious factor is the extraordinary visibility of the staff, comparable to staff living in residential facilities. More important, however, is the amount of time spent with these youngsters in the milieu where their performance is visible to all; relationships to their supervisors and to other youngsters individually and in groups is closely scrutinized. There are multiple helpers present, and the staff member is obviously part of a team in which functions are to a certain extent interchangeable according to the situation. The presence of a child psychiatrist and the coordinator of the program, who both partially participate as members of the milieu staff, affords a living demonstration of how adults deal with authority figures and their own rivalries. In turn, staff members are seeing youngsters in a variety of situations in which they observe and deal with behavior within a group as well as in an individual context. While originally this complicated decisions on appropriate interventions, in the long run, it has aided the development of criteria for storefront or alternative interventions. The result has been greater clarity of interventive expectations as well as awareness of limitations for change both intrapsychically and environmentally.

Necessarily, the focus in this setting has to be on observational data, with some information from parents and the school in particular cases. This provides an appraisal of current ego strengths and ego deficits, as well as superego functioning. As noted, inferences are made from observable behavior, and this fact is underscored at the clinical conferences repeatedly. Thus, interventions are based on what is possible, given the nature of the situation (the open setting, self-referral), the nature of the population, the availability of data, and the accessibility of parents when indicated. This contrasts with customary clinic routines of securing psychosocial histories or developmental data before initiating interventions.

John, Susan, and Tom

To illustrate specifically the range of therapeutic interventions and the diversity of the youngsters served, let us look at three fairly typical cases.

John, age 18, is a Black, Spanish-speaking youngster from the Dominican Republic. He became known to us four years ago at his school, located next door to the walk-in clinic, when he participated in group meetings led by a storefront staff member. He is the oldest of ten children from an intact, working-class family. His mother is extremely passive and withdrawn, and completely overwhelmed by the violent and aggressive behavior of her husband. John was terrified of his father and dealt with this by becoming subservient to him. When the physical abuse became too great, he went to the maternal grandmother for protection. The latter relationship has remained a very positive one.

Initally, John was an extremely frightened youngster, with many anxieties and fears of physical illness and the overt fear of being forced into using drugs by peers. He had also become very involved with a particular male teacher with whom he was extremely ingratiating and conforming. This was in marked contrast to his behavior with other teachers with whom he was quick to anger and react negatively to their demands. It was clear that he saw the world as a threatening place and was in a panic over his forthcoming entry into senior high school.

After his group was terminated at school, we had very little contact with him for some time. Concerned, we decided to reach out to him, making a home visit to invite him to come to the storefront. We then learned that daily he had enormous difficulty getting out of bed, had been truant, and appeared clinically depressed. He began appearing briefly at the storefront and gradually we learned more about him and his family. He was extremely concerned about being seen as masculine and would react with anger and aggressive behavior if faced with any of his passive, dependent needs. He would view expressing these needs as being a "faggot." He would periodically place himself in situations where he would fear being overwhelmed by a stronger male figure and would become agitated and aggressive.

Staff concern was heightened by his propensity to act out his impulses instead of verbalizing his feelings. He was quick to take offense and at the same time exhibited poor impulse control over his aggressive drives. Staff were also concerned when he took to carrying a gun for "protection." While it was not possible to do a formal diagnostic study, it was clear that he was functioning on a borderline level, was severely depressed, and was prone to homosexual panics.

When he originally started coming to the storefront, he avoided other youngsters but would talk with individual staff members. He was very self-deprecating about his ability when an attempt was made to involve him in any activity. Gradually, he began to show some interest in table games, which were used to help him relate to other youngsters and to staff. Staff attempted to use these games wherever possible in order to address themselves to John's low frustration tolerance and his feelings of incompetency.

For the next two years he came to the storefront on the average of three times a week for a few hours each time. Staff observed that John did not seem too threatened by one of the storefront staff, a male MSW social worker who was assigned to give him individual attention. Brief sessions were held in a corner of the open milieu room, in the corner luncheonette, and on walks. What emerged dramatically was John's overriding fear of not being "manly" enough and his need to react violently when he felt threatened. His worker was not able to deal directly with the issue of homosexuality in view of the extent of John's defensiveness, but he did deal with how John could not express himself in other than physical ways.

While John was unable to tolerate the tension and anxiety caused by attending high school and dropped out fairly quickly, he increased the amount of time spent at the storefront. With the support of staff he soon returned to night school to study for the high school equivalency examination and he would often bring his books to the storefront and allow staff to go over his homework with him. After successfully completing his highschool equivalency, he became a teacher aide at the junior high school he had previously attended and concurrently undertook a work-study program at a local university. During this time, he continued to come to the storefront for brief periods and saw his special job there as taking care of the plants and being an "assistant" to the staff. Occasionally, he exhibited some regressive behavior, particularly when he would want to physically attack youngsters who were giving staff a difficult time, but he was able to control such impulses. John is presently continuing to function well, both on the job and at school.

Susan is a 15-year-old Black youngster who was raised from birth by her maternal grandmother and uncles in Mississippi. At age 12, after a number of years of increasingly aggressive behavior towards peers and an incident where she attacked her grandmother, she was sent to live for the first time with her mother in New York. Staff has tried unsuccessfully to contact the mother and through community contacts it was learned that she is constantly on the move and probably has been or is a prostitute.

Self-referred, Susan appeared to be very depressed, angry, and limited intellectually during her first visits to the walk-in center. She pushed for friendships with peers in an almost frantic fashion. With staff members, however, she was extremely provocative and hostile, particularly with the two female Black members of staff. During the first six months she showed up daily and began to make friends even though she instigated many fights.

After a time, she began relating to Judy, a young, attractive, White paraprofessional who learned something about her background and her motivation for coming to the storefront. She felt very much alone in a strange city, without friends or a connection to the community. She was able gradually to share her difficulties at school and her fear and confusion about life in a large urban inner city. When Susan began bringing her homework to the storefront, Judy discovered that what had appeared over a period of time as dullness and limited intellectual capacity was in fact a facade—Susan was quite bright!

In the next six months Susan joined a girls' rap group held in the group room at the walk-in center. There she shared her fears and concerns about her "preoccupation" with sexual thoughts and feelings. Extremely primitive beliefs about sex emerged, which Judy was able to deal with in subsequent individual contacts. During this time she also began associating with two girls at the storefront who were engaged in serious delinquent behavior. At one point she also ran away from home after an argument with her mother.

Faced with an escalation of Susan's self-destructive behavior, a conference with the psychiatrist and the rest of staff was held. By this time, the staff knew that Susan was not psychotic and had enough ego strengths to be capable of controlling her own behavior. Because of her good relationship with Judy and the rest of the staff, Judy confronted her with her self-destructive behavior and with its obvious consequences. These discussion did not bring in the unconscious identification processes at work in relation to her mother, but rather remained on an ego level.

Judy's expression of concern and interest appeared to reach Susan, who gradually began doing better in school and moved away from her more overt delinquent behavior. Other staff began commenting to her on this turn of events and praised her explicitly for her improved grades. During this period, it was discovered that Susan had an interest in dance, although she was completely unknowledgeable about it. Judy helped her explore possibilities for taking lessons and then in applying for a scholarship with a dance company, which proved successful.

Although Susan now lives in another part of the city, a considerable distance from the storefront, she visits once a month to relate her progress. Of particular interest here was how Susan, a Black youngster, was able eventually to use Judy, a White paraprofessional staff member, as a role model. Apparently she was unable to do this with the two Black women staff members because she had put them in the maternal role which recapitulated her earlier struggles with her mother and grandmother.

Tom, now 16, is the youngest of four boys from a Black working-class family. He has a two-year history of aggressive behavior in school, hard drug involvement, and stealing. Well known in the school and the community for this behavior, he has been coming to the storefront over the past four months. As is true of many of the youngsters who come, it was not possible to secure developmental data, history, or any information regarding his family. However, it was learned that the parents had a very ambivalent and hostile relationship to each other and that Tom appeared to be caught in the middle.

At first Tom appeared childish and immature and made contact rather readily in a clinging, dependent fashion. However, he also demonstrated extreme lack of impulse control, low frustration tolerance, and poor judgment. With peers, he evidenced openly sadistic, aggressive behavior which many times threatened serious physical danger to them. With staff, he was emotionally labile, moody, and constantly threatening physical violence as well as flaunting weapons. Over a number of months, none of the staff felt that they had made any real contact with him and in fact saw him as very unrelated. Tom himself described his difficulties in concentrating, his feelings of being depressed and bored, and his inability to control his behavior. He made a special point of emphasizing the deep resentment he felt toward his father whom he saw as restrictive of his freedom.

After having observed him for a period of four months, staff agreed that all attempts at individual relationships and working with him in the milieu had proven unsuccessful, and that he was progressively escalating his acting-out behavior. This concern was shared with his parents, whom Tom had earlier given staff permission to talk with. His mother refused to accept that Tom had any problems at all, and his father, while somewhat more realistic, was also reluctant to act. Eventually, the father was helped to go into family court to secure a Person In Need of Supervision petition so that Tom could be referred for a more definitive workup and possible placement.

Conclusion

The obvious question here is whether such a storefront, walk-in facility really works and can help youngsters. While systematic research methodology has not yet been applied to all of the storefront's interventions, criteria have been developed for deciding whether the walk-in clinic is appropriate for particular youngsters. It is now apparent that (1) many youngsters previously considered inaccessible come frequently and regularly to the storefront in time of need, and (2) so-called hard-to-reach parents frequently approach staff for help with their children. It is felt that this is due to the high visibility and accessibility of the service in the community where the youngsters can actually see their peers with storefront staff, and parents can see their own and neighbors' children in the storefront milieu. The willingness of youngsters previously thought inaccessible to come to the storefront has been brought about by the creation of an accepting climate within a convenient facility. There youngsters who were suspicious and negativistic have learned to trust adults and to relate to them as parent surrogates who are interested and concerned about them. It is equally apparent that some youngsters, like Tom, are responsive neither to individual or group milieu approaches nor to a variety of helping roles and require more structured work-up and placement in residential treatment or hospital settings.

Training for both professionals and paraprofessionals has enabled staff to tune into the specific as well as the general maturational and developmental needs of each youngster. Their firsthand observations of the youngsters in the milieu and their knowledge of peer and familial relationships as well as of school functioning enables them to make accurate assessments and to evolve appropriate therapeutic interventions inside or outside the walk-in clinic.

Therapeutic intervention is not seen as formal psychotherapy but as using a range of techniques, services, and social learning resources in the lifespace to encourage the youngsters' own strengths and impetus toward greater mastery. The staff is the critical factor in the environment and the instrument for change. The ability of staff to help youngsters in this setting depends on their achieving a disciplined use of self, creatively adapted to the youngsters' lifestyles and aspirations. Here again another myth was confronted—that the spontaneity and usefulness of staff, especially indigenous staff—would be destroyed by training. It was found, on the contrary, that the conscious spontaneity that grew out of greater self-awareness was the most therapeutic lever staff had.

Discussion of issues in delivery of mental health services would not be complete without some further consideration of the implications for preparation for working in this type of practice setting. We have seen a move recently toward the newer, more innovative approaches and techniques, with "innovative" being considered synonymous with "better." Much of the early training (in the late 1960s and early 1970s) was found to be overly general and lacking a comprehensive blend of sociocultural and psychodynamic knowledge. In effect, educators got caught up in the same myths as the practitioners and lost sight of the need to retain what was sound and effective in the curriculum—themes like knowledge of stages of the life cycle, the processes of engagement of client, mutual goal-setting, and handling many types of resistance within and outside of individual and group relationship configurations.

We cannot hope to provide high quality comprehensive care

unless the schools equip their graduates with a combination of sound theoretical knowledge and beginning clinical skills, integrated into a broad ecological systems framework. A sound academic background, maturity, and emotional stability are prerequisites for any professional in the mental health field. In addition, environmental factors such as the role, quality, and standards of grade school and high school teachers, school administrators, and peers must be studied as crucial forces in determining youngsters' coping capacities. Not only the youngster's symptoms in the familial context but the possibility that school or peer systems are inducing symptoms and behavior must be more systematically addressed, as youngsters refer themselves or are referred to mental health services.

Effective delivery of mental health services for children requires that we look at the child, family, and community and the provider system as an organic whole. It is within this framework that alternative services have to be designed to meet unmet needs. To be truly effective, these services should be based on the actual nature and needs of individuals within their community rather than on stereotypes and myths about a particular population. We also need to look at our own professional biases regarding public versus private facilities, modalities, and theories of treatment, kinds of settings, or locations of facilities, and professional versus paraprofessional staff. Rather than focus on any one of these factors in isolation, we need to see how they can interlock with each other to make a viable and effective delivery care system.

Bibliography

Cumming, Elaine and John Cumming. *Ego and Milieu,* New York: Atherton Press, 1962.

Freud, Sigmund. *Group Psychology and the Analysis of the Ego,* Authorized Translation by James Strackey, London: Hogarth Press, 1948.

Gottesfeld, H., C. Rhee, and G. Parker. "A Study of the Role of Paraprofessionals in Community Mental Health", *Community Mental Health Journal,* Vol. 6, August 1970, 285-291.

Gottesfeld, Harry. *The Critical Issues in Community Mental Health,* New York: Behaviorial Publications, 1972.

Hearn, Gordon. *The General Systems Approach: Contributions.* (NY: CSWE, 1971).

Jones, Maxwell. *The Therapeutic Community,* New York: Basic Books, 1953.

Parad, H.J. *Crisis Intervention: Selected Readings,* New York: Family Service Association of America, 1965.

Pearl, A., and F. Reissman, ed. *New Careers for the Poor,* New York: Free Press, 1965.

Redl, Fritz. and David Wineman. *The Aggressive Child,* Glencoe. Illinois: Free Press, 1957.

Simon, Herbert A. *Administrative Behavior,* Free Press, New York, 1965.

Sobey, Francine. *The Non-Professional Revolution in Mental Health,* New York: Columbia University Press, 1970.

Stanton, A.H., and M.S. Schwartz. *The Mental Hospital,* New York: Basic Books, 1954.

9

The Group Home Experience

MARY FUNNYE GOLDSON and ATKINS PRESTON

Recent developments in the group home model of care show an exciting potential as a resource for the dependent and delinquent child. This chapter illustrates an advance in the development of a community based group home for teenage boys within a large urban social agency. It presents the objectives, the process of planning for the group home, and the advantages and disadvantages of the approach.

Highlighted are the steps in the helping process at the practice level, the transactions between staff, teenage residents, their families, and the larger community. The impact of the program is illustrated in the life of one 15-year-old youth.

PUBLIC social policy has long struggled to find the best possible ways to care for children who come to the attention of the public child care agencies when their families have difficulty in carrying out their nurturing responsibility. The large institution under both public and private auspices was an early but inadequate response. Institutional arrangements were later supplemented by foster boarding homes, private families who volunteered to care for one or more children in their homes. This arrangement gave the child the critical intimacy of family life with all its individualized attention that is essential in emotional and character development.[1]

In New York City, for example, institutional care for the neglected, dependent child was the only option until 1853 when the Children's Aid Society was established and a system of boarding children out with foster families was set up through the work of Charles Loring Brace. Professionals in the child welfare field came to respect foster family care as a sound alternative to institutional care for children.[2]

The Group Home Concept

The concept of group homes has roots in the turn-of-the-century work of Lillian Wald, founder of New York's Henry Street Settlement. Her sense of the positive role of small group life in the development of young children first led her to explore the small group experience in summer camps. Other experiments followed, but it was not until after the Second World War that the small group pattern of care for neglected and dependent children became widespread.[3] Over the past two decades, group homes have been established in rapidly increasing numbers by both public and voluntary child welfare agencies, providing a valuable alternative for helping children who, for a variety of reasons, cannot be cared for in their nuclear families.[4]

Three group care arrangements are now recognized by New York State Social Services Law: (1) the agency operated boarding home, (2) the group home, and (3) the group residence.[5]

The agency operated boarding home, like the foster boarding home, can serve at most six children. Exceptions can be made for large sibling groups, but there are no exceptions to the rule permitting no more than two children under the age of two. The agency home operates in a facility acquired for the purpose, with a paid staff. The foster boarding home is a private family offering its home for the care of children. The foster boarding parents receive funds from the publicly financed child welfare department.

The group home serves from seven to twelve children. The New York State Board of Social Welfare requires that all children be over the age of six, but exceptions are granted to sibling groups.

The group residence serves from thirteen to twenty-five young people.

All these group care facilities may share assets and problems. We will, however, focus our attention specifically on the group home as a child care resource. The small group care setting provides an opportunity for individual attention not possible in a large institution. At the same time, the emotional intensity of family living can be appropriately diluted without the stigma of failure for those youngsters who sometimes have difficulty in coping with closeness.

The small group setting makes it possible to care for large sibling groups without separating them. It provides a more neutral alternative for adolescents in care whose normal growth pains and identity search create longings for the natural parents and make sustaining a substitute family situation with a foster family very difficult. Further, the group home setting, regardless of the age group served, offers an opportunity for sustained but uncluttered involvement of the natural parents with the child in care. Competition among parental figures for the child's loyalty is much more accessible, and can be dealt with by a professional seeking the best interests of the child. Thus, the group home can be a middle way between the more intimate relations possible in the foster family and the extreme of disinterest frequently experienced in the large institutional setting.

Increasingly, the group home model of care is being developed for delinquent youth as well as for those with mental health problems. Our focus however will be on the group home as a resource for helping dependent children, although they may often be adjudged delinquent as well.

A major contrast between the group home facility and large institutions is the home's presence as an integral part of a community. This makes it possible for the young people under care to interact with routines of community life, partake of its institutions and services, and contribute in an ongoing way to the life of their surroundings. They gain early experience as valuable contributing members of the real world and as partners in the development of their immediate environment. This assertion of the potential for growth and development in a community based group home does not assume that problems will not develop. From the outset, it can be anticipated that problems will indeed develop, but they can be dealt with where they occur, utilizing the full resources of the community to assist the youngsters in a crisis in developing the most constructive way of coping and problem solving.

Of the substitute care arrangements for children in need—which include the foster boarding family with its parallels to the natural family, group care arrangements for varying numbers of children, and the large institutional settings—the community based group home arrangement stresses the maximum levels of contact with the natural families. The rapidly mushrooming numbers of group homes must be seen not as a new panacea but as one of several viable options available to meet the multiple needs of dependent, neglected, and delinquent children and their natural families. The task is to choose the right option for the individual being evaluated.

At least one community in the New York metropolitan area has moved ahead trying to consolidate their resources in planning for and providing services to children and their families. The Lower East Side community—including both professionals and community residents—has supported the establishment of a community based child welfare agency known as the Lower East Side Family Union. The major community agencies have agreed to turn to the newly created Family Union wherever specific child welfare situations develop and to make it the central integrating and monitoring agency for specialized services already in existence. This will insure joint planning for any new child welfare resources entering the community. This approach has been a major step toward an integrated direct service approach to a social problem in a specific geographic region. As a result, the Lower East Side community is advancing significantly in the use of the integrated community based service model.

The Development of a Program

The introduction of a group home into a community must be carefully planned. Skillful phasing in will take into account, first, the dynamic balance achieved by the communities' existing residents and institutions, and, second, the modifications and shifts that will be necessitated by any new and conspicuous entity. This attention to the dynamics of community life allows the professional to make provision for both the positive and the negative aspects of change in the established rhythm of the society. Planned entry into a community also must be carried out through coordinated planning so that group homes can in fact fill a necessary role in the range of available child care arrangements. The group home, like any given resource, must be directly related to the continuous assessment and reassessment of shifting child care needs in a given urban community. If needs are systematically and professionally linked to resources, the best interests of the child can be kept in the forefront, and the striking temptation of available funds for new programs will not distort the pattern of service.

The group home experience can provide an excellent opportunity for the child to develop in relation to natural family ties while reducing the need for permanent substitute child care arrangements.

Organization of Group Homes

Group homes operate today under both voluntary and public auspices. With the agency operated group home, the sponsoring agency, organization, or institution may rent or purchase a separate facility which is not physically a part of the sponsoring unit. Child care staff are hired by the sponsoring agency, which also carries responsibilities for administrative, supervisory, and direct service operations.

In New York City, the Special Services for Children division of the Department of Social Services—the public agency mandated to oversee the placement and care of neglected, dependent, and delinquent children—has also moved into direct service on a limited basis through sponsoring, staffing, and operating group home facilities.[6]

While voluntary and public group home facilities may be physically located in a given community, they differ significantly from the third type, the community-based group home. This type of home may be financed privately or publicly, or jointly by both sectors. It is an integral part of the community life, and its services are highly visible and directly relevant and meaningful to the community. The community based group home is unique in the following ways: (1) community residents participate in the planning with the facility's sponsors, (2) community residents have a role in policy making through membership on the governing board, (3) community influence is provided for at administrative and direct service levels of staff, and (4) the community takes part in monitoring the program and in evaluating the effectiveness of the program it set out to provide.

Such a voluntary, public, and community sponsored group home may initially encounter some sharp questions locally, but the community based structure in time can achieve the closest and most constructive partnership with the community. It creates a setting in which negatives can be dealt with openly.

A Community Based Group Home

The emotional atmosphere within the group home is intimate, with all residents contributing actively to the choices and decisions which create the home's way of life and ambience. The fact that the residents themselves determine the mood and expectations insures that the closeness is real and not mere conformity to a predetermined expectation. Demands for closeness, expressed or implied, can overwhelm individuals as they work and struggle to find their unique place in the group. Where a large siblings group resides in a home, there is obvious potential for reframing the family model so that it furthers nurturing and growth. Increasing numbers of a selected adolescent population are being referred to the group home because its structure is most appropriate for people in this phase of development. The quality of family life and belonging can be sustained by the counseling staff while the adolescent has the benefit of a healthy distance from the adult figures who serve alternately as models to emulate and authorities to rebel against. The group home is well adapted to facilitating emancipation from the role of a child in the family and entry into the early phase of adulthood.

The community based group home represents an extension of the natural resources for child care available to individual families residing in a community, and in this its relationship to the community differs from those of past group homes.[7] The community based group home is located physically in the community where great need for such a resource exists; the service provided is not alien to the immediate survival of the community. While priority may be given to the requirements of community residents, the group home facility can also serve children in need from other communities where a group home does not exist.

The location of the group home in the community, where it plays an integral part of that community's life, means that family ties can be maintained even when placement of a child outside the home is indicated. Children in such a placement situation have available to them the vast professional resources of the group home staff to assist them and their families in coping with the circumstances that led to placement. Work can then begin immediately with the family as well as with the child, preserving a place for the child in the natural family so that once the critical problems have been dealt with, the child's reentry into the natural family remains possible.

While the child placed in a community based group home may suffer as a result of the separation from the natural family, he is not at the same time stripped of all that is familiar to him— relatives, neighbors, associates, schools, and familiar surroundings. As far as the family is able, its members can be encouraged to work with the staff of the group home to provide for the continuing emotional and developmental needs of the child. The child, although out of the natural home, does not have as great an opportunity to develop self-destructive and self-defeating feelings about himself as a bad person, banished totally from the intimacy of all that has been familiar and significant in the evolution of his sense of self. Family members are in a position to help preserve important cultural and ethnic features which give depth to a child's developing life.

It would be unrealistic to assume that the community based group home has no negative features. First, any substitute care arrangement involving nonfamily members is unusual and unnatural. In addition, many of our current practices are rooted in an attitude which sees families who need help with their nurturing role as failures. In subtle ways, the families undergoing stress in their child rearing functions often reveal that they share these same judgments. Under such conditions, families confronted with their inability to care for a child may find it initially easier to have the kind of physical distance not afforded by the community based home, so that they will not have to deal actively with the guilt, anger, shame, frustration, and humiliation of the crisis. The child also is confronted with the necessity of developing ways of dealing with these complicated feelings while interacting with his family, community, and staff. With the child nearby in the community, none of the family members are left free to suppress these very strong emotions but are held face to face with this difficult new reality. They must develop ways of coping that will strike the minimum blow and leave them at their highest possible level of functioning.

The demands on staff in the community based group home are vast. They must first struggle to recognize the strengths in the families and provide the bridge from child to family at a time when emotions are most volatile. They must bring strength to the family and child by being "nurturing partners" while remaining flexible enough to withdraw as the natural parents increase their capacity to give to their children emotionally.

The program in a community based group home must be prepared to deal with all the marks of poverty that surround children in need of care. The group home must have vital links with other institutions serving the child and family. Their success in challenging and holding these institutions to fulfil their responsibilities to the children and their families will benefit the total community by assuring the availability of an early handle for grappling with other similar crises. The need for a group home in a community therefore does not suggest inferior quality in other services, lack of opportunities for the child and family, nor a saturation of social problems. It offers a way, with other professional efforts, to combine public and voluntary as well as family resources in tackling specific problems as they emerge.

There is a strong temptation to treat the group home as an isolated resource and to locate it in communities free of negative environmental factors such as crime and delinquency. While these sort of positive surroundings are most desirable in planning for children and their families, the benefits are often offset by separation from all the major supportive networks discussed previously. A difficult reality, which does not vanish even when group home facilities are located in a middle class physical environment, is the fact that the child does very early develop significant emotional ties to parental (child caring) figures regardless of their level of functioning. The child then is an integral part of this emotional environment, having developed reciprocal patterns of interaction which have helped to mold and shape him. However attractive the surroundings of a group home, these emotional factors must be dealt with, as they even affect the child's ability to utilize an improved environment.

Where to put a group home is one necessary decision. As important is the decision about those who can be best served by the group home resource. Once we move beyond size of sibling group, as in the case of large families requiring placement, and the adolescent whose developmental needs can often be met very adequately in such an environment, we are confronted with more refined choices. Needs must be carefully assessed to achieve the best possible fit, given existing resources. Here we are confronted with the youngster who may have suffered serious emotional trauma and damage. How much will he benefit from an open setting that utilizes the basic educational, health, religious, recreational, commercial, and employment facilities in the community? No single group home facility anywhere, however well staffed, can be expected to meet the needs of the wide range of children and families that may come to its attention. A community-based group home does offer advantages, however, as its easy accessibility and open communication with its consumers can provide early signals about diverse needs. Because the community expects that the group home will act either directly or by calling on other resources, it is in a good position to insure that a response is made to the newly identified need.

An open intake policy in a group home facility is realistic only if a network of resources for meeting specialized needs are available as part of a common service system in the community. The public-voluntary agency cooperative role is critical here in the development of community based diagnostic intake centers supported by a cluster of cooperating community based group care facilities. Not only does this approach offer an opportunity on the direct service level for immediate and realistic responses to shifting community needs, but the presence of the public-voluntary joint ventures offers an additional opportunity for working out patterns for sharing specialized staff among the various facilities, sharing administrative costs that often make operating a single facility prohibitive, documenting the economics (monetary and emotional) of public funding patterns to permit flexibility of visits to the natural families, and provide avenues for community input at the decision making level in the services.

Experiences of the Henry Street
Settlement Group Home

One community based group home which we may examine is the Henry Street Settlement group home located in the Lower East Side community of New York City. The Settlement is located in a poverty area populated primarily by Blacks and Puerto Ricans, with an expanding Chinese community. The community also has a middle income Jewish population residing primarily in high rise cooperative apartments.

The Henry Street Settlement group home is an integral part of the total Settlement program that includes a mental health unit, special school, recreation and arts program, and camps, as well as an Urban Family Center—a special program providing tempo-rary housing and comprehensive social services to families. The group home is located on the third floor of one of the Settlement's multipurpose facilities, occupying space that once housed young people who chose to live in the community and work as volun-teers. When the agency began several years ago to consider new ways of using the residence space, a group home for teens came under immediate consideration by the board and staff. Essential in this planning phase was a community meeting to demonstrate the agency's readiness to explore new programs. In the meeting the staff at the outset shared with the community the preliminary thinking that had given top priority to a group residence. The staff then sought initial reactions and explored additional alternatives proposed by residents of the community. After much negotiation, the idea of a group home was agreed upon. While the agency now felt able to take the necessary steps with the public agencies to establish the group home, it also felt constrained to continue to deal with many of the reservations expressed by community resi-dents, board members, and Settlement staff. Some of the con-cerns included reluctance to bring more problems into an already overburdened community; concern that parents would be ex-posed to neighbors as "bad parents" if their child needed to be placed in the home; concern that resources in their own commu-nity might be inferior to those elsewhere; and concern that, as a family with a child in placement, they would be forced by the authorities to be involved beyond their capacity or their desire. The staff experienced all of the concerns as real issues, compli-cated by their own feelings of frustration and their inner doubts about the child care system and their capacity to accomplish change in themselves and in the children.

In recognition of the expressed concerns and in a genuine effort to provide a realistic and workable arena for the continuous interplay of community residents, professionals, and others committed to providing a quality community based service, a governing board for the group home was set up that included representation from the several constituencies. Supporters of the group home applied for and were granted separate incorporation as a not-for-profit agency. The board structure of this independent service unit clearly allowed for ongoing community input at the policy making level and insured a direct mechanism for monitoring the quality of service. The inescapable high visibility of a community based agency makes it possible for community residents not only to be involved with the program but also to raise questions. This combination of community residents on the board, neighborhood people observing the workings of the program, and consumers' direct experiences with the services makes for a solid and effective monitoring system.

Screening for the first residents of the group home sought out, first, young people from the community already in the child welfare network who might benefit from this resource, and second, youth just entering the child welfare network from the Lower East Side community. There was also provision for parents from the community to approach the group home staff directly. The emphasis on serving youth from the neighborhood strengthened the Henry Street facility's community based status. However, appropriate referrals of youth from throughout the city were welcomed. Thus, the program includes a mixture of neighborhood and nonneighborhood youth.

There is serious commitment to use of community and professional resources and strengths to complement the work in the group home. The staff, which includes residents from the community, gives particular attention not only to existing supportive networks in a family unit but to those within the larger community as well. Finding the positive possibilities in the child's home and community situation is a part of the effort to see each child's set of needs as unique and to arrive at a plan specifically tailored for him. The diagnostic and evaluative procedures have a central goal: the direct involvement of the child and family in determining whether this community based group home or another alternative will best supply the help needed.

Clarity of objectives within the group home and clear lines of responsibility are essential if the growth needs of these youngsters and their families are to be met. In the instance of the Henry Street Settlement group home, this means that the focus is on turning the powerful potential of the collective strengths in the community, which far outweigh any difficulties which predictably may emerge in meeting the needs of its children, into specific actions. The particular character of the necessary active response begins to emerge even at the early phase of problem definition. Specifically, whatever stress is being felt by the child or however intense is the crisis in the family unit, the workers must see them as part of a larger picture, not as isolated conditions to be dealt with separately. Although we may not fully understand it, we know a good deal about the past history of these children and their families. At Henry Street, the program is the pivot for the future. In problem definition then, the worker will consider not only what is going on with individuals and in the family structure but also relevant influences from the immediate environment, the impact of institutions attempting to meet needs of the family, and the significance of ethnic and economic factors.

At the Henry Street Settlement group home, the director carries full responsibility for the overall management and quality of care. A professional social worker implements the day-to-day program. Other resources—such as psychiatric, psychological, medical, dental, educational and recreational—are available through the Henry Street service system.

Once a child comes to the facility, the social worker and the child and family together identify needed achievements. A mutually agreed upon definition of the problem allows the worker and family to move together to the next step of setting priorities for the work, exploring resources to determine those most effective in minimizing or resolving the problem. Throughout, the worker continues to be attentive to the broad based approach to direct service, joining his technical skills with those strengths that the child and family can muster and linking them to the total resources of the Settlement and the community. The social worker always is the integrating force, providing either alternately or simultaneously direct service and monitoring of the contributions of other resources.

The Use of Structure

In any problem solving relationships in the human services, the helping process demands that all parties concerned invest active energy in dealing with the identified difficulty. The responsibility of the professional worker is to keep these energies directed precisely at the priority that he and the client have agreed to deal with, whatever multiple resources are called upon in the problem situation. The worker must always remain alert and spell out in accurate detail the descriptions and dynamics of his observations as he works with the client systems in tandem and with other resources drawn upon.

Defining the problem and setting priorities is a never-ending process. Every event in the experience of youth and families using the facility may become a key ingredient in the helping process. Choices must be made continually by staff, families, and young people concerning which events to focus on and which developmental ends to pursue. For the group home to function as this kind of dynamic, helping unity, all the persons involved must have some grasp of the structure of the program.

The group home experience at Henry Street suggests that the essential elements in the program structure are the events (transactions) that occur within the program involving staff, residents, their families, and other elements in the larger community. The Henry Street group home serves teenage boys. It is generally recognized that during the adolescent phase of development, the most significant influences come from peer contacts. It is essential then that a primary objective of a group home serving this population be to enable the adolescent to most constructively influence self and other residents. The necessary continuous feedback is illustrated by following diagram:

Staff/Staff	1	2	Staff/Resident
Resident/Staff	3	4	Resident/Resident

While the above flow evolves, input from the family and other key influence persons (with an emphasis on peers of the residents) are fed into these interactions by the residents and staff.

Preparing the Staff

A basic requirement for the effective functioning of a group home is preparation of staff to bring into play their combined resources and to mobilize the strength of the group system on behalf of the youth under their care. All training experiences must deal with the staff's attitudes toward the youth with problems and toward the neglecting or abusing parent. The best training approach is through specific family situations which allow the worker to see the impact of his attitudes in a given situation and to begin developing work strategies that focus on top priority factors. A serious problem in helping relationships has been contamination of communications channels because of the workers' different economic and ethnic backgrounds. The training experience can help the worker anticipate the impact of these differences on himself as well as on the client. Once the workers move through their initial training experience, they are much better prepared to face cultural and expectational differences in a less primitive and defensive manner.

On yet another level, the training experience can also prepare workers to be alert to combinations of dynamics and events that hinder productive work with a given client or with other systems. Knowing about and respecting the role of the social climate helps the worker to face even these difficult situations with a problem orientation rather than an emotional one. The worker trained to recognize a wide range of obstacles to the work can make efforts to deal with them within the work relationship and respect the multiple dynamics when breakdown occurs, rather than fall back on the somewhat simplistic view that sees problems as primarily reflecting client readiness.

Another critical area in staff training is achieving mutuality in all work. While the training experience can assist in preparing workers to hear and respond to the needs of youth and their families, yet another level is needed if the diagnostic assessments are to be based not only on the individual and his unique internal systems but also on the external systems—the family, other small groups, and the community—as they specifically affect his life. The worker learns that, with this perspective of problem definition, his repertoire of helping skills must allow for work directly on a problem with an individual client or with a representative of the systems touching a given difficulty. Therefore, it is essential to teach workers, first, how to help enhance the coping capacity of individuals and to utilize knowledge of group dynamics in assisting families and other small group systems in achieving their specific goals and fulfilling their mutually agreed upon purpose, and second, how to facilitate the appropriate connections among the several appropriate systems in a given problem situation.

Throughout all this work, workers must keep in mind the necessity for developing specific working agreements as they explore and plan with any person or family needing help. The skills necessary to arrive at a working agreement can be spelled out and related to methods of achieving the ends of such an agreement. It is clear that staff members in a group home must develop skills not only for working with individuals and family groups but also with diverse social systems.

Impact of the Program on a Resident

While we may see the potential of the group home as a unique community of residents, counselors, and other staff, its impact does not become evident until put to the challenge. For 15-year-old Peter, entering the Henry Street Settlement group home from the Lower East Side community was a particularly difficult experience that he was reluctant to accept. Peter, a very bright Black youth, lived near the Settlement with his mother and siblings. He had a long, traumatic history of encounters with the courts and a variety of social agencies, was experiencing difficulty in school, and was rapidly exhausting his mother's ability to handle him. His mother sought help at the Settlement and she, Peter, and the agency agreed that the group home would be a good resource since it would allow him to struggle in a community with many of the problems that were making life difficult in the natural family. Peter went willingly and almost enthusiastically into the group home, but immediately found himself torn between longing for home and rejoicing in being away. The proximity of the natural home and family and the staff's deliberate effort to keep the natural family active in his life sharpened for Peter the reality of these two major forces.

Peter was encouraged to talk about how he experienced this situation in the nightly rap sessions. When he was reluctant, other residents taking part were encouraged to share their experiences, thus helping Peter to see that he had much in common with the others. Experiencing and accepting this commonality of problems helped prepare Peter to use the group home resource in concert with the natural home on his own terms, while consistently evaluating the outcomes of his actions. Thus Peter was able to experience regularly his own power in shaping the environment. After nine months, he could be depended on to lend his own energies to those of staff and other residents in the group home in defining the role of the group home in his life and applying its resources to developing his special potential.

Peter's experience illustrates use of the AIM (Achievement In Me) agreement. The AIM agreement has the characteristics of a contract. It specifies areas where achievement is desired by the youngster. It further indicates the resources available through the agency and community to facilitate these achievements and the commitment by the youth to specific efforts that can, when joined with the resources, make these achievements possible. The agreement highlights two important ingredients necessary for Peter to be helped: (1) the helping potential of the resources available through the agency, community, and natural family; and (2) the active role of Peter himself in all aspects of work dealing with his situation.

In most group home structures, the staff in close contact with the youth are called counselors or, in some instances, house-parents. The Henry Street staff uses the counselor label and they may be residents of the Lower East Side community. The counselors are the adult figures against whom is focused the adolescent's struggles. As counselors, they are not in competition with the parental role. Their more neutral and yet strong and consistent adult presence is critical in the development of the troubled adolescent. If a youth's own emotional needs make it important and necessary to relate to the counselor as an actual parent, this is possible. This need is most prevalent among youth whose natural parents are not active in their lives or who have suffered serious and sustained early emotional deprivation. With the youth who tends to respond to the counselor as if he were the real parent, the staff is encouraged to see this as part of a growth continuum. The work emphasis is then placed on helping the youth experience the warmth and closeness necessary to taking the next step in his own development toward young adult life.

We earlier mentioned that the combined energies of clients, workers, and other resources must be focused upon a commonly agreed problem if the helping process is to proceed. This basic foundation of mutuality is essential during all phases of the helping process. In the beginning phase, the client presents his view of the problem. The worker is directly involved in this process, skillfully raising questions, seeking clarifications, and mirroring contradictions—checking these growing observations against what he knows about human behavior, the impact of economic and social conditions, and the ethnic experience, and sharing his impressions with the client. Through this process the client and worker arrive at a mutually agreed upon initial definition of the problem and priorities of work. This process is repeated throughout as reassessments are made.

In the middle phase of work, the actual problem solving phase, the client also participates actively. Movement to next steps is clearly related to evaluation by the client and worker of the effectiveness of current helping strategy. Once a strategy is mutually agreed to be on target and effective, the foundation for ongoing work is strengthened and there is a basis for proceeding to next steps.

In the final phase of work, termination, the worker, client, and mutually agreed upon significant others take a close look at the entire problem solving process. Particular attention is given to the overall effectiveness of achieving the mutually agreed upon goals. The presence of the agreed upon others (such as consultants, supervisors, board members, community residents, and researchers) can provide some objective balance. The size of this group, as well as the role of its members in the meeting, must be carefully considered beforehand.

Separation of these steps as well as the earlier steps in the helping process is not as sharp as it sounds here. Drawing structural lines enables us to examine the process with greater clarity, but even as we diagram, we must take into account the changing quality of the human experience and the unavoidable interplay of all experiences.

In moving mutuality from the conceptual frame into working reality, the experiences open to the youth at the Henry Street Settlement group home are relevant.

The youth entering the group home has an opportunity to talk about this new experience directly with the executive director, his counselor, and his social worker. In the discussions with his social worker, he takes a look at his total situation and begins to identify specific areas he wishes to work on. Through the AIM program, he is able to write down these specific areas of work so that the initial understandings and goals are clear. While living in the group home, he earns points as he begins to achieve these goals that can be exchanged for some tangible benefit to him.

Once a part of the group home community, the youth meets weekly with his social worker or with the frequency dictated by his situation. In addition to his individual contacts, family group meetings may also be planned if they would seem helpful to the youth. The group home residents (twelve at full capacity) are assigned in groups of four to a counselor. These subgroups allow for a greater level of individual attention. Meeting once a week, they discuss the members' problems, the program in the group home, and aspects they wish to see changed or developed. The several teams rotate responsibility for home chores.

Youth in the group home meet with the executive director every two weeks. This gives them a direct link to the decision making level. The youth have also met with the board of directors to discuss their ideas and concerns about the group home.

Once each month a house meeting is convened by the social worker. Present are the young residents, the line staff, the executive director, and representatives from the board of directors. Content may include any aspect of life in the group home, with all participants free to submit a specific agenda item.

The nightly rap sessions led by a counselor are attended by all youth in the group home. Here they review their day, share common concerns, and reach out to help each other with unresolved issues before settling down for the evening.

All of the experiences of a youth in this group home require his direct participation and shared responsibility in decision making. Morale and participation runs high. Where breakdowns occur, the staff is able to return to the early working agreement between the youth and the group home, where he stated in writing his willingness to participate actively in dealing with his own situation and set out his AIM agreement.

The group home structure as illustrated in the foregoing example opens up a wide range of helping modalities and incentives to change. Taken separately, each of them has been tried in a variety of settings. The importance here is the integrating force of "what works for the youth." Mutuality in all phases of the work enables the workers to be more confident of "what works" than in programs differently conceived. On this foundation individual, family, and group services are based and are most appropriate and effective. Aspects of behavior modification, as in the AIM program and the psychosocial approach of the counseling, can coalesce with effective outcomes under the same program umbrella. Additionally, the group structures that bring consumers together with service providers and policy makers has special meaning; through this task oriented group, the young people in residence gain unique experience and new skills in negotiating on their own behalf in the real world. This structure has sound mental health components that help the youth deal constructively with the frustrations and anger formerly expressed in negative ways that were costly to self and society.

Effectiveness of Group Home Experience

The group home that keeps an ear continuously attuned to the shifting needs of the youth in care has made a critical programmatic commitment to quality service. Community based group homes function as open settings where the youth in the home can draw on the already existing educational, health, and recreational resources in the community. In fact, when group homes are planned, the open setting gives rise to very cautious intake policies. The youths with more complicated and difficult problems, who could function in the open setting if services were carefully tailored to their identified needs, are often denied this opportunity. Shortages of professional personnel and of funds for agencies that serve youths whose needs are extensive also result in excessive caution at intake and limit the overall effectiveness of the resource. Continued responsible screening for group home residents is absolutely essential, but we must be prepared to take a second look at those rejected and see if on balance the decision is just. We know that large numbers of older youths remain in need of care and cannot often be located with foster families. There is general agreement in the field of child welfare that the large institutions, even at their best, are less than desirable. The challenge for the professional social workers working with the group home resource is to join with youths and families in need of the services, with community residents, and with other professionals in exploring and testing specific structures and combinations of resources to permit a wider range of youth to be served by the group home.

Summary

The group home must be considered as one of several resources and not as an answer to the ills of many other patterns of substitute child care. A group home can be an exciting resource in the community and will function at its highest level of effectiveness as part of a network of child care services that have specific links to an identifiable community.

The majority of group homes as presently operated do allow for more individualized care of the resident youths. We must, however, begin to look for additional ways to connect the potential of this resource to the shifting developmental needs of youth and care.

Notes

1. Anna Freud and Dorothy Burlingham, *Infants Without Families* (New York City: International University Press, 1944), chap. 1.
2. Marge Benjamin and Louise Murray, *Group Homes in New York City: A New Concept in Child Care,* City Planning Commission, New York City, October 1973, p. 17.
3. Ibid.; Lillian D. Wald, *Windows on Henry Street* (Boston: Little, Brown and Co., 1934).
4. Gula Martin, "Group Home: New and Differential Tools in Child Welfare Delinquency and Mental Health," in *Group Homes in Perspective* (New York City: Child Welfare League of America, 1964 and 1972).
5. New York State Social Services Law, Article 6, § 374 (b) and (c).
6. Benjamin and Murray, *Group Homes in NYC,* p. 20.
7. Irving Rabinow, "Agency Operated Group Homes," in *Group Homes in Perspective.*

Bibliography

Benjamin, Marge, and Louise Murray. *Group Homes in New York City: A New Concept in Child Care,* City Planning Commission, New York, October 1973.

Billingsley, Andrew, and Jeanne M. Giovannoni. *Children of the Storm,* Harcourt Brace Jovanovich, Inc., New York, 1972.

Freud, Anna, and Dorothy Burlingham. *Infants Without Families,* International University Press, New York, 1944. *Foster Care Needs and Alternatives to Placement: A Projection for 1975–85,* edited by Blanche Bernstein, Donald Snider and William Meezan, (NY: Research Dept, Center for NY City Affairs, New School for Social Research) Prepared for State Board of Social Welfare, Nov. 1975, with supplementary report, *A Plan For Action.*

Goldstein, Joseph, Anna Freud, and Albert J. Solnit. *Beyond the Best Interests of the Child,* The Free Press, New York, 1973.

Group Homes in Perspective. Child Welfare League of America, New York, 1964 and 1972.

Group Methods and Services in Child Welfare. Child Welfare League of America, New York, 1963.

Lawder, Elizabeth A., Roberta G. Andrews, and Jon R. Parsons. *Five Models of Foster Family Group Homes–A Systematic View of Foster Care,* New York, Child Welfare League of America, 1974.

New York State Social Services Law, Article 6, § 374(b) (c).

Pearson, John W. "A Differential Use of Group Homes for Delinquent Boys", *Children,* Vol. 17, No. 4, July–August 1970, pp. 143–148.

Wald, Lillian D. *Windows on Henry Street,* Little, Brown and Co., Boston, 1934.

10

Evolving Roles and Services in Abortion Counseling*

FLORENCE HASELKORN

The new human service of abortion counseling, based on a social policy of legalized abortion, provides an opportunity for social workers to help high-risk populations with an age-old social problem.

The author reviews the knowns and unknowns of the psychological impact of abortion and looks at the importance of the milieu. Highlighted are those core tasks performed by the social work practitioner before, during, and after the abortion experience.

She considers the important issue of who does what in the abortion counseling team. A primary prevention, health promotion model that includes in addition to abortion counseling, focus on human sexuality, family planning, and fertility concerns, is projected for practice in the future.

ADVANCES in contraceptive technology, a social policy mandating the delivery of family planning services, changing sexual mores, the shifting cultural role of women, and, finally, the historic decision to legalize abortion, have put us at the threshold of an era of discretionary parenthood. Freud's vision is becoming fact: "it would be one of the greatest triumphs of mankind, one of the most tangible liberations from the bondage of nature to which we are subject, were it possible to raise the responsible act of procreation to the level of a voluntary and intentional act, and to free it from its entanglement with an indispensable satisfaction of a natural desire."[1] Although pregnancy prevention is by far the preferred approach to voluntary procreation, abortion is being seen as a necessary backup service to family planning.

* I wish to express my appreciation to Bayla Silbert, my former student, for her helpfulness.

Abortion counseling emerged as a new human service following the liberalized abortion legislation in the late 1960s. The implications for policy and ethics are not yet clear and years of legislative tinkering and court controversy will precede the establishment of norms. Trends and patterns of counseling services are barely discernible and are likely to undergo considerable modification with accumulated experience. Knowledge about the meaning of abortion to the woman and to those attending her is only now being developed in this new area of unprecedented social responsibility. Whatever direction is taken by the evolution of the service, however, the knowledge, experience, values, and interventive repertoire of social work are certain to remain highly pertinent to abortion counseling.

Revolution and the Growth of a Service System

The reform and repeal of restrictive abortion statutes in several states in the late 1960s, culminating in the dramatic Supreme Court ruling in January 1973, precipitated a mushrooming growth of medical and nonmedical abortion services. Medical services are provided by public, voluntary, and proprietary hospitals and their outpatient departments and by nonprofit and profit-making, free-standing clinics. The clinics developed because of the difficulty in monitoring abortion procedures in doctors' offices. They are operated by private physicians either as individuals or groups or by Planned Parenthood affiliates. These clinics service women in the early period of gestation and have back-up arrangements with nearby hospitals for emergencies.

Early developments in abortion service delivery were uneven and marked by bureaucratic snarls. Hospitals set up their own regulations and eligibility criteria, largely on the basis of the state and local political and religious climate, and staff attitudes toward abortion. In the earlier era, access to abortions was marked by socioeconomic inequality. While abortions are now supposedly available equally to those in need, statutes alone do not insure implementation. Maldistribution of services within and between states continues. Geographic and financial barriers, waiting periods, and other institutional obstacles still confront mostly poor and low-income women. Medicaid coverage for abortion is highly variable across states and is now threatened by legislation at the federal level. It covers those defined as poor but excludes the nearly poor—once again discriminating against low-income women. Social policy advocacy for adequate financing of abortion care is receiving the attention of social work.

Nonmedical abortion services are diverse in their auspices, personnel, and functions. Counseling services are provided by hospitals, clinics, and clearing houses for abortion; information and referral are sponsored by health departments, Planned Parenthood clinics, church groups, women's groups, crisis telephone lines for youth, college peer counseling services, and profit-making referral agencies. The latter have been banned in some states but continue to flourish in others. Counseling personnel include psychiatrists, gynecologists, nurses, social workers, clergy, nonprofessionals, and volunteers. In the absence of professional role models and standard job descriptions, diverse personnel patterns have developed as various professions in the field have staked out professional claims; self-ascribed roles have been defined by each profession's knowledge, values, and skills; moral and political commitments and the availability of manpower and funding. While expedience largely explains the wide-spread use of nonprofessionals and volunteers, it is also true that the professionals were slow to sanction and to move into an area beclouded by moral, religious, and political controversy. More significant perhaps, is the lack of agreement about the need for academic credentials for rendering the service.

Information and referral centers are largely staffed by volunteers and nonprofessionals. Free-standing clinics employ young college women whose chief qualification seems to be that they too have had an abortion. They also depend upon paraprofessionals and volunteers who may be recruited from professional groups. Position statements of National Association of Social Work chapters and guidelines of standard-setting agencies call for "certified social workers" or "trained counselors" or "professional staff." The number of social workers currently employed by free-standing clinics is estimated to be only 10 percent of the total staff.

In voluntary and public hospitals, however, social workers have traditionally contributed psychosocial perspectives to health care and carried direct service roles. It is in these settings that professional social workers are now providing abortion counseling, supervising beginning level bachelor's degree and master's degree level social workers, training paraprofessionals, and providing consultation to other team members. The use of nonprofessionals in abortion counseling is controversial and the issue is further complicated because interventive tasks have not yet been specified and allocated. Roles and tasks can be delineated only when the nature of the abortion stress and client needs are understood. Hence the knowns and unknowns about the psychological impact of abortion need to be briefly reviewed.

Psychological stress and counseling

Pregnancy has been viewed as a developmental crisis that is exacerbated when the pregnancy is unwanted. Those holding this view, that a request for an abortion always signifies a life crisis, argue that "abortion without counseling is unethical and will hopefully some day be considered malpractice."[2] In this vein, some suggest that abortion is rarely required for medical reasons but rather for social and psychological reasons; they urge psychosocial assessment of women who seek abortion, believing that "concern for human well-being mandates its (counseling) availability at the highest level of competence possible."[3]

Others emphasize the social aspect of reproductive behavior and the abortion experience. Social conditioning is seen as the crucial shaper of attitudes. When the opprobrium of illicitness and danger are removed from abortions, the moral and legal climate of censure and disapproval eliminated, and the status of women no longer defined by the maternal role, it is believed that most women will negotiate the experience with the aid of the ego's self-restorative process. In this view, abortion is a situational stress that falls within the range of normal expectable human difficulties and calls upon the usual coping mechanisms. Most women will need only simple practical information, good routine medical management, institutional supports in the milieu, and emotional and social supports in the primary social network.[4] At present, most women appear to rely more upon husbands, boyfriends, and relatives for emotional support than upon professional counseling. Although they tend to talk through the decision with social network figures, in the final analysis, they appear to make the decision themselves. The counseling process generally includes testing for ambivalence and most women have reached a relatively firm decision to abort when they apply. On the surface, it would appear that women who lack social and emotional supports or who are in marked conflict about the solution to an unwanted pregnancy are relatively few.

It is reported, for example, that approximately a third of the women who apply for abortion resist supplying more than the necessary minimum of information about themselves and do not avail themselves of the opportunity to discuss their situation—this need not necessarily imply that adaptive problem-solving resources are available.[5] Some reasons for resisting involvement in the counseling process are:

1. Anticipation of judgmental attitudes of the counselor toward sexual lifestyle;
2. Perception of the counselor's exploration as a lack of trust in the client's capacity to decide to abort;
3. Anxiety masked by magical thinking, avoidance, or denial;
4. A civil rights stance that interprets the counselor's exploration as an infringement on the client's unquestionable right to abort.

Once legalization is no longer a new phenomenon, some of these resistances can be expected to diminish.

Most women experience varying degrees of guilt and ambivalence related to the abortion experience as well as the inevitable fear of the threat to body integrity. For some women the pre- and post-abortion experience can be emotionally hazardous and crisis producing. But many unsupported generalizations and passionately held opinions about the sequelae of abortion are current and contribute to the difficulty in making sound judgments about service needs. Should services, for example, be designed for all women who face abortion, as a social provision integrally linked to medical care? Should services be mandatory or available? If women are not aware of their need for service, can service be imposed? Must counseling be freely entered into in order to be effective? On one hand, a physician writes, "The sad but historically necessary misuse of the psychiatric interview to 'prove' emotional 'disease' in order to 'qualify' for an abortion is still too much with us and warns against any form of mandatory counseling program."[6] On the other hand, NASW recommends that the "organization should take appropriate action to see that professional counseling be guaranteed by law or ordinance."[7]

Not even research findings are fruitful sources of the hard data about the nature of the abortion stress and its emotional outcome needed to determine interventive tasks and to guide differential use of personnel. Is the abortion experience, now that it is legal, a simple elective medical procedure, or is it fraught with potential for lifelong guilt, shame, and depression? Follow-up studies in the past have provided few clear-cut answers. Findings have tended to confirm beliefs already held; as one writer observed, "evidence is wedded to ideology."[8] Much of the available research was conducted in an era of illegal or therapeutic abortions and may not be relevant to today's context of shifting moral, legal, and health policies. Other shortcomings in existing research include inadequate and inconsistent follow-up, lack of precision and agreement about definition of symptoms included in psychological sequelae, and insufficient attention to the preabortion mental health status.

Abortion research faces two inescapable limitations. First, the consequences of an abortion cannot be isolated from the web of circumstances in which both the pregnancy and the abortion take place. Second, the consequences of an abortion cannot be evaluated without reference to the consequences of not having an abortion, and this kind of control study is hardly possible. Still, whatever the uncertainties of extrapolating the effect of not having an abortion upon individual women, social workers have had abundant experience with the social and psychological consequences of large family size, premature marriages, unmarried motherhood, unwanted children, and child abuse.

There is reason to believe that the inevitability of depression and guilt has been overemphasized.[9] According to one investigator, "Initial reactions were uniformly positive. In a subsequent effort to assess long range adjustment, none of the women reported symptoms of impaired functioning, e.g. work, school or marital difficulties and all denied feelings of regret about the abortion."[10] Others report similar findings. Depression, when it occurs, is usually mild and self-limiting and has been compared to the post-partum blues where similar hormonal changes occur. Anxiety and other symptoms of distress more often accompany the confirmation of an unwanted pregnancy and the search for an abortionist. The abortion itself is usually followed by spontaneous remission of symptoms and a great sense of relief. Aftereffects of guilt and remorse are often related to such contextual variables as a premarital sexual relationship or to failed attempts to force a marriage or bring a husband closer.[11] The sense of loss experienced by some teenagers is often more related to the loss of a boyfriend than the loss of a baby. It seems to be the abortions performed under the pressure of husbands, boyfriends, or parents that are liable to be associated with feelings of loss, anger, and impaired interpersonal relationships.

Vignettes from postabortion counseling sessions point up the idiosyncratic and social situational factors that affect how the abortion experience is perceived.

I feel blue and sad. The abortion was the least of my troubles. I was so scared of having the baby alone. What made the whole thing awful was not the abortion, but when I told my boyfriend I was pregnant, he said it wasn't his problem and that I should do what I want. I told him he should marry me, but he said forget it, and then stopped coming around.

There were such complications that I think if I survived the panic of finding out I was pregnant, I'll survive anything. You see, the father is married and of another race. It would have been an impossible situation and ruined me and the child, and I would have had to drop out of college. How could I possibly have any misgivings?

The reaction of a 22-year-old Irish Catholic young man as described by his fiancee illustrates how resolution of the crisis depends not only on an individual's coping responses but on others in the interpersonal network.

When he came to the hospital he kept saying "What have I got you into?" We went to a party a week after the abortion and he got drunk and flirted with my best girlfriend, and then told me it was because he couldn't face me after he got me into trouble. Later he began having nightmares in which Satan kept chasing him. He went to the priest and explained the whole story but now, five months later, he still has those dreams. He wakes up in a cold sweat feeling he did something awful, killed his child. He tells me to go out with other boys and feels I could never respect him after this. I can't seem to convince him that sleeping together was a joint decision.

Antitherapeutic attitudes of physicians, interns, nurses, admitting clerks, and other personnel can be injurious to women's sense of worth and dignity. Such attitudes may affect her capacity to deal with the abortion experience and to manage the ambivalent feelings that may follow. A nurse's revulsion when removing the expelled fetus of a patient who has undergone saline induction, the placement of teenagers on maternity wards, the requirement that fetal death certificates be signed, nurses' buttons that read "Thou shall not kill," and comments such as "You've had your fun, now you'll pay for it," are examples of noxious factors in the caretaking environment that increase the difficulty of coping with stress. It seems entirely likely that maladaptive responses to the abortion experience have more to do with the societal and service milieu than with the personality of the individual. Teen-age clients often report encounters like these:

> People look down their noses at you, make you feel like you're a slut or a tramp.
> The nurse told me I should have used pills and not been so stupid as though I had deliberately planned to have sex.
> The lady in the clinic said, "What do you mean you *need* an abortion?"

Although arbitrary assignments of personnel to abortion services are not uncommon, medical supervisors increasingly recognize that personnel who have strong antiabortion feelings should not be expected to work in these areas. Adverse staff attitudes may also stem from unresolved feelings about sexuality or intolerance of differing sexual and cultural life styles. They often reflect the staff member's inadequate education in human sexuality.

Under favorable circumstances the health care environment can provide what women need biologically and psychosocially to avert the disequilibrating effects of stress. Some women are surprised that medical care for abortion is now safe and efficient, that personnel are sensitive and humane, and that waiting rooms and recovery rooms are physically attractive. So simple a measure as serving cookies and coffee in the recovery room conveys a sense of institutional caring.

Under benign circumstances, young women may achieve greater maturity from their experience of responsible decision-making and successful mastery of a stress situation. For example, a 15-year-old used the experience to reflect on her self-defeating behavior and to come to grips with the developmental tasks of adolescence:

> The experience smartened me up. Before I wasn't sure I wanted to stay in school. Now I want to graduate and get a decent job. How could I have raised a baby when I'm not raised yet myself? Everybody was so great and kind to me and gave me so much attention. Now I care for myself and my future. I'm not going to get mixed up with boys who just want to make out and don't care anything about me.

The questions remain: Did all or some of these women require counseling? Should significant others be included in any counseling? What *is* abortion counseling?

Abortion Counseling

Counseling is an imprecise term used to cover practices ranging from advice to psychotherapy. Its ambiguity of meaning is pointedly expressed by a British observer who notes that "abortion counseling both here and in the USA is at present somewhat unevenly suspended between psychotherapy and contraceptive instruction, and in practice it will depend largely on the counselor where the emphasis is placed."[12] Use of the generic term *abortion counseling* obscures the multiple purposes and differing complexities of the activities thus described. Clinic counselors, for example, often carry heavy clerical responsibilities and a number of paramedical tasks, including assisting with the medical procedure and laboratory work. Their counseling tasks may sometimes be peripheral or perfunctorily discharged.

The term *abortion counseling* is unacceptable to some. *Pregnancy counseling* is preferred, to avoid suggesting a pro-abortion bias that would preclude consideration of other options in dealing with a problem pregnancy. (Services may utilize such titles as Pregnancy Interruption Clinic, Pregnancy Options, and Family Advisory Counseling and Treatment Services that suggest a range of options and are less likely to offend sensibilities.) Because language may be part of the problem when task delineation is unclear and the qualifications and training of personnel are at issue, we shall return to the subject of terminology at several points in the discussion.

Although abortion counseling seems to cover a multiplicity of tasks and eludes precise definition, its aims are reasonably clear. Broadly stated, these are:

1. To help women make informed decisions about unwanted pregnancies;
2. To prevent the emotional disequilibrium and unfavorable outcome to which women under stress may be vulnerable;
3. To prevent future unwanted pregnancies or abortions.

These purposes seem guided by value judgments that women have basic human rights to informed consent about procreation, to comprehensive health and social services, and to respect for their dignity and personal worth. Differences in the priority given to each of the varying purposes and the range of content, process, and structure of counseling make description or identification of patterns difficult. It is possible, nonetheless, to identify a number of core tasks in the process.

1. Information and referral

This includes the simple practical information required by most women concerning resources, fees, legalities, procedures, and referral and follow-up. It is a service largely provided by volunteers and nonprofessionals, often through innovative service structures developed as statutes were liberalized. The task calls for up-to-date knowledge of resources, ordinary human warmth and empathy, respect for people, and emotional neutrality about abortion. The use of the term *counseling* for this essentially pragmatic level of service is perhaps confusing. If this is counseling, information provided by telephone about a Wasserman test could be called premarital counseling.

Since many information and referral services developed in response to needs as they existed before the Supreme Court ruling on abortion in 1973, they may gradually disappear as medical services become more available. Ideally, information and referral should become part of the network of human service organizations and especially those serving youth. If the continuous updating of knowledge of resources required of agency social workers proves to be not feasible, however, an extensive public referral service may offer a way to serve all women, including those not known to social agencies.

2. Preparation for surgery and psychological support

This includes the distinctive knowledge and skills that have long been the contribution of social work in the health field. Fear of pain, helplessness, body damage, and death are experienced by all people entering a hospital. These anxieties take on particular meaning when surgery is associated with sexuality and reproduction. Preparation should include information and education, anticipatory guidance and psychological support to reduce anxiety and strenghten the individual to deal with a temporary disorganizing experience. Counselors may explain medical procedures, give specific information about when patients will be medicated, what anesthesia will be used, who will be present, how long it takes, what the possible side-effects of anesthesia may be like, and so forth. There may be opportunity in individual or group sessions for reality-based discussion of questions and fears about the effects of abortion on sexual pleasure, physical scars, pain, possible sterility, or medical complications.

In responsible practice, special attention is given to preparing patients who must undergo saline induction, in which an injection through the abdomen and uterine wall induces labor and the expulsion of the fetus. This procedure can be emotionally disturbing unless sensitively managed, both because of the procedure itself and the likelihood that there may be more emotional attachment to the fetus after the first trimester of pregnancy. The presence of the clinic counselor in the operating room during the induction, in the recovery room at the side of the patient, and in visits to patients during their hospitalization are important for psychological nurturance and emotional support. Cooperation with the doctor is facilitated and the pain and trauma of surgery reduced.

Some clinics supply factual information about abortion procedures and contraception in small orientation groups ranging from four to ten patients, followed by a private interview where desired. Other facilities attempt to see all patients individually if only briefly. In both the voluntary and public hospital, a nurse is likely to be the one who provides information, but experimental efforts are being made to find the most effective pattern of service. Social workers who co-lead groups with nurses find that the focus tends to be limited to medical and practical aspects when the nurse is present. Some researchers are exploring the advantages or disadvantages that follow initial contacts made by social workers and those made by nurses.[13] When the counselor is a social worker, the subjects covered tend to be more open-ended and to deal with emotional aspects such as ambivalence and guilt, relationship with sexual partners, reactions and possible pressures for or against the abortion by significant others, feelings of hurt and abandonment by boyfriends, confusion about sexuality, causes for the unwanted pregnancy, and the possible emotional consequences of the procedure.

The use of the small group setting to provide information, opportunity for emotional release, and psychological preparation for surgery developed out of necessity since the number of women appearing in a single day could not be handled singly by available staff in some facilities. Necessity turned into a virtue because of the power of the small group to give mutual support, dilute anxiety, and combat self-devaluation, isolation, and alienation. Some worry about the heterogeneity of the groups, however, observing that the group approach is primarily acceptable to adolescents who welcome peer support. These workers believe that older and married women usually want privacy to discuss intimate matters.

Another unsettled issue is whether diversity of social class and cultural background among the participants will impair the small group's effectiveness. The use of the small group is sometimes criticized for its lack of individual focus; participants' concerns are seen as being dealt with superficially and incompletely. This criticism seems to me to be misdirected, whatever the need for further refinement of methodology. When the use of the group is considered not as an economy measure but rather as a preventive approach, the rationale becomes clearer. Intervention at the level of primary prevention is directed not to individuals but rather to the population of women who may be vulnerable to the potentially emotionally hazardous event of abortion.

3. Contraceptive information

Heavy emphasis is placed by most clinic counselors on preventing future unwanted pregnancies. Much of what is called

counseling is actually education about contraception. The introduction of contraceptive information is justified on the grounds
that women are as susceptible to influence about contraceptive
practice while under stress relating to abortion, just as they are
when they are post-partum patients on maternity wards. Several
follow-up studies using effective contraception as the criterion for
successful counseling reported marked improvement in contraceptive practice following abortion.[14] While not disagreeing
with the objective, some social workers are wary of an excessive
emphasis on contraception. They see more promise in utilizing a
broader psychosocial and psychosexual framework. They are
concerned that discussion of contraception when the request is
for abortion will seem to be a latent message, "Don't get into
trouble again." It may cause some women to feel that obtaining
an abortion is dependent on their promising "to be good girls and
protect themselves."[15] This is a dilemma, since a good abortion
service works to eliminate itself by promoting prevention rather
than terminations of unwanted pregnancies. Lectures, visual
aids, and pamphlets are widely used and are effective with
women whose inefficient use or avoidance of contraception is
caused by lack of knowledge, lack of access to services, or failure
with a particular method. Indigenous family planning aides are
utilized by many hospitals to promote contraceptive use. They
are especially effective in reaching clients of ethnic minority
groups. The extent to which women with more complex motivations for "unwillful exposure to pregnancy" can be reached by
mass educational techniques, however, is open to question.

Women with sexual identity problems sometimes seek evidence of their fertility but interrupt their pregnancies because
they do not wish to bear a child. Abortion is sometimes an attempt to satisfy masochistic strivings. Some women do not practice contraception, using fear of pregnancy to avoid sexual advances of husbands, and then have unwanted pregnancies. Others use pregnancy to punish a parent or to force a marriage.[16] For
the unmarried whose sexual activities are unplanned and
sporadic, the pill seems an expensive and inconvenient nuisance.
For adolescents especially, use of contraception implies a commitment to sexual activity that most find unacceptable. Conflicting value systems and ambiguous societal norms discourage the
open planning of sexual activity by young people. Sexual activity
that just happens can be more easily rationalized and is accompa-

nied by less guilt. A prevalent postabortion attitude among young single women is denial that they will engage in sexual activity again. No mere provision of the "hardware and gadgetry" of contraception without attention to the individual, including consideration of sociocultural and psychosexual determinants of contraceptive behavior, is likely to help resisting or inefficient users achieve competence in family planning. Following the abortion, individualized family planning and sexual counseling to at-risk women and, for adolescents, sex education programs geared to their developmental needs are necessary if these women are to be helped to achieve responsible sexuality.

4. Postabortion counseling

Patterns of follow-up vary widely, where it is built into service at all. Personal interviews, telephone contacts, or group sessions are used to help women sort out their feelings about the abortion and clear up areas of confusion about sexual functioning or contraceptive practice. These procedures are also used to spot pathogenic reactions and to identify the need for social supports from community resources or more extended social treatment. Often members of the family, boyfriends, and close personal friends may be present when the session is held immediately following surgery. Some counselors report a high degree of success with postabortion counseling but note that some time must elapse before women are ready to deal with their feelings. The question of appropriate timing for the nonmedical follow-up has not been settled and practice varies from two to several weeks following the abortion. Many observe that clients are more willing to examine problems related to the unwanted pregnancy or other areas of social functioning after the abortion than during the preabortion sessions. Anxiety runs high during the initial session and the client's purpose is to get the abortion over.

Other women are unresponsive to the offer of follow-up and wish to forget the whole experience. Whether suppression, repression, or denial of affect are maladaptive mechanisms in the case of abortion or necessary and adaptive for ego functioning is a matter of conjecture—we lack access to this group of women. Often, counselors agree, "a judgment of what is evasive and what is adaptive perception must be made with tenderness of spirit on the part of the practitioner."[17]

5. Screening

Whether they are labeled initial screening, informational counseling, or first line counseling, or not differentiated from other levels of counseling, there is general agreement that the components of service described above should be available to all women who apply for abortion. Situations of obvious psychological or social complexity requiring skilled intervention are referred to a psychiatrist or social worker. The arguments advanced for using nonprofessionals at this level of service echo the larger debate about manpower issues and are explored fully in other contexts in the literature.[18]

Feasibility, or insufficient professional manpower, limits abortion counseling just as it does the large-scale delivery of other human services. Another argument is based on the belief that the tasks can be discharged by nonprofessionals and volunteers selected for personal qualities rather than academic qualifications. Grassroots counselors carefully selected for empathy, nonpossessive warmth and genuiness, and emotional neutrality about abortion, have demonstrated competence and effectiveness after adequate training. "Adequate training," however, is a vague concept; depending on the intensity of the instruction, it may imply less than one week to about one month, with the proviso that "experienced personnel be available for consultation on a continuing basis."[19] Early surveys of services indicate that the training component is often weak, consisting only of several days of induction to the role or even a two-hour orientation session with a gynecologist. While some facilities do have more adequate provision for staff training and ongoing consultation, it is largely in the hospitals that supervision and consultation are routinely available.

The feasibility argument is a cogent one. Until further advances in contraceptive technology provide a simple, inexpensive, completely safe and effective long-term protection, demands for abortion are likely to increase. It is estimated that the number of legal abortions will rise to 1.6 million a year, or roughly four abortions for every nine births. Because of changed legal and moral sanctions, a greater number of normal women, those not requiring the

services of highly trained professionals, will be among those seeking abortions.

There is sharp debate whether nonprofessionals have the
screening skills to identify the clients who require crisis-oriented,
goal-limited intervention or to detect early any high-risk women
whose problems require referral for psychiatric or social treatment. Some social workers believe the screening task requires
rapid and highly refined assessment and cannot be left to the
random and haphazard skills possessed by nonprofessionals.
These workers point out that it is the usual practice to put the
most experienced staff at intake.

While many remain committed to professional delivery of direct services, the realities are that there is widespread use of
paraprofessionals in abortion counseling. It is not yet possible to
be dogmatic about the level of competence needed or the amount
of training required. Moreover, if the purpose of abortion counseling is considered to be mainly prevention of unfortunate reactions, then the use of paraprofessionals follows. Social responsibility for reaching large target groups for health promotion and
prevention, funding realities, limitations in professional manpower, and variations in the complexities of the tasks required—
these are factors supporting the use of paraprofessionals. There is
strong evidence that barriers of social distance are reduced
through the use of noncredentialed helpers and that effectiveness
of interpersonal helping with the socially and economically disadvantaged is increased. Clearly, however, social work in
employing people with less training has the responsibility to be
sure that they are prepared to identify high-risk women and perform other appropriate screening tasks. The need to work col-
laboratively in teams consisting of professionals and workers of
varying degrees of training is as much an imperative in abortion
counseling as it is in other health delivery services. It may be the
only way to meet the concern for standards while providing
widely needed service.

There is little question that some direct services should be
carried by graduate social workers, because some situations do in
fact require skilled crisis intervention rather than advocacy, linkage services, contraception education, and simple supportive
care. In an area as new as abortion counseling, it is also important
that some professional social workers continue to be involved in

direct service for demonstration, teaching, and knowledge building purposes. Since the two patterns of personnel utilization coexist at present, objective means for specifying effectiveness criteria and evaluating comparative effectiveness are needed.

6. Population-at-risk

We are beginning to witness a number of systematic efforts directed at finding efficient ways to identify the high-risk patients among the total population group of abortion patients served. One approach has been at the level of theory. Drawing upon crisis formulations, Rapoport and Potts offer hypotheses about the key psychosocial coping tasks that must be mastered by the client if the abortion experience is to be one of growth and maturing.[20] The tasks are notably specific and are useful for screening, assessment, and intervention. It should be possible for practice to test and build upon these formulations and to feed into further theoretical developments.

Another approach to structuring services draws upon the public health concept of epidemiology. It uses self-administered questionnaires for quick identification of women who should be seen for further evaluation and attention. In general, questions are designed to ascertain feelings about the pregnancy, to learn which network figures are aware of the pregnancy and their reactions, and to determine emotional health before and during the pregnancy (as indicated by poor appetite, trouble in sleeping, feeling irritated, feeling sad, and so forth). Other question areas include the client's decisions regarding the pregnancy, adoption, termination, use of contraception or reason for nonuse; plans for contraceptive practice after the present pregnancy; and interest in talking over her decision with a social worker. A number of hospital social service departments and several independent investigators have been conducting small scale studies seeking to identify the demographic characteristics of groups who may be at special risk.[21] The list of indices vary but generally include—

> Women with marked indecision
> Women under 18 or over 35
> Late aborters
> Repeated aborters
> Woman with multiple unplanned pregnancies and unwanted
>   children

Women with unstable marriages
Women who appear under pressure from others
Victims of sexual assault
History of severe ego disturbance or characterological
    problems

It may be that the conviction that only professional social workers are qualified to do abortion counseling is based on experience with a somewhat different sample of abortion patients. Of women who have abortions in public hospitals or as ward patients in voluntary hospitals, a higher proportion may fall within the high-risk group than do those who have abortions in clinics and come to the attention of peer counselors. For example, women with unwanted pregnancies who are institutionalized (in correction agencies, residential treatment and drug abuse centers, or mental hospitals) or who are AFDC mothers or adolescents in AFDC or public assistance families generally tend to be referred to hospital social services departments rather than to free-standing clinics.

7. Crisis intervention

Finally, for women who have marked ambivalence about the solution to a problem pregnancy or who request abortion but do not really want it, pregnancy precipitates a crisis accompanied by both potential hazard and opportunity for growth. This group consists largely but by no means exclusively of teenagers and young women whose unplanned pregnancy is compounded by the developmental crisis of adolescence. Since abortion has become available, fewer choose to continue the pregnancy. Of those who do carry the pregnancy to term, more young women, especially whites, are keeping their babies rather than using adoption as a solution. This probably reflects changing cultural attitudes toward unmarried motherhood.

Most counselors appear to assume that the client has not come for psychotherapy. They do not delve into deep-rooted personality deficits presumed to lie beneath the problem pregnancy. The counseling process is basically a reality-oriented, problem-solving process directed toward reducing nonrational and irrational factors in decision making. The focus is on the here and now and the situation itself. Chronic or underlying pathology is viewed as separable from the immediate crisis. The purpose is clearly to help women weigh the various alternatives available and to arrive at informed autonomous decisions. Confusion under stress is lessened as the woman is helped to examine the options—adoption, carrying the pregnancy to term, foster care, maternity home care, or abortion—and their impact on her life. Finally, she is given help to implement her decision.[22] The process is not designed to be a challenge or stress situation to make sure the client knows what she wants. As one client put it, "for every argument, I was presented with a counter-argument. The presence of a warm ally who helps the client manage her feelings, permits her to discharge her tension, and reduces her anxiety, confusion, and helplessness serves to free the client's problem-solving energies.

Conflict and problems often arise as much from the pressures and coercion of relevant others as from personal ambivalence of the client. A small pilot study of a group of poor Puerto Rican and Black girls, for example, found cruel, guilt-provoking confrontations with parents and boyfriends about having committed "murder" to be a common experience.[23] Others who want their babies may be pressured by parents, boyfriends, or husbands to have an abortion when the relationship is unstable. Whatever action is taken may provoke rejection and recrimination by others in the close interpersonal network. The importance of including sexual partners (and parents, when this is emotionally tolerable to minors) in conjoint interviews is recognized by most counselors. It is difficult, however, to know the extent to which actual practice includes dyadic or family interviews. Writers seem to agree that the counselor should act as advocate for the client when there are opposing pulls, but also recognize the need to intervene in dysfunctional transactional processes: "Finally, the counselor must be able to tolerate ambivalence, uncertainty, and ambiguity. Many counseling situations will not be clear-cut, and the decision reached will be an imperfect one resulting from a compromise of needs and pressures."[24]

The hazards of imposing or intruding the values, biases, and other subjectivities of the counselor are obvious. Together with insufficient attention to cultural value orientations, the counselor's attitudes can affect a decision having far-reaching consequences on a person's life, including medical risk. A line of inquiry covertly attempting to divert a youngster from behavior that appears destined to start her on the downward spiral of un-married motherhood can be dysfunctional. Using the social control function in a personal effort to reduce illegitimacy and economic dependency, or allowing nonverbal communications of anger and punitiveness to reach the abortion repeater are among the pitfalls for the counselor who lacks self-awareness and self-discipline. If paraprofessionals are to engage in this level of counseling or crisis intervention, their training must be directed toward self-awareness as well as knowledge and skills.

Staff training in human sexuality, including problems of pregnancy, abortion, and family planning, is being increasingly employed to counter the inadequate preparation of many would-be helping persons in sex-related areas of practice. Such programs are emerging in departments of social services, family and children agencies, and in the health care system.[25] Formats vary but generally include basic information about sexuality and its affective dimension. They range from intellectualized discussions of feelings to experiential learning aimed at reducing anxiety, shame, disgust, hostility, and judgmentalness.

In one training program, nurses were helped to confront the fact that their professional role had shifted from helping to bring life to interrupting pregnancy. They experienced a kind of culture shock that stirred up intense emotions.[26] Especially emotional areas are recidivism, teen-age sexuality, and saline induction, where nurses attend the expulsion of a relatively well-formed fetus. Many have found the experience of self-confrontation worthwhile, despite the accompanying anxiety. The "sensitivity training" approach has also met with resistance. Feelings of inadequacy at recognizing antitherapeutic attitudes, combined with the anxiety inherent in the subject of sexuality, can pose a threat to the helping person. Our limited experience shows that these programs, with their spirit of experimentation and attention to a neglected area, hold great promise.

The Problem with Words

At several points in our discussion, the usual terminology has proved inadequate or misleading. The diversity of tasks performed in abortion services cannot be neatly covered by the one word, *counseling*. This is not mere semantic quibbling. The words we use have a way of exerting influence on the direction services take. *Counseling* does not sufficiently describe the range of ecologically-oriented indirect services that are needed at the interfaces between individual and environment. The term obfuscates the aspect of social work activities that aim at programmatic changes in the delivery system and include consultation with other personnel. The term may retard the development of conceptual clarity and precision in setting out the necessary tasks. Social workers should really have no need for the term *abortion counseling*. As one social worker observed, "We do not refer to 'hysterectomy counseling' or 'tonsilectomy counseling'; why not call it social work practice with women with problem pregnancies?"[27]

Conclusion

Beset by unanswered questions, the search for a model of abortion counseling is underway. It may prove fruitful to utilize preventive theory, as a conceptual framework for designing a model for practice.[28] Analysis of the services now being delivered suggests that we are offering primary prevention, a basic mode of health promotion for a large target population. There is also service at the secondary prevention level for relatively fewer people—screening for early detection, assessment, and brief goal-limited intervention. Since preventive techniques are not yet fully developed, we should encourage flexibility, experimentation, and inventiveness in practice. Similarly, we should continue to employ personnel with different levels of education in order to further empirical discoveries. Social work can extend its contributions in education, supervision, and consultation beyond the hospital system to the free-standing clinics. As abortion becomes emotionally defused and enters the mainstream of comprehensive health care, there may ultimately be no need for career specialists in abortion counseling. Clients with fertility-related concerns are known to all fields of social work practice, and reproductive decisions are linked to family welfare and social functioning. In a time when social work seeks to fulfill its preventive functions, family planning, which includes abortion, merits our serious attention.

Notes

1. Sigmund Freud, "Sexuality and the Aetiology of the Neuroses," in *Collected Papers* 1 (New York City: Basic Books, 1959): 238.

2. H. G. Whittington, "Role of the Counselor in Abortion," in *Abortion Techniques and Services,* Excerpta Medica, 1971.

3. Franklin C. Cohen and Reva King, "Experiences with and Observations of Abortion Counseling," *Counseling in Abortion Services: Developing a Model for an Interdisciplinary Approach to Counseling in Abortion Services,* proceedings of a conference, Continuing Education Program, Columbia University School of Social Work, 1973, p. 41.

4. Lydia Rapoport and Leah Potts, "Abortion of Unwanted Pregnancy as a Potential Life Crisis," in *Family Planning: A Source Book of Readings and Case Materials,* ed. by Florence Haselkorn, Council on Social Work Education, 1971.

5. Madeleine Simms, *Abortion Counseling* (London: The Birth Control Trust, June 1973).

6. John D. Asher, M.D., "Abortion Counseling," *American Journal of Public Health* 62 (May 1972): 686–88.

7. Adopted by the 1971 NASW Delegate Assembly for inclusion in the publication, *Goals of Public Social Policy.*

8. Betty Sarvis and Hyman Rodman, *The Abortion Controversy* (New York City: Columbia University Press, 1973); see also Joy D. Osofsky et al., "Psychological Effects of Legal Abortion," *Clinical Obstetrics and Gynecology* 14 (No. 1, 1971).

9. J. Kummer, "Post-Abortion Psychiatric Illness—A Myth?" *American Journal of Psychiatry* 119 (1963): 980–83; see also Leon Marder, M.D., "Psychiatric Experience with a Liberalized Therapeutic Abortion Law," *American Journal of Psychiatry* 126 (March 1970).

10. Elizabeth M. Smith, "Counseling for Women Who Seek Abortion," *Social Work* 17 (No. 2, 1972).

11. Natalie Shainess, M.D., "Abortion: Social, Psychological, and Psychoanalytic Perspectives," *New York State Journal of Medicine* (1 Dec. 1968), p. 3072.

12. Simms, *Abortion Counseling.*

13. Etta Sherman, "Social Work Counseling in Abortion Services," *Counseling in Abortion Services: Developing a Model for an Interdisciplinary Approach in Abortion Services,* proceedings of a conference, Continuing Education Program, Columbia University School of Social Work, 1972.

14. Christopher Tietze, "Two Years Experience with a Liberalized Abortion Law," *Family Planning Perspectives* 5 (Winter 1973); see also B. Dauber, M. Zabar, and P. J. Goldstein, "Abortion Counseling and Behavioral Change," *Family Planning Perspectives* 4 (April 1972).

15. Sherman, "Counseling in Abortion Services," p. 25.

16. Eugene C. Sandberg, M.D., and Ralph I. Jacobs, "Psychology of Misuse and Rejection of Contraception," *Family Planning: A Source Book of Readings and Case Materials,* ed. by Florence Haselkorn, Council on Social Work Education, 1971.

17. Norman A. Polansky, *Ego Psychology and Communication* (New York City: Atherton Press, 1971), p. 76.

18. See, for example, Francine Sobey, *The Nonprofessional Revolution in Mental Health* (New York City: Columbia University Press, 1970), and Robert L. Barker and Thomas L. Briggs, *Differential Use of Social Work Manpower* (New York City: National Association of Social Workers, 1968).

19. Asher, "Abortion Counseling," p. 687.

20. Rapoport and Potts, "Abortion of Unwanted Pregnancy," p. 261.

21. Alma T. Young, Barbara Beckman, and Helen Rehr, "Women Who Seek Abortions: A Study," *Social Work* 18 (May 1973); see also "Correlates of Abortion Seeking Behavior Under a Permissive Law," Research Project, NICHD, Columbia University, 1971.

22. For a fuller discussion, see Leah Potts, "Counseling Women with Unwanted Pregnancies," in *Family Planning,* ed. by Haselkorn.

23. Helen Dudar, "Abortion for the Asking," *Saturday Review* (April 1973).

24. Asher, "Abortion Counseling," p. 687.

25. Florence Haselkorn, "Are Social Workers Ready for Family Planning?" *Human Needs* 1 (April and May issues, 1973); see also Michael Carrera and Gary Rosenberg, "In-service Education in Human Sexuality for Social Work Practitioners," *Journal of Clinical Social Work* 1 (Winter 1973); and Haselkorn, "Human Sexuality and Social Work Education," Proceedings of the Symposium "Human Sexuality and Fertility Services . . . Social Policy and Social Work Education." Canadian Association of Schools of Social Work, October 1972.

26. Frances Katz, "Nursing Counseling in Abortion Services," *Counseling in Abortion Services,* proceedings of a conference.

27. Ruth Breslin, personal communication.

28. Gerald Caplan, *Principles of Preventive Psychiatry* (New York City: Basic Books, 1964).

11

Changing Orientation to Alcoholism

BERNICE SHEPARD

A major thesis of this chapter is that in order to understand current approaches to the treatment of alcoholics, it is necessary to know the unique history of alcoholism in the United States, with its century of neglect of alcoholics and their families.

Not until the early 1970s did large scale possibilities for comprehensive treatment of alocholics and their families emerge through federal legislation and funding. A nationwide network of services has just recently made the alcoholic populations visible. An eclectic array of behavioral, cognitive, and group therapeutic approaches are being utilized to help both previously known and newly identified alcoholic populations, and counseling goals are being rethought.

A major new role for Master's level social workers, highlighted in this chapter, is that of team educator, supervisor, and program director in programs of alcoholism counseling, with a staff composed of Bachelor's and Master's level social workers. Undergraduate social work programs are seen as ideal for alcoholism counselors. For a variety of educational levels within social work and for professional disciplines such as nursing and medicine, suitable academic and on-job preparation for work with alcoholics is in an early stage of development.

Looking to the future, we can predict greater integration of alcoholism counseling with other substance-abuse programs in a national health service system.

THE main difference between alcoholics and other drinkers is the purpose for which they drink. Many uses of alcohol in both ancient and modern times have been considered legitimate or even required. Alcoholic beverages are an element in religious rites, ceremonies, and social activities. They are used as food and drink, or taken for warmth and medicine (they long served as tranquilizers and anesthetics). All of these are reasons for drinking. All have been advanced by the alcoholic at some time or other, but none of them is the reason that alcoholics drink. They drink because they have to. The thought of facing life without alcohol is beyond consideration. So, whatever definition we give to alcoholism, and there are many, we must essentially deal with a person who cannot stop drinking.

Inability to stop is not unique to the use of alcohol. People use all kinds of substances—gas, liquid, or solid—for all kinds of effects. The substance can be any chemical that combines with the body chemistry to produce an effect. In the course of history, humans have learned which chemicals have pleasurable effects and, being human, have gone back for more. Since tolerance develops with the use of some substances, in order to get the desired feeling, amounts are used that are harmful to the body. This is the "chemical trap," a phrase used by Gordon Bell in developing his theory of alcohol addiction.[1] It is a process of substance abuse in order to ward off physical or psychic pain. It is characterized by dependency to a point affecting physical, social, or emotional functioning. Of course, the Women's Christian Temperance Union was wrong in their belief that every drop of alcohol was poison. If that were so, we would have very few alcoholics—at least, very few live ones. The real trap is that it takes a lot of alcohol over a long period of time to produce an alcoholic. The confusion is that we are dealing with the abuse of a drug whose use is socially accepted and approved.

The Temperance Movement

To the early colonists, beer was food and an ingredient of meals and festivities enjoyed by everyone, including the children. The conversion to "ardent spirits" (brandy, rum, and gin) took place in the eighteenth century and by the time of the Revolution had created a quite different social pattern. Hard liquor encouraged all-male drinking and led to the establishment of saloons. There drinking was removed from the family dinner table and converted to a concentrated, thriving, and often rowdy activity. During and after the Revolution, thoughtful people attempted to control the use of distilled beverages and persuade drinkers to return to beer and wine. This was quite literally a "temperance" movement—it was composed of organizations that advocated the temperate use of alcohol. The groups began to form about 1810, usually under the leadership of the clergy and including businessmen, farmers, and physicians, to persuade adults to give up distilled spirits. They were particularly concerned about children and developed educational projects to discourage children from starting to drink hard liquor. This early movement, led by the American Temperance Society, was male-dominated, lasted about twenty-five years, and was over by 1835.[2]

In this early period there were some physicians who were concerned about "inebriety," for which the usual care was the insane asylum. Efforts to establish a medical model began in 1841 with the opening of Boston's Washingtonian Home for the treatment of alcoholics. It was closed a few years later and, although subsequently reopened, it had a rocky career. However, the doctors connected with it were convinced that there was an illness to deal with and that the prevailing use of insane asylums for alcoholics was not the answer.[3] The first attempts to define the medical aspects of alcoholism appeared in medical journals of the period, but the 1840s were already too late. A rational approach to inebriety was no longer possible.

At its second convention in 1836 in Saratoga, the American Temperance Society reorganized, changed its name to the American Temperance Union, and declared for total abstinence.[4] The groups that took over came from a quite different power base. The radical elements for social change in the 1820s and 1830s were concerned with world peace, the rights of labor, child labor, universal education, and the rights of women. Within this larger movement, a hard core of women picked up the slogan "drink keeps the working man down" and gradually became focused exclusively on alcohol, dropping their other causes one by one.

The philosophy of the later American Temperance Movement was not temperate at all. They believed that the use of any alcohol was evil and led to individual and social deterioration. Spiritually it was sinful, physiologically it was poison, economically it was wasteful and reduced job potential, and psychologically it affected rationality and judgment to the point of insanity. Legally, therefore, it should be criminal. Their goal was to eliminate alcohol in the United States. Their immediate objective was to limit its availability wherever possible. All users of alcohol were condemned and children were to be educated to hate and fear alcohol.

A long period of intense campaigning and structural change finally culminated in the founding of the Women's Christian Temperance Union in 1874. Their organization was fantastically good. They were mostly women and they were efficient, persistent, and innovative, with high morale and good leadership. There were units of the WCTU at all levels—town, county, state, and national. Their promotional material was magnificent. They dealt out pamphlets, journals, speeches, plays, songs, sermons, biographies, and confessions. They planned parades and demonstrations. Their philosophy was firmly entrenched in the emerging public school system.

A century of conflict

Their main weapon was legislation—to obtain laws controlling the availability of alcohol. During the first wave of pressure that hit the states from 1843 to 1855, nineteen states passed prohibition laws, all of which were later repealed. Some states passed and repealed or vetoed the laws several times within a few years.[5] A second wave developed in the 1880s, during which three-fourths of the states and territories grappled with forms of prohibition. Yet only six states emerged with prohibitory laws and three of those were soon repealed. In the early 1900s a third wave got underway, and by the time the Eighteenth Amendment was passed in 1919, thirty of the forty-eight states already had prohibition laws. The Eighteenth Amendment became law in January 1920 over President Wilson's veto. It was a divisive issue to the bitter end.

The National Prohibition Party ran candidates for sixty years, into the 1930s. When Carey Nation came on the scene around the turn of the century, members (mostly men) of her Anti-Saloon League signed pledges to a lifetime of sobriety amid scenes of women breaking down saloon doors. They worked closely with Sunday schools and churches. They published a year book which was an encyclopedia of facts and figures testifying to world-wide progress toward prohibition.[6] In 1920, the temperance movement proclaimed that since women had finally won equal suffrage, the repeal of prohibition "is next to impossible".[7] Alas!

With repeal in 1933, the spirit went out of the movement. The WCTU struggled on with local control laws but, although remnants of the struggle continue to the present decade, the century of power was over. In the 1970s in scattered localities, the electorate is still called upon to decide such issues as "sitting or standing" (at bars and cocktail lounges) and Sunday drinking. Many places are debating whether the drinking age should be lowered with the voting age, and drinking drivers are a thorny and continuing enforcement problem.

The temperance movement during its hundred years was totally successful. That is, the philosophy was totally accepted. It had a profound effect on law, medicine, education, and social and penal institutions. It changed and solidified American attitudes toward drinking, drunkenness, drinking by teenagers, alcoholism, drunken driving, and tax policies. It did not stop people from either drinking or abusing alcohol. Americans were always a drinking people. They still are. The temperance legacy is that many Americans were and still are anxious, confused, and guilty about their drinking. Contemporary public attitudes toward teenage drinking display confusion and anger on the part of parents and public officials. Americans are secretive about their drinking. In some circles they are even secretive about their nondrinking.

During this hundred-year period enormous social readjustments took place in almost every aspect of American life—except in our attitudes toward alcohol. Social reforms swept the country. Cities grew to contain most of the population. Science revolutionized our social and health institutions. Even our drinking habits changed. In the early twentieth century, there was a return to drinking at home with the increased use of beer and wine. Yet, in these hundred years, American attitudes toward drinking did not change.

This century-long campaign had its opposition, mostly articulated by the beverage industry. While the counterattacks became increasingly aggressive and hostile as the campaigns became more intense, industry spokesmen did not develop a positive point of view toward drinking; their efforts were concentrated on attacking the extremes exemplified by the "hatchet women." For the most part, responsible citizens played no part in the wet-dry controversy, and their denial affected the country in very dramatic ways.

Societal Denial of the Problem

The most obvious denial was the refusal to recognize, discuss, or act on the serious problem of alcoholism. The sick and anguished people who had this illness were met with insensitivity, rejection, and indifference. Alcoholics who were too visible were put out of sight in jails, workhouses, and mental hospitals where they could be successfully ignored.

The above analysis of the Century of Temperance was first developed by Seldon Bacon and has become the classic in the field for the social interpretation of the neglect of alcoholism.[8] Bacon's premise was that American society refused to deal with an overpowering loaded issue, with the effect that a whole complex of American institutions developed and were modernized without taking account of alcoholism.

Hospitals commonly refused to admit alcoholic patients. No records of alcoholism were kept on hospital patients with other illnesses. Medical and nursing schools did not teach anything about it. The bylaws of social agencies prohibited treatment of alcoholics and sometimes of their families. Agencies justified their position by saying that they did not know how to treat alcoholism, which was a self-fulfilling approach since the schools of social work did not teach it. Public health agencies did not recognize it as a public health problem. Public welfare was often denied to families where there was a drinking problem. Legal institutions offered no protection and took no interest. There was a hundred years of legislation to control alcohol, but no exploration or legislation tackling the problem of alcoholism.

Early twentieth century university and foundation research in the fields of health, welfare, and education did not deal with alcoholism. *Middletown,* a landmark sociological study of Middle America published in 1929, mentions the problem once in a revealing footnote: "It is a shortcoming of this study that it did not consider more directly the drinking habits of Middletown before and after the coming of Federal prohibition."[9]

Out of the early efforts of the Washingtonian movement, a

number of attempts arose to define the medical aspects of inebriety. In 1904 an American Medical Association Committee for the study of inebriety and narcotics was organized. It is interesting that physicians saw the connection between alcohol and other drugs, and in their *Journal of Inebriety* reported on medical studies and discourses (often from other countries) about the general problem of addiction.[10] This medical effort ran into a wall. The temperance movement attacked the medical group on the grounds that doctors were dignifying a vice by calling it a disease. Professional men of stature quickly backed away from the field. Nevertheless, the medical model persisted and by the 1950s two major agents for change held out the possibility for a serious attack on a major health problem.

One of the dramatic sources of change was Alcoholics Anonymous, which came into being in the 1930s and encouraged new thinking about alcoholism and a new feeling about helping alcoholics and their families. With its stress on self-help and anonymity, AA was able to avoid the social obloquy that still persisted. Their dedication and sense of group solidarity produced a subculture into which the helpless and the hopeless could be absorbed apart from the hostile community. In this insulated environment the alcoholic could survive and consider a life without alcohol, which is the prerequisite for rehabilitation. Here, finally, was the first effective effort to cope with alcoholism, not with alcohol. The National Council on Alcoholism, one of a number of offshoots of the new movement, started to bring public attention to this illness in 1944, urging cities, states, and the federal government to accept alcoholism as a disease and to set up special facilities for treatment.[11]

The second source of change was the federal government through its social and health institutions. Wherever programs developed to help people out of mental institutions, prisons, and off the welfare roles, a residue of alcoholic people remained. The techniques that helped institutional wards return to community life did not work for alcoholics because they were in the wrong institutions in the first place. In the 1960s, stimulated by pressure to transform these public institutions and fortified with substantial federal funding, public programs for alcoholism began to come into their own. Among the many heavy prices paid for the century of neglect was that the professionals entered the field as learners and the afflicted were the teachers.

New Possibilities for Treatment

Under the leadership of Senator Harold Hughes of Iowa, himself a recovered alcoholic, Congress enacted legislation in 1971 that provided for the development and servicing of alcoholism treatment centers throughout the country. Despite disastrous cutbacks in federal funding of many health programs, the Hughes law continues to be funded (as of fiscal 1976) and continues to stimulate state and local participation. It is administered by the National Institute on Alcohol Abuse and Alcoholism, which has set in motion a program of research and a network of services that have at last made the alcoholic population visible. Nobody knows how many people in the 1970s are alcoholic, but estimates range from five to nine million, one-third of whom, according to the National Institute, are women. Only a fraction of the estimated alcoholic population are in treatment or participating in AA.

A striking new figure which has emerged from a recent national survey by the Institute is that 28 percent of American teenagers are now considered problem drinkers.[12] While this is consistent with teenage assimilation of a variety of adult behaviors, including smoking, fast driving, and sexual activity, it points to a new population for which drinking has become a problem and for which treatment must be designed.

In the search for appropriate modalities to treat alcoholism, it is unlikely that any one approach will be found that will work for such a huge cross-section of Americans. Some researchers suggest that there are a number of alcoholisms, each requiring different treatment.[13] Clinical treatment has drawn on several major resources, predominantly AA, psychoanalysis, behavioral and cognitive approaches, and group therapy techniques.

Alcholics Anonymous

The fellowship of Alcoholics Anonymous is still the most frequent and successful route to recovery. Its success relies on the transfer of dependence from the drug to the group. In the early stages of abstinence, whenever the craving to drink occurs, the alcoholic can reach his "sponsor," day or night, and talk through his compulsion. If he goes on a binge his sponsor will collect him at the bar, get him to a doctor, a hospital, or an AA meeting, or all three in turn. He can and often does spend days, nights, and weekends "talking his 'pigeon' around." Sponsorship, known within the fellowship as "twelfth step" work, is demanding, dedicated, tough, and disciplined. It is also reinforcing and rewarding for the sponsor. The regimen of attendance at meetings develops group solidarity and reliance on the group for self-control, understanding, and a social life without alcohol.

Advanced alcoholics are isolated people. The AA meeting is often the first social experience in many years. It is a wonder and a joy to an alcoholic who has taken his first tentative step toward sobriety to meet healthy, well-dressed, employed people whose attitudes do not exclude him and who consider him worthy of redemption. The stories of members' struggles with alcohol and recovery in AA make up the content of most AA meetings. Much of this content deals with the scorn and abuse suffered by the sick alcoholic. With good cause, the alcoholic has learned that the nonalcoholic world is not to be trusted. The stories document the ignorant and pitiless treatment by hospitals, doctors, and other professionals, and the acceptance, help, and protection of AA which made recovery possible. The AA member never considers himself cured. He is always "one step away from a drink and a drunk." His security lies in his continued connection with and reliance on the group. Alcoholics Anonymous holds meetings in almost every county in the United States; in the major cities an AA member has a choice of meetings to attend every night of the week.

A parallel fellowship known as Al-Anon provides spouses—mostly wives—an opportunity to help themselves and their families. Much stress is placed on reorganizing the family system toward more independence and more attention to the neglected needs of other family members. Through meetings and discussions, wives are encouraged to reevaluate their familial roles and to move out of the skewed and destructive patterns common to alcoholic families. In many cities, Al-Anon sponsors teenage discussion groups, Ala-teens, for AA members' older children.

The success of AA has been dramatic and outstanding. With the advent of professional referral services, however, there began to be discovered thousands (or millions?) of alcoholics who have not been able to recover through self-help.[14] Many who seek professional help have tried AA. Many are able to use its supportive approach in conjunction with or after a period of clinical therapy. Observers have noted that much of AA's success is achieved because its structure supports many of the needs of the alcoholic. Its sheltered social group provides the alcoholic with a nurturing, family-like milieu, with accepting yet responsible personal relationships, and with emergency care to meet his dependence needs, denial, and hopelessness.[15] With those whose needs are different—among them women and the newly emerging young population of drinkers—AA's record is not as impressive. It is perceived as sluggish and rigid, tending to invoke dogmatic formulas not compatible with the changing lifestyles of young people and women.[16]

Psychoanalysis

Psychoanalysis as a treatment approach had discouraging results in its early attempts. It was rare to find an analyst who would give serious attention to an alcoholic patient, or at least to the patient's drinking. It was possible for the patient to go through several years of analysis without mentioning drinking, by dealing with the "more basic" disturbance. Alcoholics are not famous for their tolerance for anxiety, a necessary element in psychoanalytic treatment, as they have a built-in solution for anxiety. "They escape into the drug which brings relief and sedation, whenever anxiety is mobilized and the analytic going gets rough."[17]

Although there is no general agreement that a typical alcoholic personality exists or that there are clear-cut dynamics associated with alcoholism, the more traditional view holds that alcoholics suffer from acute dependency conflict.[18] They simultaneously experience their dependency and inability to cope, and at the same time they are reluctant to consciously admit these needs and seek a way to feel powerful, capable, and even omnipotent. According to this analysis, "the alcoholic's reluctance to admit his dependent needs and his tendency to cling to fantasies of omnipotence and self-sufficiency probably constitute some of the main obstacles to his treatment."[19] On the other hand, there are observers who feel that there is not one typical alcoholism and many studies have failed to find personality differences between alcoholic and nonalcoholic persons.[20]

In any event, case histories suggest that psychiatry has more recently had a measure of success. Certainly the stories of alcoholics in AA now frequently recount a period of therapy before or along with AA. However, definitive surveys on recovery solely through psychiatric intervention have not been reported. As in other fields, evidence tends to record those who remain ill rather than those who recover.

Behavioral approaches

Some psychiatrists who were more behaviorally oriented came to recognize that no patient could seriously enter therapy until drug-free. Ruth Fox, an early pioneer in psychotherapy with alcholics, held that the first task was to deal with the drinking and with the behaviors that resulted from the drinking.[21] Her introduction of disulfiram (antabuse) in this country, as a device to maintain sobriety during therapy, was a major breakthrough.

Therapists who have been open to experimentation, using the best of many approaches, have found new and rewarding techniques. The work of Adler, Harris, Berne, and others have contributed to a new look at alcoholism as a kind of substance abuse and the alcoholic as a patient susceptible to change. Behavioral therapists have done considerable research into the antecedents of alcohol abuse and on the response of alcoholics to various treatment techniques. For example, different forms of aversive conditioning have been explored, but outside the laboratory situation, these approaches have not been effective.

Most of the speakers at the Conference on Behavioral Approaches to Substance Abuse at the University of Washington in July 1975 concurred that alcoholism is a complex phenomenon for which simple conditioning methods are insufficient.[22] Alcoholism is currently seen as a learned response, for which effective treatment requires teaching the alcoholic alternative ways of coping with the social and emotional components of alcohol abuse. Some researchers are studying the possibility of teaching controlled drinking to certain groups of alcoholics, notably failed abstainers. This promising avenue of research is discussed below.

For the larger group of alcohol abusers, Peter Miller and others are advocating a broad spectrum approach, a focus on a whole range of behavior rather than solely on drinking.[23] This includes systematic desensitization and medical care, training in new skills in the areas of job, family, and other interpersonal relationships, and therapeutic attention to rearrangement of the ecological situation of the alcoholic. Access to these new skills would be gained through nondrinking.

The use of contingency contracts (specification of reciprocal behaviors on the part of the alcoholic and, for example, his wife or his employer) initially negotiated by the therapist are being developed by Miller and others using behavioral approaches. "Assertiveness Training" is another treatment possibility being developed, based on behavioral research on antecedents (precipitants) of heavy drinking. Investigation indicated that one frequent trigger of alcoholic bouts was the individual's inability to express anger in some daily life situation. Learning more appropriate assertive behavior could eliminate or reduce the destructive alcoholic response.

Another pair of behavioral therapists, Linda and Mark Sobel, have been working on a model that they call "Skills Training in Problem Solving," which may be useful to nonbehavioral practitioners as well.[24] The model asks clients to (1) define the setting and events (antecedents) in a drinking episode, describing them specifically and concretely; (2) delineate behavioral options to the event; (3) evaluate the possible consequences, short- and long-term, of each outcome; (4) rank order the outcomes; and (5) practice the option(s) with the best probable outcome.

Although behavioral approaches to helping remain controversial, the emphasis at the recent Conference on Behavioral Approaches on broad spectrum intervention and on assessment and individualized interventive programs, differentially tailored to meet individual needs, suggests closer links between behavioral and more traditional social work approaches.

Another subject of controversy, treatment approaches based on cognitive theory, has also been recognized as appropriate with alcoholics and may be employed concurrently with medical or pharmaceutical treatment and with behavioral modification techniques. The cognitive focus is on thinking rather than the unconscious as a determining influence on emotions, motives, and behavior. Three basic premises underpin this theory: (1) emotions, motives, and behavior can be altered by change in perception;

(2) goal change can be especially influential in altering behavior; (3) perceptions can also be changed by new kinds of behavior and new activities. These approaches require that individuals assume responsibility for their thinking, motives, and behavior. They are encouraged to determine how their behavior should be altered, to establish a plan to achieve their goals, and to initiate steps toward a different lifestyle, developing skill in managing anxiety-provoking situations, and embarking on new ventures through which their needs may be fulfilled.[25]

Recent work in the behavioral sciences, combined with the lessons of AA, have led inevitably to use of group psychotherapy with alcoholic patients. Most of the clinical work is now in groups, with one-to-one interviewing conducted concurrently or as needed. This approach draws heavily on the field of social work for basic skills and techniques.

Implications of current experience

Experimentation is currently going on with all of the modalities described above. Contrary to common belief, treatment is often successful. In a Rand Corporation study of forty-five comprehensive treatment centers, nearly 70 percent of NIAAA clients were in remission after treatment, with the highest rate among those who remained in treatment for more than five sessions.[26] A significant number of alcoholics recover without entering treatment or after leaving it—including AA. Probably the study's most controversial finding is that while some clients remain abstinent, others are able to resume normal drinking without ill effect.

The full implications of this study, which was sponsored by the National Institute, have not yet been explored, but some of its most significant suggestions should be mentioned here. In addition to the pragmatic definition of alcoholism as functional breakdown commonly used in the field, alcoholism may be accepted as an instance of addictive substance abuse, a concept that I believe would open many new prospects. Seeing alcoholism in its personal and societal context as a chosen, culturally determined substance abuse showing a stress- and anxiety-releasing pattern relates it to our wider experience of today's society. Stress and anxiety levels change as life situations change, permitting some alcoholic people to regain control. Further, the goal of abstinence might be seen as transitional, a necessary forfeit while the patient learns other ways of dealing with stress. The rigid adherence to abstinence is probably yet another hangover from the century of temperance. Many more alcoholics may be willing to enter treatment if the goal is more clearly defined as social adjustment rather than abstinence. Modalities such as the Sobels' Skills Training and cognitive theory may have even more validity in this revised framework. The counselor's role may become that of helping the patient outgrow the need to drink rather than to give up drinking forever.

Goals of Counseling in Comprehensive Alcoholism Centers

With the advent of public funds, comprehensive alcoholism services have developed in most major cities, opening a new field for personnel at all levels. These services, delivered in treatment centers, are usually hospital-based and provide detoxification facilities and outpatient clinical services as well as long term inpatient rehabilitation for those who need it. More recently, sobering up stations, community crisis, and vocational centers have been added. The practical goals for these programs are threefold.

The first objective in most treatment clinics is abstinence. While the recent research quoted above suggests that abstinence may not have to be life-long (permanent), its clinical significance will remain because the patient needs a period of sobriety in order to begin treatment. Also, we still have no way to predetermine which sick alcoholics will be able to return to normal drinking. Some clinics, however, have seen the value in a more pragmatic approach. If modified drinking is all that can be achieved, it is worth striving for. If an alcoholic can become sober enough to work, even part-time, or to participate in family life even some of the time, his contributions can be important for the family and for himself. It is often family and community attitudes that make it possible for him to return and continue functioning. Once the attitudinal barrier is down, this process begins to resemble that of other chronic illnesses that are subject to relapse and require medication, therapy, and perhaps brief hospitalization to be stabilized.

The second objective is interim survival, by which is meant helping the patient to live through the first painful period after detoxification. During this difficult period, preliminary to therapy, counseling is focused on help with jobs, living arrangements, welfare, and whatever else helps the patient bridge the gap from alcohol dependence to the beginning of a functioning life. The experienced clinical worker expects a high dropout rate from hospital to clinic, which can be reduced with careful planning for continuity of program, including carryover of staff.

The third goal of counseling is reintegration into community life. Vocational counseling is an important adjunct in which skills and potentialities are explored and evaluated. Rechanneling interest, sometimes including retraining, is often recommended. The skill level at which an alcoholic returns to the labor market is an issue for which there is no pat answer. Availability of jobs is one side of the problem. Another is the question of how much responsibility the newly returned patient can manage. Either way, his frustration level is low and his self-reliance very limited. The patient can look much better than he feels. The clinic counselor learns to watch for reawakening and to encourage assessment of life goals. This phase of counseling may be the patient's first experience in many years of thinking unclouded by an alcoholic haze. Family problems are explored in this phase, including the readjustments in the family system if one still exists or the acceptance of alternatives. Family counseling can begin.

Underlying these specific goals are the two-fold concepts of helping the patient to build self-esteem and helping him develop personal and communal relationships. The ultimate goal is, of course, that the patient be able to deal with himself and the world on his own.

Counselors for the Alcoholic

What characteristics are needed in counselors in order for them to work with alcoholic patients toward these goals? A study of the results of therapy specifically with alcoholic patients summed up these qualities as "a positive relationship between [the alcoholic] and his therapist whatever the orientation or training of the latter."[27] The researchers, working in a treatment setting for alcoholics, were in fact verifying the characteristics identified by

Truax and Wargo as accurate empathy, genuineness, and non-possessive warmth.[28] Not surprisingly, all kinds of people have been found to have these qualities, including, but not exclusively, social workers. Academic credentials provide other assets, as we will see, but the quality of rapport, so essential to the helping process, can be nurtured or acquired without formal education.

Generally the counselor who is a recovered alcoholic has a special commitment to the recovery of the patient and will extend himself in ways that the nonalcoholic is not likely to do. He has "accurate empathy" by definition. The recovered alcoholic should have had some work experience outside the field of alcoholism before becoming a counselor as evidence of his ability to interpret the goal of independent functioning outside the subculture. Some balance is necessary between recovered alcoholics and nonalcoholics so that the team itself can be a role model for the outside world. A life style compatible with the patient population and some college-level work (or at least the potential for it) are also appropriate credentials for alcoholism counselors.

Organization of Hospital-Based Treatment Programs

The following description of how some of the new comprehensive hospital-based alcoholism programs in New York City were organized is intended to indicate the structure of the programs, the team approach of the counseling staff, and the means by which the counselors were trained. Originally the program director was a physician, usually a psychiatrist, and graduate level social workers made up the senior staff of supervisors, casework specialists, and clinic coordinators.[29] More recently, a few programs have been directed by MSWs. Together with the director, social workers trained the counseling staff. Training utilized the MSW's ability to interpret behavior, the nature of resistance, unevenness in progress, and the inevitable complications of relapse. They guided staff in the use of community resources and intervened directly in difficult cases.

The usual team of psychiatrist, psychologist, and social worker served as specialists, with the social worker organizing the clinic, assigning cases to counselors, and taking responsibility for teamwork. The internist and nurse on the team concentrated on treating the secondary illnesses in addition to the alcoholism. This was in line with the trend toward treating the whole patient in the alcoholism clinic rather than referring him to the hospital's clinical services for other medical attention because of the bearing of the total experience on motivation and engagement.[30] The professionally trained staff functioned at the specialty level of their disciplines while giving support, supervision, and direction to a cadre of counselors who were the treating agents.

For the most part, counselor training took place on the job. There were good reasons for this, aside from the lack of schools for alcoholism counselors. The training could be tailored to the particular alcoholism program and to the particular abilities of the counselors who were encouraged to develop their individual counseling styles, an important consideration for counselor-level staff who come to the job without generic conceptual education.

Demonstration of counseling skills and techniques and the study of alcohol and alcohol abuse were the two major training components. Instructors were drawn from the psychiatric and graduate social work staff. Where practical, clinics joined in organizing training for their counselors. Courses in counseling skills and techniques covered three main areas: one-to-one interviewing, group counseling, and counselor adjustment on the job. For one-to-one interviewing, the technique used was the observed interview in which a counselor brought a patient to the class to be interviewed by another counselor. The kind of material elicited was often startling and quite dramatic. In one training course a patient who was asked how he came to seek help described waking up in the gutter being pushed by the broom of a sanitation worker. When he protested, the sanitation worker declared that he was sweeping him up with the rest of the garbage in the street. A more classic instance of "hitting bottom" could not be devised. The patient went on to recall the mixture of shock and despair that motivated him to find a hospital.

When the patient left the training session, the trainees pieced together a psychosocial history and formulated the case. The counselor who brought the patient then read back his own psychosocial history and the class, guided by the instructor, began to evaluate and sharpen skills and develop discipline in interviewing. The format was somewhat similar to that used at the graduate level, but the stress was on use of self, comfortableness with what each had to give, and acceptance of difference in style and approach. The benign atmosphere of these sessions made it possible for counselors, new to their jobs, to risk exposure to criticism.

Group counseling was taught by a skilled group therapy instructor working with the class as a demonstration group. Most of the counselors were even less familiar with group techniques than with individual interviewing. The instructor took the class through the process of forming and solidifying the group, beginning with simple exercises and introducing others as the class could absorb them. Some clinics also offered counselor training in case finding and in family group counseling. The objectives were increased insight and self-awareness in addition to the development of specific techniques.

The rising incidence of alcoholism in children and adolescents has become a pervasive problem faced by large urban mental health clinics and hospitals. In a typical situation, the adolescent's problem often involves an objective or subjective deprivation and an identification with alcohol abusing parents as well. Across the country, the professional consensus is that it is difficult to help anyone in this age group without outreach counseling of immediate or extended family or within a system such as school or church. Extended hospitalization and psychotherapy can seem to the adolescent to be a stigma and a burden. Vigorous and aggressive outpatient treatment, including family counseling if possible, is felt to be the most desirable course. Since family cooperation cannot always be relied upon, however, the counselor may have to be able to devise imaginative methods to compensate.[31]

Inevitably in team training programs, adjustment problems surface. One successful device has been a workshop that is part of the training program and runs concurrently with it. In small groups of eight to ten, counselors meet with a group leader, skilled both in alcoholism and in group leadership, who is not from their own programs. This arrangement makes possible an unloading hour. There are no supervisors or directors in attendance and therefore no authority links with their own programs. No judgments or evaluations are made. As trust in the confidentiality of the workshop develops, counselors deal with their work problems. High on the list are feelings about recovered alcoholics working with nonalcoholic colleagues. A typical high voltage session can take place when the recovered alcoholic is faced with getting paid to do what may be viewed as "twelfth-step" work. In a similar vein, nonalcoholics are faced with their very basic feelings about "drunks." Much confusion comes out about accepting and using supervision, which for untrained people of all backgrounds is a new and sometimes uncomfortable experience. Peer competitiveness can be revealed and examined. Another source of grievance is the higher status and pay of the rest of the clinical team while counselors at the bottom feel that they do all the work. The task of the group leader is to keep the group focused on the issues so that the sessions do not become analytic periods for individual participants. Much depends on the leader's competence in dealing with personality, relationship, and the clinical helping process, in addition to understanding alcoholism and the self-help concept.

Another aspect of on-job training is a knowledge base in alcohology—the study of alcohol and alcohol abuse—which is not currently taught at most colleges or universities. Most counselors know very little about the field, while the knowledge base of recovered alcoholics is usually limited to their own experience. This gap can be filled by a series of sessions that present some of the basic body of knowledge about the field of alcoholism. There are a number of conflicting views and theories and, since most courses are geared to specific treatment programs their approaches are generally pragmatic.

A broad approach that seems to me consistent with contemporary American drinking patterns has been mentioned previously. It sees alcoholism as substance abuse, with ethyl alcohol as the drug of choice. The choice is conditioned by cultural and historical inheritance; this heritage in a drug society encourages alcoholism. In this view, addiction-prone people become ill in a variety of ways, suggesting again that there is probably not one but a variety of alcoholisms.

Academic Preparation of Alcoholism Counselors

Academic credentials for counselors have not been stressed in most of the existing programs, yet some of the newer programs are now requiring a BA in health-related fields and developing plans for meaningful career ladders at all entry points. A question of growing importance is: in what ways and at what levels can the schools prepare people to enter this field?

Several universities have collaborated in on-job training of alcoholism counselors. The pioneers in the field were the Baltimore Training Program at Johns Hopkins University and the Rutgers Center of Alcoholic Studies. University sponsored on-job training has been extremely useful for newly organized programs.

Undergraduate programs in social work and health care are ideally suited for alcoholism counselor training. Wilmar State College in Minnesota was the first to experiment, and the University of Iowa is one of the few other colleges to try such a program. Most undergraduate curricula in counseling make little or no reference to alcoholism. Old prejudices die hard! It would appear appropriate for the BS social work programs, which offer psychology, sociology, and casework, to offer a sequence in alcoholism that might include individual and group techniques with alcoholic patients, field placement in an alcoholism setting, and a course in alcohology. Clearly there are growing opportunities for graduate social workers as educators in the field at the college level. Some of the content they will be expected to deal with are: knowledge and ability to deal with mood-changing drugs, particularly ethyl alcohol; understanding of the cultural implications of substance abuse; and the dynamics of subcultural life as demonstrated in the self-help fellowships.

The Future

The graduate social worker in alcoholism enters the field as supervisor, teacher, and program director. This departure from the traditional expectations for the beginning graduate social worker has definite implications for the curriculum of the graduate schools of social work. At present, the MSWs in alcoholism treatment centers, like the counselors, have needed to continue learning on the job, whatever credentials they bring with them.

The organization and funding for alcoholism treatment came from special interest groups who saw the need for a specialized attack on a major health problem. As a result, the alcoholic population in all its complexity and enormity is becoming visible at last. As with other health problems, specialized facilities encourage experimentation, research, and documentation. Eventually, this approach holds the possibility for a major breakthrough to the etiology of alcoholism. Isolation of the patient population and earmarking of alcoholism funding guarantees that attention will be paid, that efforts and resources will not be dissipated, and most important, that deeply rooted attitudes toward alcoholics may be changed. Those who take this view see the possibility of merging the treatment of alcoholism with other drugs as a danger.

In the last decade, we have seen an increasing number of patients addicted to alcohol and other drugs. The process of detoxification and treatment is becoming infinitely more complicated. The decision to refer a person to an alcoholism clinic or to a hard drug clinic is not always easily made. The judgment has to do with the patient's self-image, age, lifestyle, and relation to the law. It is possible that as the treatment of all drug abuse becomes a more standard division of mental health care, the criteria for separating alcoholism treatment will appear less appropriate and even artificial. As the country moves toward a national health system, there may emerge a more permanent and integrated base for the treatment of all addictions within the traditional health system. Inevitably, training for the health services will have to be more appropriately integrated into the educational system.

Finally, the impact of ecology has barely been felt in the health services. The human use and abuse of the earth's substances is only beginning to be explored.

Notes

1. R. Gordon Bell, *Escape from Addiction* (New York City: McGraw Hill, 1970), pp. 11–14.

2. Seldon D. Bacon, "The Classic Temperance Movement in the U.S.A.," *British Journal of Addiction* 62 (1967): 5–6.

3. E. M. Jellinek, *The Disease Concept of Alcoholism* (New Haven: Hillhouse, 1960), p. 2.

4. Ernest H. Cherrington, *The Evolution of Prohibition in the United States of America* (Westerville, Ohio: American Issue, 1920), p. 119.

5. Ibid., pp. 134–39.

6. Ernest H. Cherrington, ed., *Anti-Saloon League Year Book* (Westerville, Ohio: American Issue, 1923).

7. Cherrington, *Evolution of Prohibition,* pp. 174–75.

8. Bacon, "Classic Temperance Movement," pp. 5–18.

9. Robert S. Lynd and Helen M. Lynd, *Middletown* (New York City: Harcourt, Brace, 1929), p. 277.

10. Jellinek, *Disease Concept of Alcoholism,* pp. 2–7.

11. Thomas F. A. Plaut, ed., *Alcohol Problems: A Report to the Nation by the Cooperative Commission on the Study of Alcoholism* (New York City: Oxford University Press, 1967), pp. 25–27.

12. "School Study Calls 28% of Teen-Agers 'Problem' Drinkers," *New York Times,* 20 Nov. 1975.

13. E. Monsell Pattison, "A Critique of Alcoholism Treatment Concepts," *Quarterly Journal of Studies in Alcoholism* 27 (1966): 49–66.

14. Alcoholism Recovery Institute, "Annual Report of the Information and Referral Service," New York City, 1969, 1970.

15. "Descriptions of A.A.," *Psychiatric Annals* 5 (Marcy 1975): 56.

16. "A Critique of A.A.," *Psychiatric Annals* 5 (March 1975): 15.

17. Margaret B. Bailey, "Treatment of the Alcoholic," in *Alcoholism and Family Casework* (New York City: Community Council of Greater New York, 1968), p. 74.

18. "Dependency-Conflict Hypothesis and Frequency of Drunkenness," *Psychiatry Digest* (May 1975), p. 51.

19. Viekko Tähkä, *The Alcoholic Personality,* The Finnish Foundation for Alcohol Studies (Helsinki: Maalaiskuntien Liiton Kirjapaino, 1966), p. 222.

20. "Problems in Affiliation," *Psychiatric Annals* 5 (Marcy 1975): 33.

21. Ruth Fox, "Disulfiram (Antabuse) as an Adjunct in the Treatment of Alcoholism," in *Alcoholism: Behavioral Research, Therapeutic Approaches,* ed. by Ruth Fox (New York City: Springer, 1967), pp. 242–54.

22. Conference on Behavioral Approaches to Substance Abuse at the University of Washington, July 1975; reported by Shirley Hellenbrand, Columbia University School of Social Work.

23. Peter Miller and R. Eisler, "Alcohol and Drug Abuse," *Behavior Modification: Principles, Issues and Applications,* ed. by Kazdin and Mahoney (Boston: Houghton Miflin, in press).

24. Conference on Behavioral Approaches, U. of Wash., 1975; reported by Linda and Mark Sobel.

25. Veronica Snyder, "Cognitive Approaches in the Treatment of Alcoholism," *Social Casework* 56 (Oct. 1975): 480–85.

26. David J. Armor, J. Michael Polich, Harriet B. Stambul, *Alcoholism and Treatment* (Santa Monica, Calif.: Rand Corporation, June 1976).

27. Joseph Mayer and David J. Myerson, "Outpatient Treatment of Alcoholism," *Quarterly Journal of Studies in Alcoholism* 32 (1971): 620–27.

28. Charles B. Truax and Donald G. Wargo, "Psychotherapeutic Encounters That Change Behavior: For Better or for Worse," *American Journal of Psychotherapy* 20 (No. 3, 1966): 499–520.

29. Three of the comprehensive alcoholism programs sponsored by the City of New York are at Long Island College Hospital, Beth Israel Medical Center, and the Hospital for Joint Diseases and Medical Center. The design for on-job training of counselors was first demonstrated in these three programs in a project jointly planned by Bernard Bihari, Director of the Beth Israel Alcoholism Center, and the author.

30. Morris E. Chafetz et al., eds., *Frontiers of Alcoholism* (New York City: Science House, 1970), pp. 206–29.

31. Roche Report, *Frontiers of Psychiatry,* World Wide Medical Press.

Bibliography

Bacon, Seldon D. "The Classic Temperance Movement in the U.S.A." *British J. of Addict.* 62 (1967) pp. 5–18.

Bailey, Margaret. *Alcoholism and Family Casework.* New York: Comm. Cncl. of Gtr. N.Y., 1968.

Bell, R. Gordon. *Escape from Addiction.* New York: McGraw Hill, 1970.

Brill, Leon. "Three Approaches to the Casework Treatment of Narcotic Addicts,": *Social Work* 13 (April 1968) pp. 25–35.

Calahan, Don. *Problem Drinkers.* San Francisco: Jossey-Bass, 1970.

Caroff, Phyllis, Florence Lieberman, and Mary Gottesfield. "The Drug Problem: Treating Pre-addictive Adolescents," *Social Work,* 51 (November 1970) 527–32.

Chafetz, Morris E., et al. *Frontiers of Alcoholism.* New York: Science House, 1970.

Cherrington, Ernest H. *The Evolution of Prohibition in the United States of America.* Westerville, Ohio: American Issue, 1920.

Cohen, Pauline, and Morton Krause. *Casework with Wives of Alcoholics,* FSAA, 1971.

Cork, Margaret R. *The Forgotten Children.* Ontario: Addiction Foundation, 1969.

Corrigan, Eileen. "Linking the Problem Drinker with Treatment," *Social Work,* 17 (March 1972) 54–61.

Eldred, Carolyn A., Velma Grier, and Nancy Berliner. "Comprehensive Treatment for Heroin-Addicted Mothers," *Social Casework,* (October 1974) 470–77.

Finlay, D.G. "Alcoholism: Illness or Problem in Interaction" *Social Work* 19:4 (July 1974) pp. 398–405.

Finlay, D. "Anxiety and the Alcoholic" *Social Work,* November, 1972 pp. 29–33.

Fox, Ruth, ed. *Alcoholism: Behavioral Research, Therapeutic Approaches.* New York: Springer, 1967.

Friedman, Philip H. "Family System and Ecological Approach to Youthful Drug Abuse" *Family Therapy,* 1:1, Libra Publications, 1974, pp. 63–78.

Garard, Stephen L. "Communicational Styles and Interaction of Alcoholics and Their Wives," *Family Process,* 10 (Dec. 1971) 475–90.

Heyman, Margaret M. "Employment-Sponsored Programs for Problem Drinkers" *Social Casework* 52 (November 1971) 547–52.

Jellinek, E.M. *The Disease Concept of Alcoholism.* New Haven: Hillhouse, 1960.

Krimmel, Herman. Alcoholism: *Challenge for Social Work Education.* New York: Cncl. on Soc. Work. Educ. 1971.

Mayer, Joseph, and David J. Myerson. "Outpatient Treatment of Alcoholism" *Quart. Journ. Stud. Alc.* 31 (1971) pp. 620–627.

Miller, P., Ann G. Stanford, and Diane P. Hemphill. "A Social-Learning Approach to Alcoholism Treatment," *Social Casework* 55 (May 1974) 279–84.

Miller, Peter, and R. Eisler. "Alcohol and Drug Abuse," *Behavior Modification: Principles, Issues and Applications,* Kazdin and Mahoney, eds., Boston: Houghton Mifflin, in press.

Mueller, J.F. "Casework with Family of the Alcoholic" *Social Work,* September 1972, 79–84.

Pattison, E. Monsell. "A Critique of Alcoholism Treatment Concepts," *Quart. Journ. Stud. Alc.* 27 (1966) 49–66.

Peltenburg, Cathrin M. "Casework with the Alcoholic Patient," *Social Casework* 37 (February 1956) 81–85.

Pittman, David J. and Charles R. Snyder, eds. *Society, Culture and Drinking Patterns.* New York: John Wiley, 1962.

Plaut, Thomas F.A., ed. *Alcohol Problems: A Report to the Nation by the Cooperative Commission on the Study of Alcoholism.* New York: Oxford University, 1967.

Purvine, Margaret, ed. *Educating MSW Students to Work With Other Social Welfare Personnel.* New York: Cncl. on Soc. Wk. Educ. 1973.

Sobey, Francine. *The Non-Professional Revolution in Mental Health.* New York: Columbia Univ. 1970.

St. Pierre, C. Andre. "Motivating the Drug Addict in Treatment," *Social Work* 16 (January 1971) 80–88.

Truax, Charles B., and Donald G. Wargo. "Psychotherapeutic Encounters that Change Behavior: For Better or for Worse," *Amer. Journ. of Psychotherapy* XX:3 (1966) 499–520.

Weinberg, J. "Counseling Recovering Alcoholics," *Social Work* 18, July 1973, pp. 84–93.

Zimberg, Sheldon, Henry Lipscomb, and Elizabeth Davis. "Sociopsychiatric Treatment of Alcoholism in an Urban Ghetto" *Amer. Journ. of Psychiatry* 127: 12, June 1971.

12

From Psychiatric Hospital
to Community Team

SUE MATORIN

*This chapter illustrates what a hospital based community
mental health model of practice means for hospitalized
patients, their families, and citizens of the community.*

*For the social work practitioner, close collaboration
with new team members and a change in the focus and
the locus of treatment are among the central innovations
of practice. Case materials are given to illustrate the
roles and activities of professional social workers,
paraprofessional workers, and other psychiatric team
members. A developing eclectic approach and emphasis
on the import of the milieu is rapidly replacing the former
exclusively psychoanalytic orientation of the hospital.*

A 19-year-old Spanish-speaking woman was found wandering
in the streets by the police and brought to the emergency
room in the Washington Heights area of New York City.
Unable to speak, she remained an emigma after an overnight
stay in the hospital and a complete battery of tests.
Transferred to the area community psychiatry ward, she
could provide staff with her age and a female first name, not
necessarily her own. A professional social worker combed
area city and state hospitals to no avail. The first year
psychiatric resident, baffled and anxious, privately pressed
for a rapid discharge. The paraprofessional, on her own
initiative, placed an advertisement on a local Spanish radio
station. Identifying herself only as a mental health aide in a
major New York hospital, she asked that any Spanish family
missing a young female member contact the station. Within
minutes a frantic family was in touch with staff and reunited
with their daughter. A diagnostic puzzle was unraveled.

THIS imaginative piece of paraprofessional work is both admirable in itself and an example of the emergence of new styles of health service delivery. Further, the vignette illustrates many of the facets encountered in community mental health practice. The traditional psychiatric setting with a strong analytic flavor is being reorganized into a community mental health service, and the process presents an exciting challenge. The chemotherapy revolution opened the door to life outside an institution for numbers of psychiatric patients.[1] Such persons became accessible to a variety of psychotherapeutic approaches and social rehabilitative interventions. Rapidly, it has become apparent that personnel other than the psychiatrist are now involved in this public health issue. The new interdisciplinary team has expanded to include not only the psychiatrist or social worker but also nurses, psychologists, occupational and recreational therapists, and paraprofessionals or indigenous workers. Any review of the issues emerging in this revolution and their effect on the social worker's repertoire will delineate what has been retained or modified from traditional social work practice and what new concepts and techniques have been created. Such a review will have particular relevance for new and returning professionals.

The Washington Heights Community Service, affiliated with the New York State Psychiatric Institute, offers comprehensive psychiatric care (inpatient, day, night and outpatient) to anyone over the age of 14 within a catchment area of approximately 90,000 persons. Before the service began in 1965, area residents needing hospitalization had been transferred from the emergency room of the medical center to a large city hospital psychiatric ward. There they usually received massive doses of drugs and were rapidly discharged. Those who required long-term care were frequently removed from family and neighborhood and sent to a state hospital. The restriction of the institute's attention to those "selected" teaching patients who were useful in its training and research programs was hardly comprehensible to the surrounding community. Neighborhood resentment was probably a factor in the collapse of previous attempts to establish a community mental health center there. Psychiatric Institute, nationally and internationally renowned, had relatively few roots in its own area.

A New Patient Population

The new Washington Heights Service moved to modify the Institute's traditional psychoanalytic approach directed predominantly at the white middle class in order to reach a more varied patient population. From the beginning of the newly created service, the majority of the patients were from the lower social classes (more than 61 percent from classes IV and V on the Hollingshead scale). That trend has continued, with a particular increase in numbers of patients from social class IV. The reorganized service began to treat more blacks than previously. That trend has increased significantly, as the racial composition of the neighborhood has shifted. In addition, there are several Hispanic groups of varied origin (such as Puerto Rico, Cuba, and the Dominican Republic).[2]

What has been the impact on the professional social worker of the new dual commitment—service to a new type of population and education of interdisciplinary trainees? How have the professional social worker's traditional knowledge and skills been modified to meet the challenge? Changes have occurred in several areas: (1) greater concentration on diagnosis of the patient's social network; (2) more reliance on ego-building treatment techniques; (3) a change in the locus of treatment; (4) imaginative creation of new resources to fill societal gaps in service.

1. Diagnosis of the patient's social network

Traditionally, the social worker on an interdisciplinary psychiatric team would provide other staff members with information concerning the socioeconomic factors affecting a patient's ability to function. Now, confronted with a more diverse and harder-to-reach population, the social worker is called upon to identify the social factors in both diagnosis and assessment of ego functioning. In current practice, the social worker's ability to discern and articulate strengths and weaknesses in a patient's social network is crucial. Home visits are the social workers active diagnostic and treatment tools; they permit assessment of patients in their natural milieus and involvement in the realities of the patients' life situations. Such realities may include exorbitant utility bills, inhumane single room occupancy hotels, dehumanizing procedures in public assistance, or confusing Social Security regulations.

2. Ego-building treatment

While traditional psychodynamics remain essential in understanding the patient, many patients in this new diverse population do not have the emotional resources to invest in long-term psychological treatment or personality reconstruction. Crisis intervention and ego support are often what is immediately required. Professionals must revamp their skills to do briefer assessments with competence. They must learn to intervene rapidly and devote less time to lengthy history-taking. A variety of methods is used, including group treatment, role modeling, and formation of environmental resources to provide for clients whose needs are not met elsewhere.

3. From hospital to community

In contrast to the original, traditional structure of service—exclusive operation within hospital walls—the Institute's in-hospital clinical program now is only one aspect of treatment possibilities within a more comprehensive program. Consistent with mental health practice across the country, our staff has increasingly been compelled to find ways to offer treatment outside the structure of the hospital.[3] Our service is currently divided into a tripartite system with an intensive care unit, an expanded day hospital which offers transitional and rehabilitative care, and a large aftercare clinic. The operational philosophy is to keep the actual hospital stay brief (under two weeks if possible), with the major treatment and rehabilitative interventions provided in the day hospital and aftercare units. This change in the structure of delivery of service and type of population served has been accompanied by changes in role and function. In the acute unit, the medical model prevails with the psychiatrist's role focused on diagnosis and aggressive use of psychiatric medications. In the other sectors of the program, the psychiatrist functions as a consultant to other team members who assume primary responsibility for the treatment. The narrower role of the psychiatrist in the acute unit and blurring of roles which has occurred in the day hospital and aftercare sectors have created some challenging dilemmas in the training of the interdisciplinary team.

4. New means to meet needs for service

To foster the movement of treatment out of the hospital and to modify the psychoanalytic approach to treatment of hard-to-reach persons, professional social work staff introduced the paraprofessional program. The paraprofessional plays a key role in bringing the hospital to the neighborhood. Initially recruited to help professional staff work with Spanish-speaking patients, paraprofessionals soon demonstrated that they could be utilized to benefit the entire patient population. Their activities now include, for example, diagnostic home visits, transitional homemaker service to help a discharged psychotic mother care for her children, and advocacy on behalf of patients dependent on DSS, SSI, or job training agencies.[4]

Mrs. S., an elderly white female, was hospitalized on the Service for severe organic illness necessitating a referral to a nursing home facility. A paraprofessional was assigned to make home visits to the patient's husband. She encountered a gentleman in his 30s, highly independent and suspicious of her efforts to help because of fear of the cost. The paraprofessional found a filthy, cockroach-ridden apartment filled with collected old clothes, dirty laundry, and general junk. She described it as "really, really bad." During the paraprofessional's contact with Mr. S., his wife was transferred to a medical facility where she subsequently died. The paraprofessional, ostensibly in the home to help Mr. S. with self care and general apartment management (laundry, cleaning, shopping), gradually encouraged him to ventilate his feelings of depression following the death of his wife; he felt guilty for having delayed in hospitalizing her. Mr. S. accepted the paraprofessional's practical help and offer of friendship during a most painful time, and his depression gradually lifted. Weekly visits for six months were decreased to twice monthly and then to monthly contacts. Mr. S. is now able to care for himself and has visited one of his children in California. The paraprofessional told her supervisor, "Between you and me, he invited me to go to Europe."

Goals of Intervention

The newer patient population suffers from profound and, at times, overwhelming socioeconomic deprivations. As part of a team heavily weighted toward the psychoanalytic point of view, the professional social worker not only keeps attention directed to the patient's social network but also raises searching questions about the health care being delivered—questions such as "What constitutes mental health?" or "What are the boundaries of psychiatric intervention?" The paraprofessionals, closely in touch with the cultural values, life styles, and daily struggles of the patient population, counteract the tendency of professional staff to overlook unfamiliar realities of patients' lives. Paraprofessionals are in daily contact with bureaucracies, and through continual feedback to professional staff about service gaps and inadequacies in the community, they translate the social work concern for human dignity and social welfare into action. The paraprofessional provides rich data about the social reality of the patient population and the professional social worker conceptualizes them for the team.

In the former structure of service, social workers had been concerned primarily with the impact of psychiatric hospitalization on the family system. In current practice they confront many patients who have no intact family or social support systems. Should intervention go beyond the remission of acute symptoms? What are realistic goals for the hospital stay?[5] Should professional staff utilize hospital contact with a patient to evaluate and perhaps improve the quality of his or her functioning and life situation? In a setting where psychiatric residents are entering their first phase of work with psychotic patients, the professional social worker must stimulate these inquiries about each patient. The questions lead to painful choices about which patient or family unit is to receive attention.

Moreover, service pressures and psychiatric labels can blur clinical judgment. On an acute service with high admission rates, medication may dominate other forms of intervention. Acute symptom remission may be used prematurely as an index of psychological stability and community adjustment. The diagnostic label "chronic schizophrenic" may lead beginning therapists to assume that nothing can be done aside from medication rather than to consider the patient's individual situation. What are the patient's abilities between symptomatic episodes? What precipitates symptoms in a "chronic" patient who might otherwise live outside a hospital setting? The social worker on the team consulted for "disposition" must be a forceful spokesman and teacher so that dispositional issues are integrated into the patient's total treatment. A referral to the Welfare Department, for example, is rarely a treatment of choice but should be viewed as a temporary means of financial assistance for those patients who ultimately can return to former employment or who can benefit from a vocational program. The anxious psychiatric resident or student social worker may approach the patient with a narrow view of the possibilities. The professional social worker's careful attention to ego assets is necessary to identify those patients who might move beyond symptom remission. While time-consuming, such expansion of goals and intervention may reap long-term gains in the patient's community adjustment.

One of our professional social workers was asked to help the outpatient clinic nurse place a 59-year-old Spanish female in a nursing home. The nurse was understandably frustrated by what appeared to be her client's stubborn refusal to function in her apartment following a brief admission on the acute service. In the postdischarge period, the patient made frequent trips to the emergency room and barraged the nurse with chaotic phone calls. The patient had a long history of serious medical problems, had endured and survived considerable surgery including the removal of one eye, and in addition had been hospitalized several times for depression—on one occasion following a suicidal ingestion of prescribed psychiatric medications. At the point of consultation the patient's husband and two adult daughters, reportedly exhausted by care-taking and frustrated by the patient's histrionic outbursts, were demanding placement. The patient saw the nursing home as a place where she could be cared for and no longer burden her family.

A family meeting revealed a number of interesting factors.

1. Drawing on a bank of experience with families, the social worker evaluated the family as basically available. Though irritated by the patient, this family was able to verbalize rather than act on such feelings. Clearly committed to helping the patient remain in the community if feasible, despite their initial plea for placement, they were eager for ongoing meetings.

2. The patient was troubled by a cataract in her remaining eye and distressed about her inability to care for her husband and home.
3. She was quite lonely during the husband's working hours and saw a placement as a way of avoiding being alone.
4. She was suffering a recurrence of a urinary infection; her periodic incontinence was humiliating.
5. The patient was preoccupied with aging, loss of her youth and attractiveness, and unfounded fears that her husband would leave her.
6. The clinic nurse was unable to control countertransference reactions to the patient's infantile attempts to cope and responded with cold irritability.

Having teased out the above in a brief assessment the social worker suggested a time-limited trial of homemaker service. A person helping in the home could more objectively evaluate the patient's actual ability to do for herself (rather than to be catered to by the family) as well as the degree of visual impairment. In addition she could provide support and companionship and capitalize on the patient's underlying desire to resume care of her apartment. The social worker suggested a time frame so that the patient and family would be clear that the plan was an assessment, not a solution, with placement an alternative if necessary. The social worker assigned less burdensome tasks to each family member—one daughter would accompany the patient to the urologist, the husband would supervise medication prescribed by the clinic psychiatrist. The social worker could point to the patient's sense of humor as a positive prognostic factor ("The cost of my medical care built this hospital"). She demonstrated firm limit setting to the family and nurse when the patient began to disrupt the session with histrionic behavior.

In the postsession rehash, the social worker encouraged the nurse to discuss her countertransference and helped her see the patient's infantile manipulative behavior as a clumsy effort to deal with the normal life cycle crisis of aging.

The vignette illustrates the matrix of factors surrounding a seemingly simple request which indicate the need for a more thorough assessment, the variety of possible solutions (such as family system evaluation, provision of concrete service, psychiatric medications, role modeling, attention to the client's ego assets), and the professional social worker's particular expertise in the team effort. Social work training fosters an appreciation for the complexity of life cycle stresses, an eye for functional and dysfunctional ways of coping, and a sense of the value of a social network.

Social worker as team teacher

Throughout all these areas, the professional social worker's function as a teacher on the clinical team has been clear. Acting as an ethical compass, the social worker ensures that a patient is not fragmented by being viewed as a collection of interesting textbook symptoms, or as a welfare case. Drawing on knowledge of psychological and social dynamics, the professional social worker provides a broad framework for responding to patients as whole persons in the context of their life struggles.[6]

Paraprofessionals: Potential and Pitfalls

As mental health service has adapted to serving a more diverse patient population, the professional social worker has had to redefine the term *therapist*. Increasingly, primary responsibility for patient care has shifted to the paraprofessional. While the physician or professional social worker clearly retains full legal and administrative responsibility for clinical decisions, chart work, and the like, the paraprofessional may be the team member who develops the richest therapeutic rapport with the patient. In the Washington Heights Community Service, it has been observed that while paraprofessionals begin as auxiliary aides to professional staff, they gradually become a primary source of help to clients.[7] The two dangers in this shift are that paraprofessionals will be permitted to do too little or be asked to do too much.

Paraprofessionals' creativity may be constricted by staff's inability to utilize their talents. Administrative support and education of professional staff are necessary if the multiple talents of the indigenous worker are to be tapped. Encouraging paraprofessionals to share descriptions of their patient experiences with the professional staff is helpful. Expanding paraprofessional skills though in-service training and supervision by the professional social worker is essential. Unfortunately, to date, bureaucratic structures have not been designed to financially reward this expansion of talent with the provision of adequate career ladders. On the other hand, too much responsibility may be allocated to the paraprofessional. This is a distinct danger in a clinical setting where individuals in training may back off from client contact because of their own anxiety and lack of experience. What at first appears to be an appropriate assignment for the paraprofessional—care of a difficult Spanish-speaking patient, for example—can shallowly conceal professional abdication of responsibility in a complex clinical situation. The resident or student social worker, uncomfortable in learning how to work through a translator, can avoid contact with a psychotic Spanish-speaking patient by "delegating" responsibility. Eager to be useful, paraprofessionals may assume such responsibility without required legal coverage or appropriate clinical supervision. Nevertheless, many rewards emerge when professional staff delegates responsibility to a paraprofessional with greater care.

A Chinese-speaking widow was hospitalized for an acute paranoid decompensation. Her only available relative was a young son. Feeling burdened and resentful, he could participate only minimally in his mother's treatment. A Puerto Rican mental health aide established good rapport with this woman. Patiently and nonverbally, she reached out to this floridly psychotic woman who had entered the ward emitting blood-curdling screams of terror. The aide reduced the patient's fear of medication so that the flagrant symptomatology could be controlled. With supervision, the paraprofessional was able to take a firm line with the son concerning his responsibility to his mother while being sensitive to his ambivalence. He shared with the aide his previous negative experience with a city hospital, which had called to "announce" his mother's discharge. The paraprofessional pointed out that his simple cooperation in letting herself and a visiting nurse into the apartment to give the patient medications would free him of his mother's acute and terrifying behavior and would reduce his contact with the hospital. The patient was stabilized on semi-monthly injections of medication and functioned well in her own apartment with visits from the paraprofessional and visiting nurse.

Home visit tool

The home visit becomes a major tool in the new approach. Many professionals are anxious and uncomfortable in stepping out of the more familiar office role. The paraprofessionals' ease in home visits and their desire to teach staff its value as a diagnostic and treatment tool help dispel the anxiety and stimulate interest. Clues to tenuous ego functioning can be identified and their implications for diagnosis and intervention can be sparked by the paraprofessionals' colorful reports of home visits. Their vivid descriptions can alert professional staff, for example, to the addict's misuse of family funds or the psychotic mother's inability to dress and feed her children.

Mrs. B., employed in the Medical Center as a nurse, was hospitalized on the Service for a psychotic episode. A paraprofessional was assigned to take her home to gather clothing. Within the apartment, the paraprofessional discovered that the patient had pulled out all the electrical wiring. During the visit, the patient took a dry cell and began playing with it using a penny, while putting her hand under the faucet. Asked why, the patient responded that she "liked to feel the shock." In the aide's words, "I felt so scared. I told her she was acting improperly, that we had come there for a purpose. I grabbed the suitcase and started to pack, getting her to help and away from what she was doing." Upon returning to the hospital, the paraprofessional made an immediate report to the therapist, who had the patient placed under supervision.

Paraprofessionals may at times be intimidated by the professional's educational credentials and facility with jargon. This is another factor that can impede the paraprofessional in sharing their own expertise, which is their contribution to a clinical setting. With administrative sanction and adequate supervision, paraprofessionals demonstrate excellent judgment in dealing with psychotic patients and seeking professional help when appropriate. The supervisory task is to encourage their self-confidence so they can share their ideas.

A 55-year-old Santo Domingan woman was hospitalized when she was found to be acutely delusional and disorganized. The patient resided with her daughter, son-in-law, and three grandchildren. A precipitant was her upset about her daughter's previous suicide attempt, which had resulted in a four month hospitalization for multiple fractures. The patient was concerned about her daughter's health and worried that she herself was a burden. After electroshock therapy, she improved markedly and was able to return to the family. In the meantime the daughter, who had received no psychiatric care after her initial hospitalization, was referred to the same service for admission on the recommendation of a visiting nurse. She was later discharged, perhaps too soon.

The paraprofessional was assigned to make home visits to check on the mother. She became increasingly alarmed about the daughter's condition, "not eating, like a vegetable, speaking of wanting to die." The paraprofessional unsuccessfully pressed the doctor to readmit the daughter for a longer stay. She decided to bring the doctor into the home on her next visit. He found the paraprofessional's observations to be accurate and immediately arranged for the daughter's readmission. Throughout her involvement with this family, the paraprofessional served as translator in marital sessions between the daughter and husband and as an advocate in taking the mother to SSI, eye, and dental clinics. Her most significant contribution was alerting the professional staff to a dangerous psychological situation.

Group Treatment

The shift toward briefer hospitalization has resulted in a greater use of group treatment throughout the entire program. On the acute service, we have reevaluated the purpose and function of ward milieu groups. Initially, groups were organized to replace medical rounds and to give the psychiatric residents daily group contact with their patients. Gradually, as patients remained in the hospital for several months, the groups became interdisciplinary in leadership and psychodynamically oriented in content. The diversity of the new patient population and the rapid turnover of the patients, however, affected the trust, cohesiveness, and stability required for group functioning. It now appears that activity groups focused on self-care, personal hygiene, and tasks of daily living are more relevant to a brief hospital stay. Groups for psychologically oriented discussion are more appropriate in the day hospital or outpatient phase of treatment. It is our impression that retaining modified psychotherapy groups in brief acute care serves mainly to meet staff's need for emotional support. Postgroup staff sessions for rehash of group issues had provided an arena for developing colleague rapport and an outlet for an occasional neurotic interaction. Staff's interest in group process and technique may be met and their time utilized more effectively, however, by the use of outpatient groups. There is impressionistic evidence that this shift may fragment ward staff by removing an arena in which to meet and work. This issue will require continuing assessment.

In the day hospital and aftercare service, professional staff has become aware that the patient population, largely schizophrenic, requires an emphasis on activity and socialization skills to cut through apathy, regression, and social isolation. The paraprofessionals are particularly adept in these areas. Some of the most effective groups within the milieu are those run by paraprofessionals. The Spanish-speaking cooking group, for example, serves multiple purposes: (1) it gives staff firsthand knowledge of patient functioning during symptom remission; (2) the group's food shopping encourages individual functioning in activities of daily living; and (3) the entire patient and staff population is exposed to one culture's food preference. In the words of the husband of a hospitalized patient, "One thing I can say, you can tell me the hospital was bad for you, but one good thing you learned is to make a nice rice with chicken."

The paraprofessionals are highly skilled in forming groups by picking up spontaneously on fluctuating client needs. When a number of non-English-speaking patients are present, the aides will schedule English classes to teach basic vocabulary that will permit use of the hospital clinics, simple communication with a doctor, use of the subway, and so forth. Often the patient gains sufficient comfort to attend classes in the community. When there are a number of elderly patients, the aides will reach out sensitively and plan group recreation or an introduction and escort to a neighborhood senior citizen's center.

In our aftercare program, professional social work staff members continually reassess the clinic population to provide a variety of relevant group experiences. The professional social worker's view extends beyond individual case needs to demographic shifts. The solidity of a group for Spanish-speaking patients co-led by a professional and paraprofessional has been associated with a dramatically low readmission rate for the group's members. The paraprofessional's use of home visits and phone calls has reduced the drop-out rate in the group. The aide's ability to engage in simple activities and socialized tasks with the extremely regressed and withdrawn patients—some with years of state hospitalization histories—has resulted in an exciting open hour. The group has had striking success in engaging patients who had previously been relegated to once a month ten-minute medication clinics and to the isolation and despair of single room occupancy hotels.

Behavior Modification

Our professional staff has utilized behavioral modification concepts in order to deal more effectively with particularly regressed patients who resist other treatment approaches. Such patients frequently present behaviors that are especially repugnant in a milieu setting and frustrating to nursing staff. These behaviors, which the patients are not capable of discussing in therapy, include excessive and uncontrollable touching of people and objects; attention-seeking tantrums leading to secondary gain; and refusal to carry out self-care tasks in hygiene and maintenance of personal living space.

While the professional social worker on the interdisciplinary team need not be an expert in behavioral modification theory, familiarity with several basic concepts is useful—the use of reward as opposed to punishment, the desirability of identifying specific rewards meaningful to the patient, the immediacy of positive reinforcement of desired behaviors, and the necessity for constancy of environment requiring total staff involvement. Social workers who can grasp and acquaint themselves with these basics are assets on their teams: they can help nursing staff carry out the details of an individualized behavioral program by demonstrating their own reinforcing interactions with the patient; they can enable staff to grapple with the ethical concerns raised by questions of "manipulating" a patient's behavior. The more staff members are helped to verbalize their reservations, the less likely are they to sabotage the program. In our experience, a behavioral plan that lacks the endorsement of total staff or of the patient's therapist is doomed to fail. The social worker also can maintain constancy for the patient by teaching reinforcing techniques to the family so that the program is extended to the home. For example, the worker may instruct the family in the use of brief breathing exercises with a patient who continually somaticizes all fears; the family may be encouraged to provide immediate rewards for the patient's desired behavior.

Paraprofessionals may have difficulty in comprehending and supporting wholeheartedly a behavioral modification approach, with its emphasis on reward instead of punishment. In one case, professional staff decided to "reward" an extremely regressed young Spanish-speaking woman (diagnosed as schizoprehnic with retarded features) by giving her an extra sweet treat whenever she performed self-care tasks appropriately. The aide, angry and frustrated by this difficult patient, initially interpreted the approach as spoiling her. Discussion by the professional social worker concerning the underlying assumptions of the approach may soften the paraprofessional's resistance.

Crisis Intervention

The Washington Heights Community Service, by shifting its philosophy from long-term to brief hospitalization, has relied heavily on crisis intervention. The paraprofessional's natural style of being available to patients in the community long after discharge lends itself to a crisis model. Frequently, the paraprofessional is the first staff member to be contacted by the family concerned about an individual spiralling into psychiatric crisis. The aides' ability to respond, perhaps by bringing the patient in for a visit with professional staff, is a feature crucial to the working of our program. Frequently, however, a speedy response on the part of the trained professionals is necessary.

A staff psychologist and professional social worker received a phone call from the distraught mother of a 30-year-old male, a chronic paranoid schizophrenic, in treatment in the aftercare clinic. The mother returned home from a brief medical hospitalization to find her son extremely withdrawn and uncommunicative. Opened cans of uneaten food littered the kitchen. Drawing on their long-term relationship with the mother and son and knowing this patient's potential for aggressive acting out when provoked, the staff members responded with an emergency home visit. Each was attuned to the stress of the mother's recent hospitalization on this patient. He had been unable to visit his mother at the hospital, had failed to take his full psychiatric medications, and had missed a clinic appointment.

The staff worked in tandem. The social worker spoke with the mother and toured the apartment to view evidence of the patient's deterioration. In contrast to the rest of the apartment, his room was filthy and strewn with cigarette butts. The psychologist attempted to engage the patient despite his withdrawal. While this mother characteristically tended to deny her son's limitations and project her guilt onto the staff, on this occasion it was clear she was responding appropriately to her son's obvious regression. Weakened by her own recent hospitalization, she was less able to cope with his symptoms.

The staff was able to bring the son to the hospital voluntarily without resort to the police and despite the potential for an aggressive outburst. The following day the mother discovered his notebook containing delusional writings of psychotic and violent content. She referred to the staff as "angels" for their rapid response to her call.

Creation of New Resources

We have created supervised living arrangements where none existed before in the community—specifically a halfway house, three supervised apartments, and a family care program. Inappropriate discharge of patients from large state hospitals to non-receptive communities ill-equipped to provide care dramatically leads to incidents that highlight the absence of such supervised living facilities for isolated patients. Our clinical staff has been confronted increasingly by patients who have no family or social support and are destined for a single room occupancy hotels—

fertile ground for further psychological deterioration.

Mrs. C., a black divorced woman in her early 30s, was admitted to the Service requesting a "rest" after spending several weeks sleeping in hospital waiting rooms. We learned that Mrs. C., after a three-year stay in a large state hospital, had been discharged to a welfare center and single room occupancy hotel. It is unclear what aftercare was offered. Mrs. C. stopped medications, became frightened of fellow boarders in her rooming house, maintaining that they intended to kill her. She subsequently left the facility and frequented waiting rooms until hospitalized on our unit. She presented as a disheveled dirty young woman, friendly in a rather childlike way, completely preoccupied with tales of dead relatives, insurance claims, and fears of people out to kill her. Clearly, she was quite unable to live in the community without structured aftercare.

Having to plan individual disposition for several such chronically disabled, passive-dependent patients, one of our professional social workers began to meet with the patients as a group in the hospital. This provided an arena in which "collective egos" would ease the transition to a supervised living arrangement outside the hospital. Working with her as active participants were the paraprofessionals. They explored and located neighborhood rentals, made preliminary negotiations with landlords, and sought furnishings. Supervised by a professional social worker, the paraprofessionals eased the patients' anxiety about living outside the hospital (which was expressed as inordinate "complaints" about the lighting, plumbing, and so forth). They taught basic home care skills so that patients would not be evicted. They alerted professional staff to an outpatient's impending decompensation. The paraprofessionals, horrified at the appalling single room occupancy hotels provided by society for this segment of our population, have made alternatives possible through their resourcefulness and profound caring.

The professional social work staff has expanded on this original model to organize several additional apartments. Initial experience suggests that such facilities are more suitable for the older isolated psychiatric patient than for the younger individual with greater potential for acting out.[8] As treatment in the mental health field shifts from custodial to community-based care, professional assessments will be needed to objectify more carefully the types of patients who might respond favorably to such placements.

Placement with families

Similarly, the proliferation of family care programs, in which a community family is reimbursed by state funds for its supervision of a psychiatric patient, necessitates social work assessment. Some queries raised by our own experience with this program are, How does one identify a "suitable" family from applicants to the program? What constitutes a favorable patient-family match? What type of social work consultation-education should be available from the hospital to such families to facilitate a positive experience for the individuals concerned? At this point the program has dealt with too few patients to provide answers. Our professional social workers, however, so immersed in clinical work with a largely psychotic population, tapped different skills to launch the program. Professionals scoured the community for applicants. They felt uncomfortably like some kind of private investigators while they conducted home interviews on "nonclients," interviews necessitated by funding requirements calling for tours of physical facilities. Professional staff members have had to learn to assess the applicants' complex motivations for taking in a psychiatric patient, and to dispel distorted notions that applicants may harbor concerning psychotic patients. The professional must spell out an individual patient's needs quite clearly in order to facilitate a match with what a prospective family might have to offer.

Advocacy skills

The need for professional social work skills in advocacy remains. Unquestionably, paraprofessionals do the leg work effectively in a number of contacts. They are indefatigable in searching for employment and housing resources for clients. Nonetheless, the professional social worker must pave the way for the paraprofessional's visit, interpret agency policy, and smooth the routes of service. The professional social worker's failure to prepare an adequate referral letter, assess the patient's resources, or anticipate an agency interview with the patient has too often left the paraprofessional holding the bag when an inappropriate agency contact has resulted.

A Spanish-speaking man was accompanied to the welfare department by a paraprofessional. His psychiatric disability was a sensitive issue for him and had not been adequately explored by his therapist. When asked by the welfare investigator why he was not supporting his family, he lost control and began flinging paper and furniture around the office to the horror of all present. The highly responsible paraprofessional managed to remove him from the agency, calm him down, and call for supervisory help. It took many weeks to dispel her own sense of failure for not handling the situation more effectively. Clearly, however, the supervising professional had failed to make a thorough assessment before referral.

Liaison role

Establishing formal collaboration with the neighborhood community council for which the Service provides immediate inpatient back-up was an important part of our shift to a more comprehensive program. The social worker's traditional role of liaison with agencies becomes particularly challenging when it involves collaboration with the community group that has responsibility for delivery of health care services. The professional social worker must take the lead in clearing away cobwebs of mutual distrust and distortion as two alien structures converge on their common concern—the health of the community. Such distrust adds a new dimension to liaison work, which differs in kind from the interagency contacts with which the social worker may be most familiar. The social worker must draw on clinical skills and knowledge of individual and group dynamics to deal with defensiveness in both systems. Representing a teaching hospital, the professional social worker can set a tone of respect for different educational credentials and therapeutic styles. To the hospital staff, he or she can teach the value of the availability offered by a community storefront approach. By emphasizing the community's sense of commitment and common concern for health needs of the neighborhood, the social worker can help reduce the hospital staff's criticism and impatience with more informal referrals and occasional inappropriate requests for hospitalization. The social worker can create a bridge so that the two groups can begin to offer complementary rather than competitive care to the neighborhood residents.

Legal Issues in Treatment

The professional social worker is increasingly called on to interpret new legal guidelines concerning the civil rights of patients in current hospital-based practice. Where formerly a disruptive individual was in danger of being locked away from family and society, perhaps unfairly, the new guidelines provide stringent standards that prevent forcing patients into a hospital or other forms of treatment against their wills.[9] A wide range of disruptive behaviors may threaten the family and not result in hospitalization of the disturbed individual. In the poignant plea of one family emotionally battered by a psychotic member who refuses medications, begs food and money from local storekeepers, and provokes beatings, "Where are the family's rights?" Social workers are caught in the middle. They must support the law to protect the individual patient's civil rights, yet bear the family's despair and disbelief. They must help them understand that treatment cannot be effected against the disruptive individual's will. A similarly difficult position arises when the social worker must work with a disturbed family who intrudes in the patient's treatment plan and demands cessation of necessary medications as an "interested party." Our profession is in an ideal position to document such cases and provide pressure for legislative modification of guidelines so that the best interests of all parties can be served. On our Service, the social work staff has organized a combined program with law students. The law students are exposed to real patients and live civil rights issues; social workers gain legal advice, interpretation of current law, and fruitful dialogue.

Conclusion

In conclusion, the professional social worker in contemporary community mental health practice utilizes a wide range of skills imaginatively to deal with a psychiatrically complex and socially disorganized population. The social worker's role on the interdisciplinary team has expanded beyond diagnosing psychosocial disability and estimating ego assets. We are challenged to teach others the interface of the psychological and social problems we are confronting. We encourage team members to stretch their vision of psychiatric intervention. We attempt to create facilities where society has failed. We have developed a core of paraprofessionals who daily expose themselves to the uncertainities of working with an unpredictable population.

With little instruction, a paraprofessional was asked to accompany a patient on a home visit where he was to flush his drugs down the toilet and bring his needles back to the hospital. In the words of the aide, "I was terrified all the way and praying all the way, afraid of who was going to be there in the apartment. An old lady, his mother, came to the door, they embraced, and I came down to earth again."

The shifts in mental health service delivery are many. The demands of current practice on the professional social worker are exacting. Nonetheless, we must pause to remind ourselves of the humanity and humor within the helping arena.

Notes

1. Francine Sobey, *The Nonprofessional Revolution in Mental Health* (New York City: Columbia University Press, 1970), p. 3.

2. Social Background Record, Washington Heights Community Service, April 1968–March 1976.

3. Conference on Alternatives to Mental Hospital Treatment, sponsored by the Mendota (Wis.) Mental Health Institute and Department of Continuing Education, October 1975.

4. J. Shachnow and S. Matorin, "Community Psychiatry Welcomes the Non-Professional," *Psychiatric Quarterly* 43 (July 1969): 492–511.

5. Marvin Herz, "Brief Hospitalization and Aftercare," in *Strategic Intervention in Schizophrenia: Developments in Treatment,* ed. by R. Cancro et al. (New York City: Behavioral Publications, July 1974).

6. Genevieve Oxley, "A Life Model Approach to Change," *Social Casework* 52, No. 10 (Dec. 1971).

7. Gerald Adelson and Anthony Kovner, "The Social Health Technician: A New Occupation," *Social Casework* 50 (July 1969): 395–400.

8. Stephen Reibel, "Open Hour; Group Therapy for the Severely Impaired," unpublished manuscript.

9. *Harvard Law Review* 87 (April 1974); in the paper, "Developments

in the Law: Civil Commitment of the Mentally Ill," there is a comprehensive review of civil commitment procedures.

Bibliography

Adelson, Gerald, and Anthony Kovner. "The Social Health Technician: A New Occupation," *Social Casework*, vol. 50, July 1969.

Epstein, Norman, and Anne Shainline. "Paraprofessional Parent Aides and Disadvantaged Families," *Social Casework*, vol. 55, April 1974.

Herz, Marvin. "Brief Hospitalization and Aftercare," *Strategic Intervention in Schizophrenia: Developments in Treatment*, ed. by R. Cancro et al., New York: Behavioral Publications, 1974.

Kramer, Philip. "The Indigenous Worker: Homemaker, Striver, or Activist," *Social Work*, Vol. 17, January 1972.

Kurzman, Paul A. "The New Career Movement and Social Change," *Social Casework*, Vol. 51, January 1970.

Oxley, Genevieve. "A Life Model Approach to Change," *Social Casework*, December 1971.

Reibel, Stephen. "Open Hour: Group Therapy for the Severely Impaired." Unpublished manuscript.

Shachnow, J., and Matorin, S. "Community Psychiatry Welcomes the Non-Professional," *Psychiatric Quarterly*, July 1969.

Sobey, Francine. *The Nonprofessional Revolution in Mental Health* (New York City, Columbia University Press, 1970).

For a comprehensive review of civil commitment procedures, refer to *Harvard Law Review*, vol. 87, no. 6 (April 1974), "Developments in the Law—Civil Commitment of the Mentally Ill."

DATE DUE

MAY 10 '79	MAY 4 '79		
FEB 1 6 '84	FEB 4 '81		
GAYLORD			PRINTED IN U.S.A.